SPECTRUM SERIES PHONICS
AND
WORD STUDY

TABLE OF CONTENTS

 McGraw Hill **Children's Publishing**

Columbus, Ohio

INSTRUCTIONAL CONSULTANT
Mary Lou Maples, Ed.D.
Chairman of Department of Education
Huntingdon College
Montgomery, Alabama

EDITORIAL AND PRODUCTION STAFF
Series Editor: Joyce R. Rhymer; *Project Editor:* Suzanne Kloss; *Production Editor:*
Carole R. Hill; *Senior Designer:* Patrick J. McCarthy; *Associate Designer:* Terry D. Anderson;
Project Artist: Gilda Braxton Edwards; *Artist:* Sheila Monroe-Hawkins; *Photo Editor:* Ruth E. Bogart; *Illustrator:* Jack Wallen

Mc Graw Hill Children's Publishing

Copyright © 2003 McGraw-Hill Children's Publishing.

Send all inquiries to: McGraw-Hill Children's Publishing • 8787 Orion Place • Columbus, Ohio 43240-4027
ISBN 1-56189-946-1

2 3 4 5 6 7 8 9 10 VHG 07 06 05 04 03

The McGraw-Hill Companies

Organized for successful learning!

The SPECTRUM PHONICS SERIES builds the right skills for reading.

The program combines four important skill strands — phonics, structural analysis, vocabulary, and dictionary skills — so your students build the skills they need to become better readers.

Four types of lesson pages offer thorough, clearly focused, systematic skills practice. That means you can focus on just the skills that need work — for the whole class, a small group, or for individualized instruction.

The SPECTRUM PHONICS SERIES is easy for students to use independently.

Although phonics may be an important part of a reading program, sometimes there just isn't enough time to do it all. That's why PHONICS offers uncomplicated lessons your children can succeed with on their own.

Colorful borders capture interest, highlight essential information, and help organize lesson structure. And your children get off to a good start with concise explanations and clear directions . . . followed by sample answers that show them exactly what to do.

Synonyms

Name _____

A synonym is a word that has the same or nearly the same meaning as another word.

    big - large   bright - shiny   small - little

Read the list of words below. Then read the sentences that follow. Write the word from the list that is a synonym for the underlined word in each sentence.

| journeys | trade | simple | enjoy | major | performers |
| demands | marry | hard | twirl | remain | |

1. Circus actors and stagehands lead lives very different from most of us.   performers
2. A circus group travels from town to town for ten months of every year.
3. While traveling across the country, the circus stops in almost every important city.
4. The journey is difficult, but the circus people get used to it.
5. Many of them would not like to stay in one town for long.
6. They like seeing different parts of the country.
7. Most circus members grow up in the circus and wed other circus people.
8. Many circus tricks look easy, but the performers are highly skilled athletes.
9. Trapeze artists, for example, must be exact in every move as they hang, swing, flip, and spin.
10. The duties of circus life leave the members little time for outside friends or entertainment.
11. The circus is a way of life for these people, though, and most of them wouldn't exchange it for any other.

INSTRUCTION PAGE . . . The skill being covered is noted at the bottom of each student page for easy reference.

In addition, vocabulary has been carefully controlled so your children work with familiar words. Key pictures and key words are used consistently throughout the series to represent specific sounds. And a sound-symbol chart at the back of the text helps your students quickly recall sound-symbol relationships.

Synonyms

Name _____

Read the groups of words below. Then read the story that follows. For each underlined word, choose a list word that is a synonym. For paragraph 1, choose words from Group A. For paragraph 2, choose from Group B. For paragraph 3, choose from Group C. Write the synonym in the blank whose number matches the number of the underlined word.

Group A	caverns	stream	winds	pools	point	experience	trip
Group B	clinging	pitched	fall	enjoyed	chilly	swiftly	struggled
Group C	immediately	survived	crew	realizes	crouched	attempted	ledge

1 In June, 1985, Roman Lazowski and Michael Hall planned a (1) journey through the (2) caves of Spring Mill State Park. Both men had made the trip before, and Michael had a good deal of (3) practice exploring caves. The underground tunnel closely follows a narrow, deep (4) brook. At one (5) spot, the cave ceiling drops to four feet. After a distance, the passageway (6) turns through chest-deep (7) puddles of water.

2 At first, the two cavers (8) liked wading through the (9) cool water, but then rain began to (10) descend outside. Soon the water in the cave stream was running deep and (11) fast. The strong current (12) tossed the two men from wall to wall as they desperately (13) fought to get through the cave. Somehow they managed to pull themselves from the water. (14) Grabbing onto the tunnel wall, they thought the water would soon go down.

3 Unfortunately, Roman fell backward into the rushing water. After hitting a wall of rock, he blindly felt around and found a three-foot-long (15) shelf. (16) Stooped on the ledge, Roman watched the stream steadily rise. Michael bravely (17) tried to reach Roman, but the current quickly carried him a hundred yards downstream to daylight. Michael was rushed to a hospital (18) instantly. Two days later, a (19) team of rescuers reached Roman and pulled him to safety. Roman (20) understands he is fortunate to have (21) lived. Now every day seems especially meaningful to him.

1.   trip
2. _____
3. _____
4. _____
5. _____
6. _____
7. _____
8. _____
9. _____
10. _____
11. _____
12. _____
13. _____
14. _____
15. _____
16. _____
17. _____
18. _____
19. _____
20. _____
21. _____

REINFORCEMENT PAGE . . .
Comprehension exercises that use context as well as word-building skills help build the connection from decoding to comprehension.

Turn page for more information.

Easy to manage

REVIEW PAGES . . . Frequent reviews emphasize skills application.

ASSESSMENT PAGES . . . Assessment pages give you helpful feedback on how your students are doing.

Review and Apply: Composition

Name _____

Read the words and look at the picture below. Notice that each word contains a vowel followed by the letter **r**. Think of how you can put together at least ten of the words to make a story about the picture. Then write your story, underlining the listed words.

alarm	shirt	purse	earrings	scare
large	dirty	sure	disappear	careless
discover	store	wear	search	pair
mystery	stormy	tear	pearl	stairs

_____
_____
_____
_____
_____
_____

49

Review and Apply: Comprehension

Name _____

Read the advertisements below. Notice that many of the words contain vowels followed by the letter **r**. Use the advertisements to answer the questions that follow.

FOR SALE
Coins. Rare Spanish gold and U.S. silver dollars. Will sell whole collection for $1,000 or make fair trade. Call 555-9668 before 6:00 P.M.
Guitar. Mason and Cleary six-string electric guitar with orange hard-shell case. One year old, excellent condition. $500. 555-8298. Ask for Chee.

FOR SALE
Bedroom furniture. Pine three-drawer chest, dresser, nightstand, king-size water-bed frame. $750. Call 555-4777 Saturday only.
Be prepared for winter. Used snow thrower, 5 horsepower, 24-inch blade. 555-3838.
Pearl necklace on 15" gold chain. Matching earrings. Worn only once. $25.00. See at 128 W. Witherspoon St.

HELP WANTED
Sales Clerk. Full or part-time position selling women's footwear. Apply in person. The Glass Slipper, 150 E. Kirby St.
Warehouse Worker. Fast-growing company needs neat, mechanical person to work third shift. Must be at least 18 years old. Apply between 9:00 A.M. and 4:00 P.M., 1543 Corvair Ave.

HELP WANTED
Nurse Aide. Third-shift position open for experienced nurse aide. Top wages and benefits. Call Ms. Martinez at Oak Park Nursing Home, 555-8798.
Hair stylist. Permanent position. Guaranteed hourly wage, paid vacation, paid holidays, insurance. Applications being taken at Clare's Hair Care, 146 E. Kirby St., 555-3898.

1. What musical instrument is for sale? _____
2. What four things are being sold in one ad? _____
3. What kind of jewelry is for sale? _____
4. Is the jewelry likely to be old or nearly new? _____
   How do you know? _____
5. How is the nurse aide job like the warehouse worker job? _____
6. What is *The Glass Slipper*? _____
7. Which two businesses are near each other? _____
8. Why are no telephone numbers given for the sales and warehouse jobs? _____
9. In which street name does **r** follow a vowel twice? _____

48   Review of words containing r-controlled vowels, ar, er, ir, or, ur, ear, air, are

---

Words With More Than One Suffix

Words to use: thoughtlessness, gracefully, selfishly, courageously, comically

Name _____

A suffix is a letter or group of letters that can be added to the end of a word. Some words have more than one suffix.

hope + **ful** + **ness** = hope**fulness**   act + **ive** + **ly** = act**ively**

Read the suffixes below. Then read the items that follow. Follow the item directions, using the suffixes to form new words.

-al   -less   -ness   -ive   -ful   -ly   -ish   -ous

1. Form a new word by adding two suffixes to the word *music*. ___musically___

2. Form two new words by adding two suffixes each to the word *fool*.
   foolishly   **foolishness**

3. Form two new words by adding two suffixes each to the word *attract*.
   attractively   **attractiveness**

4. Form two new words by adding two suffixes each to the word *nerve*. Before adding the suffixes, drop the final **e** from nerve. **nervously**   **nervousness**

5. Form four new words by adding two suffixes each to the word *care*. **carelessness**
   carelessly   **carefulness**   **carefully**

Use the words you wrote above to complete the sentences below.

1. Some ___musically___ talented youngsters have begun learning to play the piano as young as two years of age.

2. The ___attractiveness___ of the store's window case caused people walking by to stop and look at the goods.

3. Shaking hands and a cracking voice were signs of my ___nervousness___ while giving a report to the class.

4. The police officer taught the children to look ___carefully___ in all directions before crossing the street.

5. Before the invention of the airplane, most people thought the idea of a flying machine was pure ___foolishness___.

6. Clothes, papers, and books were ___carelessly___ scattered across the teenager's bedroom.

ANSWER KEY . . . Gives you the help you need when you need it — including student pages with answers for quick, easy reference.

Hard and Soft C and G

Name _____

The letters **c** and **g** followed by **e, i,** or **y** usually stand for their soft sounds, as in **cent** and **page.** The letters **c** and **g** followed by any other letters or at the end of words stand for their hard sounds, as in **cat, attic, wagon,** and **bag.**

Read each set of sentences and its list of words. In each blank, write the list word that best completes the sentence.

1. How would you like to hike the mountains of _____California_____

   with a llama as your _____?

2. Llama trekking is a _____ way to see mountain

   _____ that cannot be reached by car.

3. Instead of _____ a heavy pack, you can load your
   goods on a llama.

4. These furry _____ can carry sixty to ninety pounds.

lugging
companion
creatures
great
California
country

5. Because they walk at a slow _____, you will not cover

   great _____ with a llama.

6. A _____ who has a good _____
   of forest camping will go with you and seven or eight others in a group.

7. Pine, _____, and _____ are among
   the sweet-smelling plants and trees that will delight you as you journey.

8. Be _____ where you walk, though—stepping into a

   patch of poison oak could leave you in an _____ state!

lilac
knowledge
cedar
careful
guide
pace
uncomfortable
distances

Hard- and soft-c and g words in context

Hard and Soft C and G

Name _____

Read each sentence and the words beside it. In each blank, write the word that best completes the sentence.

1. There are _____certain_____ dangers to know about while llama trekking.

   certain
   curtain

2. Rattlesnakes live in mountain _____, and _____, like other wild animals, may be unfriendly if you frighten them.

   rags
   ranges
   cents
   coyotes

3. Don't let these _____ worry you too much, though.

   creatures
   cyclones

4. A llama, when it senses _____, will give an early warning by making a sound like a siren.

   danger
   digger

5. If you journey near the rocky _____, you may be able to see the _____ Ocean from the path.

   circus
   coast
   Pacific
   panic

6. Off in the _____, in the other direction, you can view the _____ of the desert.

   distract
   distance
   edge
   egg

7. All too soon, it will be time to return to the valley, where everyday life and _____ wait for you.

   carnation
   civilization

8. When you return home, you may begin making plans for your next mountain _____.

   vacation
   vaccination

9. _____ you've traveled with a llama, you'll want to do it _____.

   once
   orange
   again
   agent

Hard- and soft-c and g words in context

OLD, OST, IND, and ILD

Name _____

The letter **o** followed by **ld** or **st** usually stands for the long-**o** sound, as in **cold** and **most**.
The letter **i** followed by **nd** or **ld** usually stands for the long-**i** sound, as in **kind** and **wild**.

Read the list of words below. Then read the sentences that follow. Write the word from the list that best completes each sentence.

winds   bold   postmarked   mild
grinding   goldfinches   childhood   northernmost

1. Our geography book shows new vocabulary words in _____**bold**_____ print.

2. Long ago, Indians used large flat stones for _____ acorns to make bread.

3. A narrow road _____ its way from the foot of this mountain to a jagged peak two miles above.

4. Winter in the northern part of our state was very _____ this year.

5. In order to take part in the race, your entry form must be _____ by midnight tomorrow.

6. Going fishing with Aunt Winona is one of my fondest _____ memories.

7. The bird watchers spotted five _____ near a sunflower in the meadow.

8. The Arctic is the _____ point in the world.

Read each clue and the list of words. Write the word from the list that matches the clue.

1. unable to tell one color from another _____**colorblind**_____

2. not tame _____

3. fuzzy growth that may appear on old bread _____

4. cloth used to cover the eyes _____

5. one of two poles on which a crossbar

    is mounted for playing football _____

6. cause a person to remember _____

7. son or daughter of one's child _____

mold

wild

remind

goalpost

grandchild

blindfold

colorblind

Review and Apply: Comprehension

Name _____

Read the television schedule below. Notice that many of the words have hard or soft **c** or **g** sounds. You will also see words ending in **old, ost, ind,** and **ild.** Use the schedule to answer the questions that follow.

Wednesday

7:00 PM

2 **Secret Agent 101**—Calvin and his grandchild uncover danger when they find bags of gold in the cellar closet.

4 **Movie: Creatures From Outer Space**—A 1960 gem! This one is certain to make you grab your chair. Special effects could be more convincing, but generally a great cast. Marge Post, Tracy Cedars, Gary Bold, and Clay Ridges.

5 **Guests in the Garden**—If you aren't wild about playing host to gophers, snails, and other creepy critters, this show is for you.

6 **Movie: General Hedges at Your Service** (1985)—You'll howl over this one! One of the greatest comedies ever! Stars Bill Bridges.

7:30 PM

5 **Big League Soccer**—Columbus Coyotes vs. Cincinnati Cyclones.

8 **The Gentle Genius**—A great mind answers the question: What is the capital of Georgia?

8:00 PM

2 **Certain Curtain**—Watch your favorite stars laugh as they battle for your applause.

6 **The Ghost With the Most**—The ghost joins a circus only to find out that no one can see his act.

8 **Go for Golf**—See some golf greats at their finest. Host: Carla Cargo.

9:00 PM

2 **The Lucy Lilac Show**—Lucy tells us how to prepare carrot cider, cactus cookies, and grape gravy.

4 **Movie: Behind the Cemetery Gates** (1986)—Scary? You guessed it! Be certain to see this with company. Be prepared to sit on the edge of your seat.

1. Which teams are playing soccer this week? _____

   _____

2. Who will be the two main characters in the spy adventure show? _____

   _____

3. What three movies are being shown on Wednesday? _____

   _____

4. Name the stars of the 1960 movie. _____

   _____

5. On which show is the major character invisible to everyone but the television viewers?

   _____

6. What valuable metal will be discovered on a 7:00 show? _____

7. The first two words in the schedule that have **ind** and **ost** are _____ and _____

Review and Apply: Composition

Name _____

You have just heard bad news on TV. Due to the carelessness of many humans, several kinds of wild animals in the western part of the country are in danger of becoming extinct. These include the whooping crane (a large bird), caribou (reindeer), wild sheep and goats, and the grizzly bear. Write a letter to a government official explaining your concern about this matter. Use at least twelve of the words below in composing your letter. Notice that each word has a hard or soft **c** or **g** sound or contains **old, ost, ind,** or **ild.**

remind	almost	certain	creatures	grizzly
convince	panic	danger	trace	caribou
wild	goats	civilization	find	edge
most	country	mind	large	crane
kind	great	old	city	concern

_____

_____

_____

_____

_____

_____

_____

_____

_____

_____

_____

_____

_____

_____

Silent Consonants: *WR* and *RH*

Name _____

In some words, two consonants together stand for one sound. The letters **wr** and **rh** usually stand for the sound of **r,** as in **write** and **rhyme.**

Read each sentence and the words below the blank. Write the word that best completes the sentence.

1. Dad used the _____rhubarb_____ from his garden to make a wonderful pie.
   (rhino, rhubarb)

2. Our team won first prize in _____ this year.
   (wrecking, wrestling)

3. Divers discovered treasure in the old remains of the _____.
   (shipwreck, songwriter)

4. The _____, which is native to Africa and Asia, is a plant-eating
   (rhinoceros, rhythm)
   animal.

5. The plumber used a _____ to tighten the water pipes.
   (wren, wrench)

6. Rock and roll music has its roots in another form of music called _____
   and blues.   (rhubarb, rhythm)

7. I hurt my _____ while playing football with my brother and sister.
   (wrist, write)

8. A _____ is a songbird that often builds its nest near a house.
   (wren, wreath)

9. There is no word in the English language that _____ with *orange.*
   (rhymes, rhythms)

10. The _____ sound of waves crashing on the shore is my fondest memory
    (rhyming, rhythmic)
    of our summer trip.

11. The hot desert sun left my skin feeling dry and _____.
    (wriggled, wrinkled)

12. A _____ is a copy of a diamond that is made of glass or paste.
    (rhinoceros, rhinestone)

13. I _____ out the wet towel and hung it on the clothesline.
    (wrong, wrung)

Words containing silent consonants in context: *wr, rh*

Silent Consonants: *KN, WH,* and *SC*

Name _____

In some words, two consonants together stand for one sound. The letters **kn** usually stand for the sound of **n,** as in **knot.** The letters **sc** sometimes stand for the sound of **s,** as in **scissors.** The letters **wh** sometimes stand for the sound of **h,** as in **who.**

Complete the unfinished word in each sentence by writing **kn, sc,** or **wh.**

1. I bruised my _____<u>kn</u>eecap when I fell on the ice at the skating rink.

2. Do you know _____ose bicycle is parked in the driveway?

3. The door _____ocker on the large house was made of brass.

4. Vera is helping the stage crew paint _____enery for the school play.

5. The _____ent of blossoms fills the country air each spring.

6. _____oever called on the telephone hung up before I had a chance to answer it.

7. This ring is too small to fit over my _____uckle.

8. The store owners can offer _____olesale prices to their customers because they buy goods to sell in large numbers.

9. A _____ientist may work outdoors, in an office, or in a laboratory.

10. These _____issors are not sharp enough to cut the thick cardboard.

11. Dan is _____itting a sweater for his mother's birthday.

12. The pancake recipe calls for a half cup of water and a _____ole cup of milk.

13. Jeanette won first prize in the photography contest for her picture of a snowy mountain

    _____ene.

Silent Consonants: CK and MB

Name _____

In some words, two consonants together stand for one sound. The letters **ck** usually stand for the sound of **k,** as in **duck.** The letters **mb** usually stand for the sound of **m,** as in **lamb.**

Read the list of words below. Then read the sentences that follow. Write the word from the list that best completes each sentence.

peacock	hammock	cricket	woodchuck
padlock	buckles	speckled	crackled

1. Looking into the sparrow's nest, I saw two tiny _____speckled_____ eggs.

2. I need a key to open the _____ on the barn door.

3. A _____ is sometimes called a groundhog.

4. Star's new coat has gold _____ on the sleeves.

5. A _____ chirps by rubbing its front wings together.

6. The burning logs popped and _____ in the flames of the campfire.

7. When spread, the feathers of a _____ look like a brightly colored fan.

8. Gina tied the _____ between two tall oak trees.

In each sentence below, circle the two words that have **mb.** Then write the word in which **mb** stands for the sound of **m.**

1. The lost (lamb) was frightened and (trembling) when we found it. _____lamb_____

2. Last December, two climbers reached Mount Runyon's peak. _____

3. The huge cedar limbs were cut into pieces and used for lumber. _____

4. We remembered to spray bug bomb to keep insects out of our tent. _____

5. A thimble is usually worn on any finger except the thumb. _____

6. Two members of my family are plumbers. _____

7. The carpenter mumbled when she hit her thumb with the hammer. _____

8. Crumble dry cereal crumbs over the casserole before baking it. _____

9. The circus clown carried a jumbo-size comb in his pocket. _____

Words containing silent consonants in context: *ck, mb*

Silent Consonants: *GN* and *GH*

Name _____

In some words, two consonants together stand for one sound. The letters **gn** usually stand for the sound of **n**, as in **sign.** The letters **gh** are usually silent, as in **night.**

Read each clue and the list of words. Find the word in the list that matches the clue. Write the word next to the clue.

1. wear away by chewing _____gnaw_____   slight

2. tallness _____   watertight

3. large snow sled _____   cologne

4. exhale a long, deep breath _____   sigh

5. not crooked _____   gnaw

6. from another country _____   sign

7. thick flour mixture used to make bread _____   foreign

8. try to get votes _____   height

9. perfume _____   campaign

10. sealed so as not to leak _____   straight

11. very small or unimportant _____   dough

12. write one's name on something _____   sleigh

13. decorative pattern _____   design

In each sentence below, circle the two words that have **gn** or **gh.** Then write the word in which **gn** stands for the sound of **n** or **gh** is silent.

1. The artist's (signature) was written at the corner of the (design.) _____design_____

2. A foghorn guided the freighter safely to the dock. _____

3. Dusty grabbed a doughnut and carried it to her doghouse. _____

4. A bighorn sheep had caught its foot between two rocks. _____

5. An SOS signal is a sign of trouble. _____

6. My assignment is to write a report about hognose snakes. _____

Review and Apply: Comprehension

Name _____

Read the groups of words below. Then read the story. In each blank, write the word that best completes the sentence. For paragraphs 1 and 2, choose words from Group A. For paragraphs 3 and 4, choose words from Group B.

Group A					
heights	scenery	sign	known	through	
padlock	wrote	who	sight	knew	

Group B					
hammock	limbs	flocks	rhinoceros	pecked	night
cricket	thought	crumbs	gnawing	scent	peacocks

1   Last summer Uncle Jake _____wrote_____ and sent a letter inviting us to his farm for an extended weekend. For someone _____ had never _____ any place but the city, it was a great thrill.

2   The _____ on the way to Uncle Jake's farm was really breathtaking. I never _____ mountains could reach such spectacular _____. Finally a _____ directed us off the busy highway, and before long the farm came into _____. Since there was no _____ on the fence gate, we drove directly _____ without stopping.

_____

3   How very strange it seemed to me being on a farm! Large _____ with their feathers spread strutted proudly about the yard. Pigs were standing in mud up to their snouts. _____ of geese _____ about for _____ of food. A black bull the size of a _____ stood _____ peacefully on a fence post. And there under the _____ of two maple trees lay my Uncle Jake swinging in a _____. I knew from the start what a great weekend it was going to be.

4   That _____ as I lay in bed, I _____ about everything I wanted to do in the next few days. But the sound of a _____ and the _____ of fresh country air soon soothed me into a deep, deep sleep.

Review of words containing silent consonants: *wr, rh, kn, wh, sc, ck, mb, gn, gh*

Review and Apply: Composition

Name _____

You have been asked to give a short speech to a group of parents at your school. It is your job to convince them of the need for some improvements around the school. Use at least twelve of the words below in writing your speech. Notice that each word contains at least one silent consonant.

know	who	thought	write
whole	knock	wrestle	might
sign	scene	limb	chuckle
science	design	rhyme	attack
dumb	rhythm	campaign	high
foreign	plumber	knowledge	taught

_____

_____

_____

_____

_____

_____

_____

_____

_____

_____

_____

_____

_____

_____

_____

_____

Review of words containing silent consonants: wr, rh, kn, wh, sc, ck, mb, gn, gh

Vowel Pairs: *AI, AY, EI,* and *EY*

Name _____

In some words, two vowels together stand for one vowel sound. The letters **ay** and **ai** usually stand for the long-**a** sound, as in **hay** and **train.** The letters **ei** and **ey** sometimes stand for the long-**a** sound, as in **eight** and **they.**

Read each sentence and notice the word in dark print. Use the sentence to help you figure out the meaning of the word. Check the correct meaning.

1. The woman had been ill so long that she looked thin and **frail.**
    ____ a. happy   ____ b. athletic   ✓ c. weak

2. I think the **beige** jacket looks best with that dark shirt.
    ____ a. light brown   ____ b. torn   ____ c. tiny

3. The hawk swooped down and, with its sharp claws, snatched its **prey.**
    ____ a. sound made by a large bird   ____ b. wing   ____ c. animal that is hunted by another animal for food

4. A **veil** of darkness settled over the quiet country village.
    ____ a. cover   ____ b. wedding gown   ____ c. bright light

5. Gregory carefully **surveyed** the theater crowd, looking for his friend Carlos.
    ____ a. applauded   ____ b. looked over   ____ c. disliked

6. Because a traffic jam **detained** him, he arrived at the meeting late.
    ____ a. discovered   ____ b. held back   ____ c. signaled

7. After hurting his foot, the boy had a slow, crooked **gait.**
    ____ a. way of walking   ____ b. sock   ____ c. opening in a fence

8. When we visit the state fair, I like to spend most of my time on the **midway.**
    ____ a. middle of a sidewalk   ____ b. rides and amusement area   ____ c. parking lot

Words containing vowel digraphs in context: *ai, ay, ei, ey*

Vowel Pairs: *AI, AY, EI,* and *EY*

Name _____

Read each sentence and the words below each blank. Write the word that best completes the sentence.

1. Many people in large cities live over an hour _____away_____ from their places
    of work.
    (await, away)

2. A worker whose job begins at _____ o'clock may have to leave home
    at six o'clock.
    (eight, eighty)

3. Because automobile traffic is so heavy, some people avoid the _____.
    (halfway, highway)

4. Instead, _____ may take an underground train, or
    (tray, they)

    _____, to work.
    (subway, survey)

5. These high-speed _____ stop often and are unlike trains that carry
    (trails, trains)

    _____.
    (faint, freight)

6. Some workers who ride the same route every day become _____ with
    one another.
    (acquainted, afraid)

7. One subway in Atlanta, Georgia, _____ airport passengers who are
    tired or hurrying to catch planes.
    (aids, aims)

8. Rushing from one end of the huge airport to another can be a _____,
    (stain, strain)

    especially for passengers who are carrying much _____.
    (wail, weight)

9. Because the train has no driver, riders must listen to and _____ the
    train's automated voice.
    (dismay, obey)

10. For example, if you stand too near the _____, the voice politely tells
    you to move away.
    (delay, doorway)

11. People who are _____ of the trains can still get through the airport.
    (afraid, unpaid)

12. They _____ ride on moving sidewalks that look like flat escalators.
    (main, may)

13. In this way, passengers can more easily catch their planes without _____.
    (decay, delay)

Vowel Pairs: *EE, EA,* and *EI*

Name _____

In some words, two vowels together stand for one vowel sound. The letters **ee** usually stand for the long-**e** sound, as in **bee.** The letters **ei** sometimes stand for the long-**e** sound, as in **seize.** The letters **ea** can stand for the long-**e** sound, as in **bean,** or the short-**e** sound, as in **bread.**

Read each sentence and the words below each blank. Write the word that best completes the sentence.

1. In order to be _____healthy_____, you need to _____ well every day.
    (heal, healthy)   (eat, speak)

2. By eating foods from each of four groups, your body can _____ what it needs for energy, cell growth, and repair.
    (reach, receive)

3. For instance, each day, you _____ four servings from the milk group.
    (need, repeat)

4. You could have two glasses of milk and two slices of _____.
    (cheese, seaweed)

5. For _____ of these, you could substitute ice _____
    (fifteen, either)   (cream, tea)
    or cottage cheese.

6. From the _____ group, you need two servings of _____
    (mean, meat)   (leaf, lean)
    meat, fish, or poultry.

7. You might decide to have chicken, pork, lamb, or _____.
    (beef, tea)

8. Also included in the meat group are _____, eggs, and nuts.
    (beans, dreams)

9. This is not as odd as it may _____.
    (seem, seen)

10. They are included because they contain a good portion of _____.
    (coffee, protein)

11. Instead of meat, you could eat _____ with peanut butter
    (bead, bread)
    _____ on it.
    (speak, spread)

Words containing vowel digraphs in context: *ee, ea, ei*

Vowel Pairs: *EE, EA,* and *EI*

Name _____

Read the list of words below. Then read the sentences that follow. In each blank, write the list word that best completes the sentence.

sweet	need	meals	peach	green
keeps	oatmeal	head	peel	leafy
really	seeds	squeezed	bread	

1. You may hear that "an apple a day _____keeps_____ the doctor away."

2. This saying is not _____ true, but it is important to eat fruits and vegetables each day.

3. A fruit is the part of a plant that contains _____, which can be planted.

4. A vegetable is any plant part that can be eaten, such as a carrot, a potato, or a

    _____ of lettuce.

5. At breakfast or lunch, you might include fresh-_____ orange juice and

    a plump _____.

6. Perhaps you'd rather _____ and eat a banana or have a serving of

    delicious _____ strawberries.

7. At dinner you may want a _____, _____ lettuce
    salad and baked potato.

8. From the grain group of foods, you _____ four servings such as bread,
    cereal, rice, or corn.

9. Spaghetti, _____, crackers, and wheat _____ are
    good choices.

10. By eating _____ that contain food from the four food groups, you can
    keep your body strong and healthy.

In each sentence below, circle the words that contain a long-**e** sound.

1. Chung (needs) a (receipt) for this dog collar and (leash.)

2. Three workers and their leader sat down to rest beneath a weeping willow tree.

3. Each member of our committee agrees that all club members should receive a newsletter.

4. That bus driver sees no need to increase her driving speed.

5. Scientists found an odd-looking creature while diving in deep seas.

Vowel Pairs: *OA, OW,* and *OE*

Name _____

In some words, two vowels together stand for one vowel sound. The letters **oa, ow,** and **oe** often stand for the long-**o** sound, as in **coat, window,** and **toe.**

Read each sentence and the words below each blank. Complete the sentence by writing the word that makes sense.

1. _____Potatoes_____ are _____ in almost every country around the
   (Potatoes, Tornadoes)   (goals, grown)
   world.

2. Worldwide, _____ produce about six billion hundred-pound
   (goats, growers)
   bags of potatoes.

3. Above ground, you might not _____ a potato plant from any other leafy
   green plant.   (know, roast)

4. _____ the ground is the part of the plant that can be eaten.
   (Below, Blow)

5. This _____, which is called a tuber, may weigh a few ounces or several
   (groan, growth)
   pounds.

6. The pink, purple, or white flowers of a potato plant have seedballs that look like small

   green _____.
   (toast, tomatoes)

7. Farmers use huge machines to plant potatoes in long, _____
   (narrow, shadow)

   _____.
   (roasts, rows)

8. When the potatoes are ready for harvesting, a machine digs them up and _____
   them into trucks.   (floats, loads)

Words containing vowel digraphs in context: *oa, ow, oe*

Vowel Pairs: OA, OW, and OE

Name _____

Read each sentence and the words beside it. In each blank, write the word that best completes the sentence.

1. Deer are some of the largest mammals that _____roam_____ the

    forests and _____ of North America.

    roach
    roam
    meadows
    minnows

2. Deer are the only animals that _____ antlers.

    glow
    grow

3. Except for reindeer, a female deer, or _____, has no
    antlers.

    doe
    hoe

4. Depending on its type, a deer's short, smooth _____ may
    be white, reddish-brown, or gray.

    coach
    coat

5. A frightened deer, running up to forty miles an hour, really runs on

    _____.

    tiptoe
    tomatoes

6. Its foot is nothing more than two _____ protected by a
    curved hoof.

    goes
    toes

7. Two toes above and behind the hoof never touch the ground but can be seen

    in tracks left in _____.

    show
    snow

8. All the contestants are ready for our town's second yearly

    _____ derby.

    soak
    soapbox

9. They begin the race near Hanby Park and _____ down
    Snowball Hill.

    coast
    coat

10. As the race cars _____ the finish line, a race official
    waves a checkered flag.

    afloat
    approach

11. Clapping _____ through the crowd as the winner crosses

    the mark and slides through a _____ puddle.

    echoes
    heroes
    hollow
    shallow

Review and Apply: Comprehension

Name _____

Read the menu below. Many of the words contain the following vowel pairs: **ai, ei, ee, ea, oa, ow, oe.** Use the menu to answer the questions that follow.

The Corner Cafe

Breakfast
Oatmeal	$1.00
Pancakes.	$2.00
French toast.	$2.00
One egg with two strips of bacon	$1.75
Two eggs with two strips of bacon.	$2.25
Hash-brown potatoes	$1.25

Soups
Ham and bean	$1.50
Vegetable beef.	$1.50
Chicken noodle.	$1.25
French onion	$1.25

Beverages
Tea (hot or cold)	$.75
Coffee	$.50
Milk	$.95
Orange juice.	$.80
Tomato juice	$.80

Sandwiches*
Chicken salad.	$2.50
Tuna salad.	$2.50
Roast beef.	$2.75
Ham and cheese	$2.75

*served on raisin, whole-grain, or white bread with lettuce and home-grown tomatoes

Main Dishes
Veal	$7.50

a lean, tender meat full of protein and low in fat

Maine Lobster Tails	$8.75

three large tails bursting with plump white meat

Stuffed Pork Chops	$6.50

overflowing with our famous cornbread stuffing

Roasted Chicken Breast . . .	$7.25

thick and tender

Shrimp Boat	$8.25

eight large shrimp served in a boat of lettuce

---

1. Which soups have meat or poultry? _____

   _____

2. If you order shrimp for dinner, how many will be served? _____

3. What hot cereal is on the menu? _____

4. Which breakfast food costs $1.25? _____

5. Name three menu items that are made with chicken. _____

   _____

6. How are the tomatoes at The Corner Cafe different from those that might be served at

   another restaurant? _____

7. What is the least expensive drink on the menu? _____

8. What kinds of bread are served? _____

9. If you were to eat lunch at The Corner Cafe, what foods would you order? _____

   _____

10. Which two menu items contain *both* **oa** and **ea?** _____

Review of words containing vowel digraphs: *ai, ei, ee, ea, oa, ow, oe*

Review and Apply: Composition

Name _____

Below are nine important steps to follow in planting a vegetable garden. However, these steps are out of order. Write the steps in the correct order. Notice that the steps you write contain words with the following vowel pairs: **ai, ay, ei, ey, ee, ea, oa, ow, oe.** Finally, circle any words you write that have one of these vowel pairs.

Before digging, indicate where each row of seeds will be placed.
Put enough dirt over the seeds so they are covered.
Purchase the seeds you will need at a nursery.
At last, you've reached your goal—eat and enjoy!
Then use a hoe to dig a straight shallow trench in the dirt.
If not, drench it every seven or eight days.
First, determine what item you would prefer to grow. Will it be green beans, sweet peas, beets, or tomatoes?
Lay each seed in a line in the trench.
If the garden receives enough rain, your work is done.

_____

_____

_____

_____

_____

_____

_____

_____

_____

_____

_____

_____

_____

_____

_____

Vowel Pairs: OO, AU, and AW

Name _____

In some words, two vowels stand for one sound. The letters **oo** can stand for the sound you hear in the middle of **moon** or **book**. The letters **au** and **aw** usually stand for the sound you hear in **auto** and **saw**.

Read the groups of words below. Then read the sentences. In each blank, write the word that best completes the sentence. For sentences 1 through 8, choose words from Group A. For sentences 9 through 13, choose words from Group B.

Group A	because	auditorium	goose	awfully	August	
	looked	school	mongoose	foot	zoo	good
Group B	choose	cockatoo	audience	Australia	macaw	squawk

1. Last _____August_____, Carmen de Molina, the manager of wildlife at the city

   _____, gave an interesting talk about animals.

2. The meeting was held downtown in the _____ of my _____.

3. As Ms. de Molina spoke, we _____ at slides of animals from many countries. They included an animal from Africa and southern Asia called a mongoose.

4. _____ of its name, I expected it to be a kind of _____.

5. But a _____ looks nothing like a goose at all.

6. Instead, it is a furry mammal, just over a _____ long, that looks more like a small beaver.

7. A mongoose can jump upon a rat or snake and kill it _____ fast.

8. In fact, it is so _____ at hunting and killing its prey the mongoose has been taken to other lands to destroy large numbers of rats.

9. Ms. de Molina showed several slides of a beautiful bird from _____ called a cockatoo.

10. Though not as bright in color, the _____ is a member of the parrot family and can be tamed.

11. Some pet-store owners _____ not to keep them, though, because they

    _____ so loudly.

12. A slide of a macaw, a South American bird, really pleased the _____.

13. Bright feathers of red, blue, yellow, and green and a long pointed tail make the

    _____ one of the most beautiful birds in the world.

Words containing vowel digraphs in context: *oo, au, aw*

Vowel Pairs: *OO*, *AU*, and *AW*

Name _____

Read the groups of words below. Then read the sentences. In each blank, write the word that best completes the sentence. For sentences 1 through 8, choose words from Group A. For sentences 9 through 16, choose words from Group B.

Group A			
hooked	claws	good	raccoon
taught	paw	looks	swoop

Group B			
shook	crawled	paused	understood
audience	applause	scooped	food	zoo

1. Ms. de Molina _____taught_____ us about birds of prey and then showed a live hawk.

2. Because it had such long, sharp _____, Ms. de Molina did not take the hawk from its cage.

3. Excellent vision allows it to spot a meal from far away and _____ down upon it with lightning speed.

4. With its strong claws and _____ beak, the hawk tears its food apart.

5. Next, we saw a young _____ that Ms. de Molina had named Bandit.

6. It got its name from the black fur around its eyes that _____ like a mask.

7. Raccoons are _____ swimmers and often eat fish they catch in streams.

8. Each _____ has four long toes, and with the front ones, a raccoon handles objects almost as well as if it had human hands.

9. In fact, when Ms. de Molina briefly turned her back, Bandit _____ across the stage and grabbed the microphone cord.

10. The mike hit the stage with a bang, and Bandit hurried toward the _____.

11. Ms. de Molina _____ that Bandit was only frightened and not really trying to get loose.

12. She quietly followed him up the aisle and _____ a box of seeds and nuts.

13. Bandit remembered that sound from his caretaker at the _____!

14. He _____, then turned around and followed her back to the stage.

15. Ms. de Molina _____ out a handful of _____ and placed it on the floor of Bandit's cage.

16. Bandit went in; the audience, in amusement and relief, cheered the pair and gave a

    round of _____.

Vowel Pairs: *EW* and *UI*

Name _____

In some words, two vowels together stand for one vowel sound. The letters **ew** can stand for the sound you hear in **news** or **few**. The letters **ui** can stand for the sound you hear in **suit**.

Read each sentence or the words beside it. Write the word that best completes the sentence.

1. Crops that cannot stand freezing temperatures are well ____suited____ to the warm weather of countries located near the equator.

   sewer
   suited

2. Bananas, pineapples, and other tropical _____ are grown in South American countries such as Brazil.

   few
   fruits

3. Citrus crops such as oranges, lemons, limes, and _____ can be grown farther north.

   cruisers
   grapefruit

4. Southern California, for example, is cooler than Brazil and sometimes has light frost, but these times are _____.

   few
   flew

5. Florida, also known for its warm weather, is a leading producer of fruit _____.

   juice
   jewelry

6. Because fruits are so easily _____, they must be harvested with a great deal of care.

   brewed
   bruised

7. As a result, most fruit farmers hire fruit-picking _____ to do the work by hand.

   chews
   crews

8. This is slow and expensive, though, so _____ machines have been developed to shake the fruit loose from the trees.

   new
   nuisance

Words containing vowel digraphs in context: *ew, ui*

Vowel Pairs: *EW* and *UI*

Name _____

Read each sentence and notice the word in dark print. Use the sentence to help you figure out the meaning of the word. Check the correct meaning.

1. The tornado left tree limbs, branches, bricks, and glass **strewn** in its path.
    ✓ a. scattered   ____ b. growing   ____ c. dead

2. A bed, chest of drawers, bookcase, and night table are included in the bedroom **suite.**
    ____ a. set of clothes   ____ b. set of matched furniture   ____ c. closet

3. The **pewter** pitcher made a clanging sound as it crashed to the floor.
    ____ a. kind of metal   ____ b. paper   ____ c. liquid

4. After our camping trip, we hung the tent out to dry so that **mildew** would not grow on it.
    ____ a. moldlike growth   ____ b. grass   ____ c. dirt

5. Dad will **brew** a fresh pot of coffee when our guests arrive.
    ____ a. cook by boiling   ____ b. refrigerate   ____ c. throw away

6. Flies were a **nuisance** at our family picnic.
    ____ a. food   ____ b. butterfly   ____ c. something bothersome

7. On week nights, my **curfew** is 8:00, but on Saturdays I don't have to be in until 9:00.
    ____ a. mealtime   ____ b. television program   ____ c. time limit for being
                                                                      away from home

8. My pen pal, who lives in Israel, speaks **Hebrew** and English.
    ____ a. softly   ____ b. a language   ____ c. coin

9. My father got seasick while he was on a **cruise.**
    ____ a. large tractor   ____ b. ocean trip   ____ c. ranch

10. The television reporter showed a **newsreel** about the disaster.
    ____ a. short movie that gives news   ____ b. tornado   ____ c. camera

11. Next week, our club will **recruit** helpers to work at the school fair.
    ____ a. fire for doing poor work   ____ b. admire   ____ c. try to get people to join

12. The police officer turned on her siren while in **pursuit** of the speeding driver.
    ____ a. automobile   ____ b. a chase   ____ c. ticket

13. I **withdrew** fifteen dollars from my savings account to pay for the broken window.
    ____ a. added   ____ b. removed   ____ c. helped

14. Since I forgot to **renew** my magazine subscription, I am no longer receiving the magazine.
    ____ a. understand   ____ b. make new or good again   ____ c. listen to

Vowel Pairs: *IE*

Name _____

In some words, two letters together stand for one vowel sound. The letters **ie** can stand for the long-**i** sound, as in **tie,** or the long-**e** sound, as in **shield.**

Read each clue and the list of words. Find the word in the list that matches the clue. Write the word next to the clue.

1.	brother's or sister's daughter _____niece_____	die
2.	film _____	believe
3.	stop living _____	grief
4.	large area of flat land with few trees _____	prairie
5.	a taking away of pain or discomfort _____	dried
6.	to think that something is true _____	relief
7.	short _____	niece
8.	having no moisture _____	brief
9.	great sorrow _____	movie
10.	cooked in hot oil _____	fried
11.	happy, content _____	untie
12.	unfasten by loosening knots _____	satisfied

In the list above, notice the sound that **ie** stands for in each word. Write the word under the correct heading below.

ie as in **tie**	**ie** as in **shield**	
_____die_____	_____	_____
_____	_____	_____
_____	_____	_____
_____	_____	

Words containing vowel digraph *ie* in context

Vowel Pairs: *IE*

Name _____

Read each set of sentences and its list of words. In each blank, write the list word that best completes the sentence.

1. Marie Curie was a French scientist who, in the late 1800's,

    _____studied_____ radioactivity.

2. During the _____, *Lassie* was a well-known television

    show about a boy and his dog, a _____.

3. The *Mona Lisa,* a painting of a woman with a puzzling smile, is Leonardo

    da Vinci's most well-known _____.

4. Though most people think of them as vegetables, tomatoes are really large

    _____.

5. Making colored circles on cloth by tying it in tight bunches before coloring

    is called _____ dyeing.

6. A king, queen, and knights are among the _____ used
    to play chess.

masterpiece
tie
collie
berries
studied
sixties
pieces

---

7. Rhubarb, which is often used to make _____ and other

    desserts, is sometimes called _____.

8. A doctor may be _____ to become a surgeon after
    receiving four to five years of special training.

9. By measuring things such as blood pressure and heart rate, a _____
    detector may help tell whether or not a person is telling the truth.

10. Shetland _____, which are only three to four feet tall,
    were once brought into the United States as children's pets.

11. Because they offer more miles to the gallon than cars that use gasoline,

    some drivers want cars that use _____ fuel.

12. Groups of _____ began California's raisin business by

    planting vines around church buildings and harvesting sun-_____
    grapes.

diesel
lie
pie
dried
priests
ponies
qualified
pieplant

Vowel Pairs: *OU*

Name _____

In some words, two vowels together stand for one vowel sound. The letters **ou** can stand for the vowel sounds you hear in **soup, touch, doughnut,** and **should.**

Read the list of words below. Then read the sentences that follow. Write the word from the list that best completes each sentence.

should	various	youth	delicious
coupon	doughnuts	couldn't	tremendous

1. This summer, our neighborhood _____youth_____ group took a trip to Colorado.

2. For three years, we've been raising money by doing _____ jobs.

3. We made a _____ amount of money by having car washes every Saturday.

4. One winter, we sold _____ books giving discounts for businesses.

5. One fall, we worked at football games selling whole-wheat _____.

6. The doughnuts tasted great. In fact, they were _____.

7. We just _____ resist eating most of them ourselves!

8. We _____ have made more money than we did on that project.

Circle the word that best completes each sentence below.

1. Last summer, my (couldn't, (cousin)) and I had a money-raising project of our own to make money for the youth group.

2. We worked on my aunt and uncle's farm picking (cantaloupes, couple).

3. Aunt Louise said that for half price, we (could, country) buy the cantaloupes we picked.

4. So each day after picking, we carried and sold melons door-to-door, charging (doughnut, double) what we had paid.

5. Lugging crates full of ten or twelve cantaloupes is a (trouble, tough) job!

6. My (should, shoulders) ached, and sometimes I thought my arms would fall off.

7. After only a week, my cousin and I decided we'd had (enough, enormous) of that project.

8. So instead, my father taught us to make and can vegetable (soap, soup).

9. A (coupon, couple) of other youth group members took orders for the soup.

10. Because there were so many of us, we were able to deliver all the soup with no (trouble, tough).

Words containing vowel digraph *ou* in context

Vowel Pairs: OU

Circle the word that best completes each sentence below.

1. Our youth (ground, (group)) was finally ready for our trip to Colorado by mid-June.

2. We departed from Saint (Loud, Louis), Missouri, thrilled and eager to be on our way.

3. We were so (jealous, joyous) at having reached our goal, we began singing and clapping.

4. Other travelers on the road must have been (curious, courageous) about us.

5. Several hours later, we crossed the (Misery, Missouri) River, the second largest in the nation.

6. By the end of the day, we had traveled (through, though) the state of Missouri.

7. We spent the next two days driving through Kansas, which produces more wheat than any other state in the (counting, country).

8. We (would, wound) like to have toured Dodge City, the Cowboy Capital of the world.

9. But since it's in the (soul, southern) portion of the state, it was too far off our route.

10. On the morning of our (fourth, found) day, we crossed the state border and proceeded into Colorado.

11. We headed toward Colorado Springs to see the most (famous, furious) mountain in the Rockies—Pike's Peak.

12. Approaching from the east, we (cold, could) see its snow-capped, 14,000-foot peak.

13. We took a railway car to the top along with other groups of (toughest, tourists).

14. My favorite spot near Colorado Springs was Garden of the Gods, an impressive cluster of (enough, enormous) sandstone rocks.

15. Several days later in Denver, we took a (tower, tour) of the United States mint, a place where American coins are made.

16. The next week, after a day in the city of Boulder, we made (our, out) way to Rocky Mountain National Park.

17. Trail Ridge Road, the most wonderful highway I've ever seen, allows visitors to enjoy the high (mountainous, monstrous) country by car.

18. Later, while walking, we saw meadows filled with blooming flowers, (should, shoulder)-high banks of snow, and Rocky Mountain wild sheep.

19. (Through, Thorough) the ages, the mountains have been cut into many different shapes by wind, rain, and glaciers.

20. For me, the breathtaking views of the Rockies were the most (mischievous, marvelous) part of the trip.

Review and Apply: Comprehension

Read the story below. Many of the words contain the following vowel pairs: **oo, au, aw, ew, ui, ie, ou.** Use the story to answer the questions that follow.

    If you've climbed one mountain, you've climbed them all. "Not true," says Reinhold Messner, master mountain climber and the first person to climb the fourteen highest peaks in the world. A mountain climber never tires of achieving that satisfying feeling of touching the skies. It's an interesting test to climb nearly impossible and dangerous cliffs. The enjoyment that comes from being outdoors can't be denied.

    Though Messner usually climbs alone, it is good practice for most people to climb in a group. Then if an accident should happen, relief would be close at hand. Since mountain country is pretty rough, it's important to have the right supplies and equipment. Rope, ice hammers and axes, metal spikes, ice screws, and other tools are important to carry. Because the ground may be loose or icy and smooth in spots, shoes with heavy spikes are a necessity as well.

    Don't forget to save room for enough food in your pack, too. Dried fruit and a few nuts will give you a tremendous boost. Water, rather than juice, is the best beverage to take. But don't attempt to haul anything too heavy, or you'll soon be exhausted.

    Any climber would agree that the sport of mountain climbing is here to stay. And the more enormous the challenge, the more fabulous the thrill.

1. Who is Reinhold Messner? _____

2. A satisfying feeling that mountain climbers never tire of is one of _____
   _____

3. Why are shoes with heavy spikes needed for mountain climbing? _____
   _____

4. What are some good foods to carry while climbing? _____

5. Because accidents can happen, what is a good practice for mountain climbers to follow?
   _____

6. What two items of climbing equipment could you pound into rock or twist into ice?
   _____

7. What will happen if you carry too many heavy objects while mountain climbing? _____
   _____

8. Write three words from paragraph 2 in which the same vowel sound is spelled by the letters

   ou, oo, and **ew.** _____

Review and Apply: Composition

Name _____

Read the unfinished story below. Then look at the list of words beneath it. Notice that each word contains one of the following vowel pairs: **oo, au, aw, ew, ui, ie,** or **ou.** On the lines that follow, write an ending to the story by using at least twelve of the list words.

When my mother couldn't locate her diamond ring last summer, she really panicked. With our loyal assistance, she turned the whole house inside out. Even the neighbors took up the search. Finally after Mother sat down calmly to retrace her steps, the pieces of the mystery began to fit together. She last remembered taking her ring off when she was outside opening a can of paint. Not wanting it to get damaged, she set her ring on a nearby windowsill.

food	trouble	took	naughty
enormous	jewelry	handkerchief	through
group	afternoon	thieves	young
tried	raccoons	knew	few
pause	lawn	crawl	believe
caught	although	would	newspaper

_____

_____

_____

_____

_____

_____

_____

_____

_____

_____

_____

_____

_____

_____

_____

_____

_____

_____

Review of words containing vowel digraphs: *oo, au, aw, ew, ui, ie, ou*

33

Beginning Consonant Pairs: *WH, SH, TH, SHR*

Name _____

Two consonants together can stand for one sound. Some consonants that stand for one sound are **sh, th,** and **wh,** as in **shoe, thin,** and **wheel.** At the beginnings of some words, three consonants together stand for special sounds, as in **shrug.**

Read each sentence and the words below the blank. Write the word that best completes the sentence.

1. Fishing crews drag nets across the ocean bottom to catch ____shrimp____.
   (shrill, shrimp)

2. James carries a _____ bottle full of hot vegetable soup when he hikes
   in the snow.   (thermos, thunder)

3. Swimmers should be careful to avoid swimming in waters known to have

   _____.
   (sharks, shirts)

4. Because _____ have lungs, they must swim to the ocean surface in
              (whales, while)
   order to breathe.

5. Plant City was having a sale on _____, so Tomás bought ten bushes.
                                    (shrubs, shrugs)

6. Dad won two free _____ tickets in our school's marble-guessing contest.
                    (theater, thermometer)

7. In the Netherlands, farmers protect their feet from the damp ground by wearing heavy

   wooden _____.
          (shades, shoes)

8. Juanita couldn't find one of the tent stakes, so she _____ one from wood.
                                                        (whittled, whistled)

9. Do not put a wool sweater in a clothes dryer, or it will _____.
                                                            (shriek, shrink)

10. When the body needs water, it sends a signal to the brain, making a person feel

    _____.
    (thirty, thirsty)

Words containing consonant digraphs in context: *wh, sh, th, shr*

Ending Consonant Pairs: *SH*, *TH*, and *NG*

Name _____

Two or three consonants together can stand for one sound. Some consonants that stand for one sound are **sh, th,** and **ng,** as in **wish, with,** and **ring.**

Complete the unfinished word in each sentence by writing **sh, th,** or **ng.**

1. Joggi_ng____ on a footpa_____ in Standish Park today, I saw somethi_____ I'd never seen.

2. In a large open area, a woman was throwi_____ a curved, flat piece of wood.

3. Each time she flu_____ it, it would spin forward, rise into the air, and fly in a curved pa_____ back to her.

4. "What is that thi_____," I finally asked, "and why does it keep returni_____?"

5. "It's a boomerang," she said. "Each side of the curve is patterned like a wi_____."

6. "By throwi_____ it with just the right motion, a skillful thrower can catch it without movi_____ from the starti_____ point."

7. "Would you like to throw it?" the woman asked. "It doesn't require a lot of streng_____."

8. I gave it a try, but with a cra_____, the boomera_____ hit a tree and landed under a bu_____.

9. "I wi_____ I weren't so clumsy," I muttered with an embarrassed smile.

10. The woman smiled and said, "Keep trying. Wi_____ a little practice, a good throw is not difficult to accompli_____."

Review and Apply: Comprehension

Name _____

Read the story below. Many of the words contain the following consonants: **sh, th, shr, ng.** Use the story to answer the questions that follow.

A shellfish is a water animal that has no backbone but has many legs. One of the most valuable of these animals is shrimp because it is a popular food. Shrimp are found in almost every part of the world in both fresh and salt water. Most shrimp have five pairs of thin front legs and five pairs of back legs. The front legs are used for walking, and the back for swimming. Unlike most animals, if a shrimp damages or loses a leg in a fight with an enemy, it can grow a new one.

The lobster, another favorite shellfish, has only five pairs of legs. Four of these pairs of legs are thin, but the fifth pair is thick. The thick legs extend in front of the lobster's head and have huge claws on the ends. One of the two claws is heavy and has thick teeth that are used to crush its prey. The other claw has sharp teeth for tearing the food into shreds. Depending on which side has the heavy claw, a lobster is either "right-handed" or "left-handed."

1. Water animals that have many legs but no backbone are called _____.

2. Name two popular kinds of shellfish. _____

3. In what kinds of water are shrimp found? _____

4. What is the difference between the front and back legs of a shrimp? _____

   _____

5. Tell about two ways in which a lobster's fifth pair of legs is different from the others.

   _____

   _____

6. What does a lobster have on each claw? _____

7. Describe each set of teeth that a lobster has, and tell how each set is used. _____

   _____

   _____

8. Write five words from paragraph 2 that end with these letters: **sh, th, ng.**

   _____

Review of words containing consonant digraphs: *sh, th, ng, shr*

Review and Apply: Composition

Name _____

Look at the photograph below and imagine what it would be like to ride the roller coaster. Then read the list of words that follow. Notice that each word contains **wh, sh, th, shr,** or **ng.** Suppose that a television reporter is interviewing you about your ride. Answer the reporter's questions. Write in complete sentences, and use as many list words as you can.

whirl	shudder	dash	screaming	thump
whoop	shriek	finish	long	whisk
shiny	shrill	path	clang	racing
shook	flash	feeling	thud	winding

1. From the ground, what does the roller coaster look like? _____

_____

2. As you were sitting in the roller coaster car, how did you feel before the ride began?

_____

3. What sights and sounds did you see or hear during the ride? _____

_____

4. What was the scariest or most thrilling part of the ride? _____

_____

5. How did you feel after the ride was over? _____

_____

6. What could be done to make the ride better? _____

_____

Sounds of *TH*

Name _____

Two consonants together can stand for one sound. The letters **th** can stand for the sound you hear at the beginning of **think** and **this.**

Circle the word that best completes each sentence below.

1. My (moth, (mother)) and (father, feather) have been running (together, tooth) for (thirsty, thirteen) years.

2. They began running as a way to lose weight and improve their (health, wealth).

3. Mom said that when she and Dad took their first run, they were (bath, both) (breathless, broth) before they had gone around the block.

4. Dad said he didn't (thin, think) he had the (south, strength) to walk back home.

5. (Although, Arthur) they were discouraged, they tried not to let their first experience kill their (either, enthusiasm).

6. They kept going out, and gradually they increased the (leather, length) of their runs.

7. After a few (math, months), it was easier to (breath, breathe), and they could go (father, farther) and farther (wither, without) getting tired.

8. (There, They've) come a long way in thirteen years.

9. Tomorrow (they'll, their) run their (teeth, tenth) marathon.

10. (That's, This) a race of over twenty-six miles! Just thinking of it is enough to make me (with, wither).

11. I'd (rather, rhythm) stick with long-distance bicycling.

12. My (bother, brother) and I are proud of our parents, (though, thought), so we'll be (theme, there) tomorrow.

13. We want to be with all the (oath, others) who'll (gather, growth) at the finish line to congratulate the runners.

Words containing consonant digraph *th* in context

Consonant Pairs: *CH* and *TCH*

Name _____

Two or three consonants together can stand for one sound. The letters **ch** and **tch** usually stand for the sound you hear at the beginning of **chair** and the end of **catch**. The letters **ch** sometimes stand for the sound of **k**, as in **chemist**. The letters **ch** can also stand for the sound of **sh**, as in **chef**.

Read each clue and the list of words. Find the word in the list that matches the clue. Write the word next to the clue.

1. break out of an egg _____hatch_____		chimpanzee
2. person in a story _____		hatch
3. small ape known for its intelligence _____		parachute
4. skydiver's equipment _____		mechanic
5. a cook _____		hopscotch
6. person who works with machines _____		champion
7. winner _____		chef
8. jumping game _____		chorus
9. buy _____		purchase
10. light fixture that hangs from a ceiling _____		chandelier
11. group of people who sing together _____		character

In the list above, notice the sound that **ch** or **tch** stands for in each word. Write the word under the correct heading below.

ch and **tch** as in **chair** and **catch**	**ch** as in **chemist**	**ch** as in **chef**
_____chimpanzee_____	_____	_____
_____	_____	_____
_____	_____	
_____		
_____		

Words containing consonant digraphs from definitions: *ch, tch*; Symbol-sound association of words containing consonant digraphs: *ch, tch*

Consonant Pairs: *PH* and *GH*

Name _____

Two consonants together can stand for one sound. The letters **gh** and **ph** sometimes stand for the sound of **f,** as in **laugh** and **elephant.**

Read each sentence and notice the word in dark print. Use the sentence to help you figure out the meaning of the word. Check the correct meaning.

1. The feathers of a **pheasant** make a beautiful pattern of bright colors.
   ____ a. fish   √ b. bird   ____ c. automobile

2. Ken filled the pigs' **trough** with corn.
   ____ a. farm   ____ b. food tray for livestock   ____ c. dairy cattle

3. The excited child tore the **cellophane** off the new toy before his mother had paid for it.
   ____ a. thin plastic wrapping   ____ b. cells   ____ c. aluminum foil

4. My older sister says that this year as a high-school **sophomore** is more enjoyable than last, when she was only in her first year of high school.
   ____ a. principal   ____ b. second-year student   ____ c. sixth grader

5. I've been buying my favorite music on tapes because my **phonograph** is broken and cannot be repaired.
   ____ a. record player   ____ b. telephone   ____ c. device that takes photographs

6. Mom is unhappy because a **gopher** dug tunnels all through our backyard.
   ____ a. insect that bites   ____ b. underground animal   ____ c. freshwater fish

7. From time to time, a snake's skin will **slough** off, and a new skin will take its place.
   ____ a. drop; shed   ____ b. jump slowly   ____ c. change colors

8. Before she began painting, the artist penciled her idea on paper as a **rough** sketch.
   ____ a. perfect; ready to be sold   ____ b. colorful   ____ c. incomplete; without detail

9. **Dolphins,** which live in salt water, can be trained to jump through hoops and catch balls.
   ____ a. intelligent dogs   ____ b. mammals that look like fish   ____ c. seashells

10. I bought a bottle of vitamins at the **pharmacy.**
    ____ a. museum   ____ b. clothing store   ____ c. drug store

11. An **oceanographer** may spend much of his or her time working on a ship.
    ____ a. person who studies oceans   ____ b. person who studies weather   ____ c. pilot

12. During the first **phase** of life, a baby is helpless and must depend on others to care for it.
    ____ a. part   ____ b. wish   ____ c. search

Words containing consonant digraphs in context: *ph, gh*

Consonant Pairs: *PH* and *GH*

<u>Name</u> _____

Circle the word that best completes each sentence below.

1. The next time a doctor tells you you're sick, you might try (cough, (laughing)).

2. It may sound strange, but scientists are discovering that (orphan, laughter) can help patients feel better.

3. Dr. Frederick Goodwin, a (physician, phone), says that jokes give many people a sense of relief and give a feeling of being able to handle frightening situations.

4. Evidence shows that even if you're having a (rough, laugh) day, making yourself smile will really help you feel better.

5. Smiling, of course, is a (trophy, tough) thing to do when you're feeling sad or angry.

6. But when you laugh, a (physical, paragraph) change takes place in your brain.

7. The body makes and uses its own pain relievers, which are called (enough, endorphins), and you begin to feel better.

Read the list of words below. Then read the sentences that follow. Write the word that best completes each sentence. You will need to use one word twice.

physically	enough	triumph	laughter
cough	laugh	pharmacy	autobiographical

1. Norman Cousins, who once suffered from a dangerous sickness, says that laughter, in part, helped him in his _____<u>triumph</u>_____ over disease.

2. Just the touch of his bed sheets was _____ to cause him great pain.

3. He had an allergy to the medicine he was getting from the hospital

   _____.

4. In an _____ account of his sickness, Mr. Cousins tells of checking out of the hospital and into a hotel. With him, he took a film projector and funny movies.

5. "I made the joyous discovery," he writes, "that ten minutes of genuine

   _____ . . . would give me at least two hours of pain-free sleep."

6. _____, of course, is not the answer to every sickness.

7. It will not cure a _____ or heal a bleeding wound.

8. Good medical care is important when you're not feeling well _____.

9. But a good rib-tickling can be healthful as well, so go ahead and _____.

Review and Apply: Comprehension

Name _____

Read the list of words below. Notice that each word contains **th, ch, tch, ph,** or **gh.** Then read the story that follows. In each blank, write the word that best completes the sentence.

earth	nothing	inch	farthest	parachuting
chase	technique	enthusiasts	trophy	
photographing	catch	tough	school	

Air sports have been popular since the 1700's, when people first began hot-air ballooning. Today the sport includes cross-country races in which the pilot who flies the

_____farthest_____ and fastest wins. In another kind of race, the hare-and-hound,

balloon pilots _____ after a balloon that has been given a head start. The

balloon that comes closest to the "hare," or first balloon, wins a _____.

Another popular air sport is skydiving, or _____. In some contests,

skydivers are judged on their form and _____ as they make daring moves

while falling through the sky. Once, for example, a team of forty parachutists formed a box

shape by holding hands as they fell. Another kind of contest rewards parachutists for landing

on or near a six-_____ circle on the ground. Although it is

_____ to do, one German who jumps has hit the mark fifty times in a row.

Because landing is like jumping from a moving car, it is easy for parachutists to hurt

themselves if they land on rough ground. Good safety rules are very important to learn in

skydiving _____.

In hang gliding, fliers hang from a kitelike wing and jump off a cliff or steep bank. They

try to _____ upward winds that will carry them through the air. One hang

glider caught the exciting feel of flying on film by strapping a movie camera to the hang glider

and _____ the flight. While some hang gliders try to beat time and distance

records, most hang-gliding _____ fly just for the fun of floating high above

the _____. Says one hang glider who used to drive race cars, "There's

_____ like it in the world. The first time I saw it being done, I knew it was

the only thing I ever wanted to do."

Review of words containing consonant digraphs: *th, ch, tch, gh, ph*

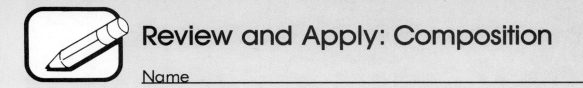

Review and Apply: Composition

Name _____

Read the paragraphs below. Then read the directions that follow.

      Wild elephants are in danger. In Africa and Asia, the human population has been growing. As a result, more and more people have cleared and settled on land where elephants once lived. The elephants are being crowded into small areas. But because elephants need large areas of land to find enough food to eat, their food supply is shrinking all the time.

      In addition, hunters anxious to make money are killing African elephants for their ivory tusks. The tusks, which may sell for over $20,000 a pair, are carved to make beautiful works of art. All the elephants in the northern and southern sections of Africa have been killed already. There are laws that forbid the killing of elephants in special areas where land has been set aside to safeguard them. But because ivory trade can make them wealthy, some hunters shoot elephants anyway.

We must find ways to make enough room for both elephants and humans to live. We must also find ways to keep hunters from killing elephants for profit. On the lines below, tell how we might be able to solve both these problems. You may wish to use some of the words listed below.

tough	population	forbid	limit
laws	protect	sale	wildlife refuge
obey	national parks	hunters	illegal
refuse	control	threaten	ivory trade

_____

_____

_____

_____

_____

_____

_____

_____

_____

_____

Review of words containing consonant digraphs: *th, gh, ph*

Vowels With *R: AR, ER, IR, OR,* and *UR*

Name _____

A vowel that is followed by **r** stands for a special sound that is neither long nor short, as in **jar, fern, bird, horn,** and **burn.**

Complete each unfinished word in each sentence below by writing **ar, er, ir, or,** or **ur.** Choose from the letters shown below the blank.

1. The h____ar____monica has been well-known in folk music since its beginning in the
    (ar, or, ur)

    early nineteenth cent_____y.
    (ar, or, ur)

2. Also called a mouth _____gan, the instrument was made in G_____many in
    (ar, ir, or)   (ar, er, or)
    1821.

3. P_____t of its appeal is its small size; it is easy to put it into a sh_____t pocket
    (ar, er, or)   (ar, ir, or)

    or p_____se.
    (ar, or, ur)

4. It's not a h_____d instrument to play; almost any boy or g_____l can do it.
    (ar, ir, or)   (ar, ir, or)

5. The harmonica is made of a wooden case with ten or more small holes. A brass reed has

    been ins_____ted in each hole so that it hangs freely.
    (ar, er, or)

6. By blowing or sucking air through the case, a play_____ can make two tones for
    (ar, er, or)
    each hole.

7. Larry Adler, an exp_____t harmonica player of the middle 1900's, became known as
    (ar, er, or)

    a harmonica st_____.
    (ar, ir, or)

8. He perf_____med in conc_____t halls and even gave one music writer an
    (ar, or, ur)   (ar, er, or)

    idea for writing a piece that Adler played with the Philadelphia _____chestra.
    (Ar, Or, Ur)

44

Words containing *r*-controlled vowels in context: *ar, er, ir, or, ur*

Vowels With *R: EAR*

Two vowels followed by the letter **r** stand for a special sound that is neither long nor short. The letters **ear** can stand for the vowel sound you hear in **ear, earth,** or **pear.**

Read each sentence and the words below each blank. In each blank, write the word that best completes the sentence.

1. When _____**Earl's**_____ science teacher told the class to write a _____
   (Earl's, Earth's)   (research, search)
   report on animals, Earl had no problem choosing a topic.

2. From the time he was two _____ old, Earl had loved_____.
   (yearn, years)   (bears, pears)

3. Until he was six, Earl's stuffed brown bear, Teddy, had been his _____
   companion.   (clearest, dearest)

4. His mother laughs when she recalls how _____ Earl always kept his bear.
   (hear, near)

5. "I couldn't _____ the two of you apart," she chuckles as she and Earl
   (smear, tear)
   remember Teddy.

6. "You once forgot to _____ your socks to school, but you never forgot to
   (rear, wear)
   take that bear," she says.

7. "I used to wonder if you'd continue to carry Teddy when you were old enough to grow a
   _____."
   (beard, pearl)

8. When Earl's mother _____ about the science assignment, she knew she
   (heard, rehearse)
   wouldn't be seeing much of her son for a while.

9. Each day after school, Earl brought home another pile of books and _____
   into his room.   (disappeared, smeared)

10. He loved _____ about his favorite animals, and in less than a week
    (learning, overhearing)
    the report was written.

11. Earl turned the report in a week _____ and _____
    an excellent grade for his work.   (early, nearly)   (earned, learned)

Vowels With *R: AIR* and *ARE*

Name _____

Two vowels followed by the letter **r** stand for a special sound that is neither long nor short. The letters **air** and **are** can stand for the vowel sound you hear in **fair** and **care.**

Read the list of words below. Then read the sentences that follow. In each blank, write the word that best completes the sentence.

air	hare	share	chair	mare
hair	dairy	nightmare	compare	stairs
repair	spare	hardware	millionaire	square

1. Milk, cheese, sour cream, and butter are products made from the milk of

   _____dairy_____ cattle.

2. I awoke suddenly last night in the middle of a horrible _____.

3. Though its body is bigger, and its ears and legs are longer, a _____ is frequently mistaken for a rabbit.

4. Mom was not amused when she had a flat tire and

   discovered that there was no _____

   in the _____ tire.

5. Before buying a set of tools, I want to

   _____ prices at three different

   _____ stores.

6. The _____ was generous enough

   to _____ her wealth with others.

7. A carpenter will _____ the

   broken banister to make the _____ safe.

8. The _____ gave birth to a beautiful

   colt with chestnut-colored _____.

9. A shape with four corners and four sides of equal

   length is called a _____.

10. Skiers ski down a slope and then ride back to the

    top on a _____ lift.

Words containing *r*-controlled vowels in context: *air, are*

Vowels With *R: EAR, AIR,* and *ARE*

Name _____

Read each sentence and notice the word in dark print. Use the sentence to help you figure out the meaning of the word. Check the correct meaning.

1. **Spearmint** has long green stems that are topped by white or light purple flowers.
   ____ a. sword-shaped weapon   ____ b. gum   ✓ c. kind of plant

2. Marcia studies at the library every evening in an **earnest** effort to raise her grades.
   ____ a. serious   ____ b. uninterested   ____ c. illegal

3. I stay out of Dawn's way in the morning because, when she is sleepy, she is a **bear.**
   ____ a. cheerful person   ____ b. bad-tempered person   ____ c. animal with fur

4. I enjoy reading my sister's funny stories because she has a real **flair** for writing.
   ____ a. flaming light   ____ b. talent   ____ c. dislike

5. When bicycling, I always carry a **spare** tire in case I have a flat tire.
   ____ a. extra   ____ b. punctured   ____ c. glass

6. I enjoyed looking through the old family photos that I **unearthed** in Grandma's basement.
   ____ a. discovered   ____ b. wrote   ____ c. buried

7. Fifth Avenue is one of New York City's busiest **thoroughfares.**
   ____ a. festivals   ____ b. main roads   ____ c. stores

8. Listening to music that is too loud can **impair** your ability to hear.
   ____ a. make better   ____ b. take away pain   ____ c. harm

Read each clue and the list of words. Find the word in the list that matches the clue. Write the word next to the clue.

1. very tired _____weary_____   rare

2. to practice _____   pearl

3. waterproof coat, umbrella, and boots _____   weary

4. fix _____   square

5. a precious gem _____   repair

6. not common _____   rehearse

7. very strong light or reflection _____ glare

8. a shape _____   rainwear

Words containing *r*-controlled vowels in context and from definitions: *ear, air, are*   47

Review and Apply: Comprehension

Name _____

Read the advertisements below. Notice that many of the words contain vowels followed by the letter **r**. Use the advertisements to answer the questions that follow.

FOR SALE

Coins. Rare Spanish gold and U.S. silver dollars. Will sell whole collection for $1,000 or make fair trade. Call 555-9668 before 6:00 P.M.

Guitar. Mason and Cleary six-string electric guitar with orange hard-shell case. One year old, excellent condition. $500. 555-8298. Ask for Chee.

FOR SALE

Bedroom furniture. Pine three-drawer chest, dresser, nightstand, king-size water-bed frame. $750. Call 555-4777 Saturday only.

Be prepared for winter. Used snow thrower, 5 horsepower, 24-inch blade. 555-3838.

Pearl necklace on 15" gold chain. Matching earrings. Worn only once. $25.00. See at 128 W. Witherspoon St.

HELP WANTED

Sales Clerk. Full or part-time position selling women's footwear. Apply in person. The Glass Slipper, 150 E. Kirby St.

Warehouse Worker. Fast-growing company needs neat, mechanical person to work third shift. Must be at least 18 years old. Apply between 9:00 A.M. and 4:00 P.M., 1543 Corvair Ave.

HELP WANTED

Nurse Aide. Third-shift position open for experienced nurse aide. Top wages and benefits. Call Ms. Martinez at Oak Park Nursing Home, 555-8798.

Hair stylist. Permanent position. Guaranteed hourly wage, paid vacation, paid holidays, insurance. Applications being taken at Clare's Hair Care, 146 E. Kirby St., 555-3898.

---

1. What musical instrument is for sale? _____

2. What four things are being sold in one ad? _____

3. What kind of jewelry is for sale? _____

4. Is the jewelry likely to be old or nearly new? _____

   How do you know? _____

5. How is the nurse aide job like the warehouse worker job? _____

   _____

6. What is *The Glass Slipper?* _____

7. Which two businesses are near each other? _____

   _____

8. Why are no telephone numbers given for the sales and warehouse jobs? _____

   _____

9. In which street name does **r** follow a vowel twice? _____

Review of words containing *r*-controlled vowels: *ar, er, ir, or, ur, ear, air, are*

Review and Apply: Composition

Name _____

Read the words and look at the picture below. Notice that each word contains a vowel followed by the letter **r.** Think of how you can put together at least ten of the words to make a story about the picture. Then write your story, underlining the listed words.

alarm	shirt	purse	earrings	scare
large	dirty	sure	disappear	careless
discover	store	wear	search	pair
mystery	stormy	tear	pearl	stairs

_____

_____

_____

_____

_____

_____

_____

_____

_____

_____

_____

_____

_____

_____

_____

_____

Review of words containing r-controlled vowels: ar, er, ir, or, ur, ear, air, are

Sounds of S

Name _____

The letter **s** often stands for the sound you hear at the beginning of **sun** or at the end of **nose.** It can also stand for the sound you hear in the middle of **treasure** or at the beginning of **sure.**

Circle the word that best completes each sentence below.

1. Where could you see dinosaur bones, an antique (sugar, suggest) bowl, and an old train?

2. If you guessed *(museum, music),* you are right.

3. You could spend many (leisure, loose) (hours, house) in one and (surgery, surely) not see everything.

4. An art museum (pressure, preserves) and (delays, displays) paintings, carvings, and other art.

5. The largest one in the United States, the Metropolitan Museum of Art, (includes, interrupts) over three million works of art in its (collections, collisions).

6. Here, you might see (vases, veins) from ancient Egypt, clay pots from (Asia, Mars), or paintings from present-day Europe.

7. A place such as this (carries, cars) a large amount of (issues, insurance) to protect against loss or damage.

8. (Becomes, Because) the price of insurance and other costs are high, some museums charge for (admission, intermission).

9. If you (vision, visit) a museum of history, you can see furniture, (tails, tools), and other things that show how people lived in the past.

10. Some museums even have old-fashioned villages or (towels, towns) from (various, vicious) times of history.

11. For example, Greenfield Village in Dearborn, Michigan, has ninety-two (blessings, buildings) and landmarks brought in from all (secrets, sections) of the United States.

12. Among these shops, homes, (miles, mills), and stores are a courthouse where Abraham Lincoln worked as a lawyer and the bicycle shop of the Wright (bothers, brothers).

13. Next door, at the Henry Ford Museum, you can see exhibits that show the (permission, progression) of transportation, power and machinery, and farming.

14. At a science museum, you can learn about machines such as (summaries, submarines) and (division, television).

15. Or, if you like, you can study plants, animals, rocks, and (Fridays, fossils).

Words containing s in context

Sounds of S

Name _____

Read each sentence and the words below each blank. In each blank, write the word that best completes the sentence.

1. Some museums have collections that cover only one _____subject_____.
    (subject, subtract)

2. The life-size figures of people at a wax museum leave you with the _____
    they are real.   (concussion, impression)

3. The Circus World Museum in Baraboo, Wisconsin, has _____ wagons,
    merry-go-rounds, and live circus acts.   (cactus, circus)

4. The Children's Museum in Indianapolis, Indiana, gives _____ to people
    of all ages.   (pleasure, pleasant)

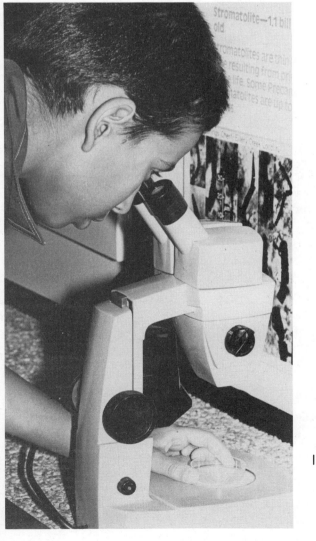

5. It _____ over 7,500
    (decays, displays)

    _____ and dolls that show how
     (toes, toys)
    children have played through history.

6. The exhibits show both old and new children's

    _____—from wooden toys of
      (tissues, treasures)
    the 1700's to today's latest space robots.

7. There are so many kinds of museums to visit,
    choosing only one could be a hard

    _____.
      (decision, division)

8. Why not start with a museum _____
    by?   (close, clothes)

9. There is _____ to be one not
              (sugar, sure)
    far from where you live.

10. If you don't have time to see all the exhibits,

    you can _____ go back to
            (airways, always)
    visit again and again.

Sounds of *TI* and *CI*

Name _____

The letters **ti** and **ci** can stand for the sound of **sh,** as in **nation** and **special.**

Read each sentence and the words beside it. In each blank, write the word that best completes the sentence.

1. When was the last time you tuned in to watch something on a television _____ station _____?

   station
   subscription

2. Chances are, while watching a half-hour show, you saw at least ten _____.

   commercials
   commission

3. Television commercials are the most important way of showing and telling about things for sale among _____ advertisers.

   motion
   national

4. One value of television commercials over other kinds of advertising is that people who watch can hear about a product and see it in _____ at the same time.

   action
   fractions

5. For example, you may _____ a Treasure Island Park advertisement more on television than on radio or in a newspaper.

   addition
   appreciate

6. On television, you could see the park roller coaster in _____ and hear the riders' screams of delight.

   motion
   notion

7. In _____ to the value of sight and sound, television commercials reach a _____ audience.

   addition
   objection
   information
   nationwide

8. Some commercials are aimed at _____ television audiences such as children, farmers, or sports fans.

   social
   special

9. As an example, think about this _____: If you wanted to sell toys, would you show them on Monday afternoon, Wednesday at midnight, or Saturday morning?

   satisfaction
   situation

Words containing consonant-vowel combinations in context: *ti, ci*

Sounds of *TI* and *CI*

Name _____

Read each sentence and the words below each blank. In each blank, write the word that best completes the sentence.

1. One way of advertising is to have a well-known or important person give

    _____information_____ about a product.
    (information, insulation)

2. A well-known rock _____ can make young people want to buy a
    (magician, musician)
    certain kind of clothing.

3. The word of a television star who plays the part of a _____ could
    cause people to buy one kind of shampoo.   (beautician, patient)

4. And who could know more about the best kind of cold medicine than a well-known

    _____?
    (physician, position)

5. Even the _____ of a favorite football player can rent cars or sell orange
    (infection, initials)
    juice and footballs.

6. In the United States, government _____ states that a well-known
    (regulation, relation)
    person must use the advertised goods at least one time.

7. Becoming known as the _____ product of some
    (glacier, official)
    _____ group or happening is another way of getting attention.
    (section, special)

8. People would like to believe that a toothbrush used by astronauts or Olympic athletes

    must offer better _____ against tooth decay than all others.
    (detection, protection)

9. One of the best ways to get people to buy a product again and again is to be sure it

    meets the customer's _____.
    (satisfaction, superstition)

10. By making a high-grade product and building a good _____, a
    (reputation, reservation)
    company can turn its own customers into walking advertisements.

Words containing consonant-vowel combinations in context: *ti, ci*

53

Diphthongs: OI, OY, OU, and OW

Name _____

The letters **oi** and **oy** stand for the vowel sound in **coin** and **toys**. The letters **ou** and **ow** often stand for the vowel sound in **cloud** and **cow**.

Read the groups of words below. Then read the sentences. In each blank, write the word that best completes the sentence. For sentences 1 through 6, choose words from Group A. For sentences 7 through 12, choose words from Group B.

Group A	wildflowers	point	enjoy	power	crowd	unspoiled	join

Group B	bounce	down	noise	without	avoid
	shower	louder	now	wow	pounds

1. Are you looking for fun? Do you _____enjoy_____ thrill and adventure?

2. Then come and _____ the wet and wild whitewater _____!

3. The starting _____ for our journey is along a quiet river bank.

4. Slide the rubber raft into the river and step inside. Don't forget to grab a paddle—this raft moves by paddle _____.

5. At the beginning of our trip, the river is quiet and smooth, so you can enjoy the view of the _____ wilderness.

6. Along the river banks, you may see beaver, deer, and _____.

7. As we float farther down the river, you may hear a rushing, roaring _____.

8. We are approaching our first set of rapids, and the sound becomes louder and _____.

9. The rushing water splashes and _____ against the rocks that form rapids in the middle of the river.

10. The raft begins to _____ up and _____ as we rush through the foamy water.

11. Don't stop paddling _____! We've got to keep moving fast to _____ flipping the raft.

12. _____! We got through that _____ dumping over, but you look like you took a _____!

Words containing diphthongs in context: oi, oy, ou, ow

Diphthongs: *OI, OY, OU,* and *OW*

Name _____

Read the list of words below. Then read the sentences that follow. In each blank, write the word that best completes the sentence.

out	bounce	voyage	choice
chow	now	join	point
avoid	around	moist	

1. Now that we're halfway through our whitewater river trip, let's paddle to the shore and have some of the _____chow_____ we brought along.

2. You have your _____ of sandwiches—peanut butter and jelly or lunch meat and cheese.

3. The person who packed the lunches in these waterproof bags was very careful. The bread is not even _____.

4. Our river guide says the most exciting part of our _____ is yet to come.

5. A huge rock in the river makes the water turn back upstream and can spin a raft around and _____.

6. In order to _____ that spot, we'll have to shoot through the roughest rapid of them all.

7. If you happen to _____ out of the raft, float on your back and _____ your toes downstream.

8. The current is too strong to swim your way _____ of it, so try to be calm and let the river carry you to the shore.

9. We'll paddle to that point and _____ you there.

10. Are you ready _____? Check your life jacket and we'll be on our way.

Review and Apply: Comprehension

Name _____

Read the groups of words below. Notice that each word contains **s, ti, ci, oi, oy, ou,** or **ow.**
Then read the story. In each blank, write the word that best completes the sentence. For
paragraphs 1 and 2, choose words from Group A. For paragraph 3, choose words from Group
B. For paragraph 4, choose words from Group A again.

Group A	grouchy	station	usually	musicians	choice	annoying
Group B	signals	confuse	explanations	sure	disguise	how	without

1   What happened while you were dreaming last night? Did you find yourself aboard a

mysterious space _____station_____? Perhaps you were the star singer with a group of

famous rock _____. Whatever you dreamed, it probably seemed very real.

2   Although you may not recall them the next morning, you have several dreams each night.

Each dream is _____ connected in some way to a thought or experience you
have had earlier in the day. It may be pleasant, adventuresome, or just plain

_____. Some dreams are so frightening or powerful that they can awaken
you in the middle of the night.

_____

3   No one knows for _____ what causes dreams. There are several

different _____. Some doctors think they are a _____
for troublesome thoughts we may be trying to forget. For example, if you are secretly
worried about something, you may dream about taking a test you have forgotten to study

for. Some scientists think electric _____ passing through the brain at night

_____ the brain. A dream, they say, is _____ the brain

tries to make sense of the signals. If you dream of being in a snowstorm _____

a coat, it may be because the covers have fallen off your bed.

_____

4   No matter why we dream, scientists have discovered that people who are not allowed to

dream during sleep experiments become _____ and nervous. We haven't

much _____ about what our dreams will be, but they do seem to be
important. So when you crawl into bed tonight, your body will be at rest, but your brain will
be at work. Sleep well, and pleasant dreamszzz

zzz

zzz

zzz.

Review of words containing *s, ti, ci, oi, oy, ou,* and *ow*

Review and Apply: Composition

Name _____

Read the article below. Notice that some of the words contain **s, ti, ci, oi, oy, ou,** and **ow.**
Use the paragraphs to answer the questions that follow.

Behind every good motion picture is a good film editor. A movie is not always filmed in the order it is shown in a theater or on television. All the scenes that take place in the same location are shot at the same time. If the beginning and ending of a movie take place in the desert, the scenes are shot one after another. Once the whole movie has been shot, film editors view it and arrange it in the correct order.

Usually, film makers shoot more film than is needed. An uncut movie might last four or five hours. Working in an office or studio, the film editors cut the film down to about two hours. They cut out parts that don't fit in especially well. Sometimes they discover parts that seem to drag. They speed up the action by shortening or cutting slow scenes. Editing a film may take several months. After all the scenes have finally been joined in the correct order, the film is ready for presentation. A film editor who has done his or her job well helps to make sure that the movie will be enjoyed by all who see it.

1. Who is the article about? _____

2. What do these people do? _____

3. When do they do this? _____

4. Where do they do this? _____

5. Why do they do this? _____

6. In one or two sentences, tell what the article is about. Include only the most important

    points. Use your answers to the questions above to help you. _____

    _____

    _____

    _____

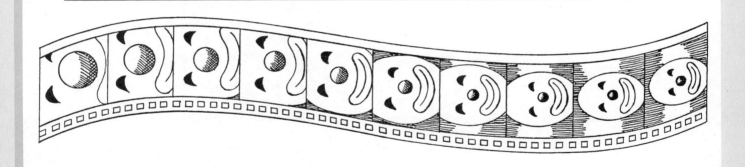

Read the story. Then, using the underlined story words, follow the directions below.

What lives in the ocean and can give you four hugs at once? An octopus, of course. Many people think octopuses are fierce animals, but they're really quite shy. When an enemy is near, an octopus may protect itself in a number of <u>ways</u>. It may hide by changing its color to match its surroundings. It can even turn two colors at once to confuse its enemy. Or it may <u>squeeze</u> its soft body <u>between</u> two rocks so it won't be noticed. If an enemy does spot it, the octopus can swim away by <u>shooting</u> water through a tube on its body. It can also send a liquid that looks like ink <u>through</u> the tube. The liquid makes a black cloud that hides the octopus and confuses the enemy.

Most octopuses are no bigger than an adult's fist. Some are very tiny, <u>measuring</u> only two inches from the tip of one foot to another. The largest ones are about <u>twenty-eight</u> feet long. The bottom of each arm has rows of small round <u>muscles</u> that can grab almost anything. On top of an octopus's <u>head</u> are two large shiny eyes. Good sight helps the octopus spot clams, small crabs, and lobsters. It catches these animals in its arms and may shoot <u>poison</u> into their bodies. The poison paralyzes the shellfish, which then becomes the octopus's <u>meal</u>. Only the blue-ringed octopus has poison strong enough to kill a person. Even though this octopus is tiny and shy, it's best to stay away from an octopus of any <u>kind</u>. So before you step into a bathtub next time, you may want to take a second look . . . just in case.

Follow each of the directions below. Number each underlined word only once.

1. Find three words in which two vowels stand for the long-**e** sound. Write **1** above each word.

2. Find one word that has the long-**i** sound. Write **2** above the word.

3. Find two words in which two vowels stand for the short-**e** sound. Write **3** above each word.

4. Find one word that has the vowel sound you hear in *joy*. Write **4** above the word.

5. Find two words that have the vowel sound you hear in *moon.* Write **5** above each word.

6. Find two words that have the long-**a** sound. Write **6** above each word.

7. Find one word that has one silent consonant in the middle. Write **7** above the word.

Assessment of phonics skills

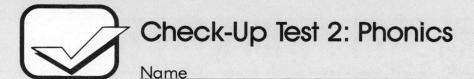

Check-Up Test 2: Phonics

Name _____

Read the story. Then, using the underlined story words, follow the directions below.

Have you ever been so angry that you "saw red"? Perhaps you've had the <u>experience</u> of "feeling blue." These <u>expressions</u> are one way that we link colors with the way we feel. Studies show that color has a <u>powerful</u> effect on our moods. When you see the color red, for example, your breathing, blood <u>pressure</u>, and pulse rate increase. This can make you feel restless or <u>excited</u>. It may contribute to your feeling angry about something that is already bothering you. Red, along with orange and <u>yellow</u>, can make us feel hungry, too. That's why so many fast-food restaurants are decorated in those colors. Wearing a red dress or shirt may also make you feel more <u>energetic</u> or perk you up when you're feeling down.

Blue, green, and violet, on the other hand, can quiet us and make us feel peaceful. They are good colors for a bedroom or any other room where you may want to rest or relax. A person who is tense or nervous may feel better by wearing one of these colors.

Our moods are not the only things that can change depending on the colors in our environment. The quality of our work can be affected, too. Experiments show that we think better and work at a more productive level when we are surrounded by colors we like. The next time you're having trouble <u>concentrating</u> on a task, take a look <u>around</u>. Are you <u>wearing</u> colors that distract you? Is the room painted in dull, drab colors? You may not be able to repaint the room, but perhaps you can wear different <u>clothes</u> or turn so that you <u>face</u> a <u>window</u>. By trying something different, you may find that a <u>change</u> leaves you feeling "tickled pink."

Follow each of the directions below. Number each underlined word only once.

1. Find two words that have a soft-**g** sound, as in *danger*. Write **1** above each word.

2. Find two words in which **s** stands for the sound of **sh.** Write **2** above each word.

3. Find three words that have the long-**o** sound. Write **3** above each word.

4. Find the word that rhymes with *caring*. Write **4** above the word.

5. Find two words that have the vowel sound you hear in *now*. Write **5** above each word.

6. Find four words that have a soft-**c** sound, as in *city*. Write **6** above each word.

Reading and Writing Wrap-Up

Name _____

A Famous Cherokee

The giant sequoia trees of California are named after a famous Cherokee Indian named Sequoya. He is also well known for something even more important.

Sequoya was born about 1760. He grew up in what is now eastern Tennessee, where his people made their homes. Most of the Cherokee were farmers and hunters, but Sequoya came from a family that was especially interested in Cherokee history and customs. Sequoya dreamed of recording this history so it would not be forgotten. But the Cherokee had no written language. Sequoya decided that he would invent a system of writing for his people. He worked on this task for twelve years, and finally, in 1821, he finished. In Sequoya's alphabet, there were eighty-six signs to represent the sounds of the Cherokee language.

At first the Cherokee refused to accept Sequoya's system of writing. They couldn't believe that their speech could actually be written down and then read by others. But Sequoya proved to them that it was true. A special meeting was held for the chiefs and leaders of the Cherokee. Sequoya had taught his daughter to read and write the alphabet he had created. At the meeting, she wrote down what the chiefs said while Sequoya was in a separate room. Then Sequoya read the chiefs' words back to them. Finally, they were convinced.

Now the Cherokee could learn to write and read in their own language. They could print their own books and newspapers. And they could prepare a written record of their history and customs to share with future generations.

Sequoya was honored by the Cherokee for his work. During the rest of his life, he worked to improve the lives of *all* Indians. A statue of Sequoya stands in the Capitol in Washington, D.C.

Social Studies

Name _____

UNDERSTANDING

A. Draw a line to connect each phrase on the left with the correct spelling on the right.

    1. a giant tree

    2. a famous Cherokee

    a. Sequoya

    b. sequoia

    c. Sequoia

    d. sequoya

B. Answer the following questions.

    1. Where did the Cherokee live? _____

    2. How did most of the Cherokee make a living in the 1700's?

       _____

    3. How many years did Sequoya work on his alphabet? _____

    4. Why did Sequoya want to create a system of writing for the Cherokee language?

       _____

       _____

    5. Why did the Cherokee refuse to accept Sequoya's system of writing at first?

       _____

       _____

    6. How did Sequoya prove to the Cherokee leaders that his writing system really worked?

       _____

       _____

    7. Where do sequoia trees grow? _____

C. Describe one way in which Sequoya was honored.

_____

_____

Reading and Writing Wrap-Up

Name _____

THINKING

A. Write the word from the box that means the same as each word or phrase listed below.

giant	convince	famous	customs	Capitol

  1. huge _____

  2. ways of doing things _____

  3. building where the government meets _____

  4. well known _____

  5. persuade _____

B. Answer the following questions.

  1. About how old was Sequoya when he finished his system of writing? _____

  2. What is the purpose of an alphabet?

      _____

      _____

  3. Why might it have been hard for Sequoya's people to accept a written language?

      _____

      _____

C. An alphabet is like a code. Make up your own alphabet, or code, and then write a message using it. Exchange messages with your classmates.

  _____

  _____

  _____

  _____

  _____

Application of thinking skills in a social-studies context

Name _____

WRITING

Imagine that written language no longer exists. You would not be able to read or write. You would have to rely on listening and speaking. Write a paragraph telling how this would change your life. What things could you still do? What things could you not do?

_____
_____
_____
_____
_____
_____
_____
_____
_____
_____
_____
_____
_____
_____
_____
_____
_____
_____
_____
_____
_____
_____

Application of writing skills in a social-studies context

Base Words and Endings: -ED and -ING

Name _____

A word to which an ending can be added is called a base word. When a word ends with one vowel followed by a consonant, double the consonant before adding **-ed** or **-ing.** When a word ends in **e,** drop the **e** before adding **-ed** or **-ing.** When a word ends in a consonant followed by **y,** change the **y** to **i** before adding **-ed.**

snap   snap**ped**   snap**ping**   save   sav**ed**   sav**ing**   hurry   hurr**ied**   hurry**ing**

Read the words below. Write the base word for each one.

1. clapped _____clap_____   5. liked _____

2. watches _____   6. hiding _____

3. carried _____   7. studied _____

4. cutting _____   8. teaching _____

Read each sentence below. Complete the sentence by adding **-ed** or **-ing** to the base word shown below each blank.

1. It was warm this morning, but the temperature has been _____dropping_____ rapidly
   all afternoon.   (drop)

2. I _____ carrots and lettuce for the salad while José began
           (chop)

   _____ sauce for the spaghetti.
           (prepare)

3. The dancers were _____ even though they were nervous about giving
                              (smile)
   their first performance.

4. _____ at her watch, Kiku _____ to get to the dentist's
        (Glance)   (hurry)
   office for her appointment.

5. Our history teacher has _____ a field trip for our class Friday.
                                 (plan)

6. Because Ms. Johnston needed a response quickly, I _____ to her party
   invitation by telephone.   (reply)

7. Phyllis _____ the tennis ball, but it landed beyond the court.
                (serve)

Identifying base words; Adding -ed and -ing to verbs in context

Endings: -S and -ES

Name _____

Often, new words can be formed by adding **-s** or **-es** to other words. To change many words, add the ending **-s.** When a word ends in **s, ss, sh, ch, x,** or **z,** add **-es.** When a word ends in a consonant followed by **y,** change the **y** to **i** and add **-es.**

laugh   laugh**s**   rush   rush**es**   copy   cop**ies**

Read each sentence below. Complete the sentence by adding **-s** or **-es** to the base word shown below each blank.

1. My neighbor, Ms. Huntington, _____studies_____ bumblebees as a hobby.
    (study)

2. She _____ bees in a glass-walled hive in her backyard.
    (keep)

3. Through the glass panels, Ms. Huntington _____ the bees as they busily
    work and communicate with each other.   (watch)

4. Sometimes Ms. Huntington _____ me over to observe the bees, and she
    (invite)
    _____ me interesting facts about their unusual habits and lives.
    (teach)

5. I learned, for example, that when a bumblebee _____ from its egg, it
    (hatch)
    _____ like a teeny white worm.
    (look)

6. During this early period of life, the wormlike bee _____ on other bees
    to feed it.   (rely)

7. As the worm eats and grows, it _____ through its outer skin and sheds
    it several different times.   (push)

8. The bee _____ this stage of life by spinning a cocoon.
    (finish)

9. After about two weeks, the bee _____ into the adult stage of life and
    (pass)
    _____ its way out of the cocoon.
    (chew)

10. Soon the adult bumblebee _____ and _____ as it
    (buzz)   (fly)
    begins to produce its delicious honey.

Endings: -ER and -EST

Name _____

In many words, the ending **-er** means "more." It is used to compare two things. The ending **-est** means "most." It is used to compare three or more things.

deep   deep**er**   deep**est**

Read the lines from newspaper advertisements below. Add **-er** or **-est** to the base word below each blank to complete the sentence.

1. Our everyday prices are even _____lower_____ than our competitors' sale prices.
    (low)

2. We strive to give you the _____ quality furniture money can buy.
    (high)

3. At Dealin' Dan's, you'll receive _____ value for your dollar than at any other car company.
    (great)

4. The Wilson Company offers the _____ customer protection plan in the business.
    (strong)

5. Our specialists are trained to use the latest methods and _____ medical equipment.
    (new)

6. At Accurite, we guarantee our prices to be the _____ in town.
    (low)

7. Does our bank pay a _____ rate on savings than yours? Check our rates.
    (high)

8. We are the city's _____ and most experienced carpet cleaning company.
    (old)

9. To find vegetables any _____ than Bean's, you'd have to pick your own.
    (fresh)

10. Shopping at Franklin's Food Store may be the _____ move you'll ever make.
    (smart)

11. Our automobile gives you more head room, better sound insulation, and a _____ ride.
    (smooth)

12. For the _____ photos you've ever seen, let Connelly Camera develop your film today.
    (sharp)

13. At Hagan's Delicious Foods, you'll get the _____ service in town.
    (fast)

Adding -er or -est to adjectives in context

Endings: -ER and -EST

Name _____

When a word ends with one vowel followed by a consonant, double the consonant before adding **-er** or **-est.** When a word ends in **e,** drop the **e** before adding **-er** or **-est.** When a word ends in a consonant followed by **y,** change the **y** to **i** before adding **-er** or **-est.**

wet   wet**ter**   wet**test**   wise   wis**er**   wis**est**   cloudy   cloud**ier**   cloud**iest**

Add **-er** or **-est** to each base word shown below.

1. hot + er = _____hotter_____
2. lovely + est = _____
3. late + est = _____
4. cranky + er = _____
5. sad + er = _____

6. brave + er = _____
7. thirsty + er = _____
8. wide + er = _____
9. lonely + er = _____
10. big + er = _____

Read each sentence below. Complete each one by adding **-er** or **-est** to the base word shown below each blank.

1. A microscope is an instrument that can be used to make objects appear _____bigger_____
    than they actually are.   (big)

2. The Sahara is the _____ desert in the world and one of the
                         (large)
    _____ places on earth.
         (hot)

3. My sister gets up _____ than I because she delivers the morning paper.
                         (early)

4. We adopted both puppies from the animal shelter because we couldn't decide which one

    was _____.
            (cute)

5. Marilyn waxed and polished her car until it was the _____ one on the
    block.   (shiny)

6. Last night's television special was _____ than the one we saw Friday.
                                          (sad)

7. Which of these two melons do you think is _____?
                                                (ripe)

Review and Apply: Comprehension

Name _____

Read the story below. Complete each unfinished sentence by adding **-s, -es, -ed, -ing, -er,** or **-est** to each word shown in parentheses.

People in the southern United States have a problem that is growing (big)

_____ bigger _____ each day. It is a hairy climbing vine called kudzu. It is

perhaps the (speedy) _____ growing of all plants, growing as

much as a foot a day. During the late 1800's, it was (carry) _____

over from Japan by people who (like) _____ its fragrant

purple flowers. They planted it in gardens and used it for (decorate)

_____ their porches. Then scientists discovered that the long

roots kept soil from (wash) _____ away during heavy rains. The
government gave away millions of kudzu sprouts and paid people to plant them
along roads. The kudzu grew . . . and grew . . . and grew. It (cover)

_____ trees, bushes, fences, houses, telephone poles, buildings,
railroad tracks, and anything else that was in its way. Today it clings to mile after

mile of forest and farmland and (threaten) _____ to choke out

even more. Cold weather is the only thing that has (stop) _____
the vines from spreading farther north. Since they can't do much about the vine,
some Southerners joke about it. One story says that kudzu creeps into pastures at

night and (catch) _____ sleeping cows. An even (funny)

_____ tale warns that if you plant kudzu, you should drop the
seed and run for your life. If you don't, the story says, the seed will sprout and
grab you before you can escape. There's not much truth to these tales, but in case

you're (plan) _____ to travel in the South, here's a word of
warning: Stay away from the kudzu, and don't stand very long in one place!

Review of words containing endings

Review and Apply: Composition

Name _____

With so much kudzu growing over the southern United States, there must be something useful that could be done with it. One scientist has suggested planting it on tops of buildings. The vines could hang down the sides of the buildings. This would help keep them cool in summer. What are some other ways in which kudzu could be used? Read the words in the boxes below to get some ideas. Add **-s, -es, -ed, -ing, -er,** or **-est** to at least two words from each box, and list your ideas in complete sentences.

fix	catch
mix	touch
miss	match
pass	scratch
crush	pinch
slash	stretch

fry	pretty
dry	sticky
bury	tasty
tiny	healthy
easy	fuzzy
carry	hungry

hang	grind
yank	thick
pick	fasten
long	gather
soak	cheap
feed	build

take	squeeze
save	trade
poke	shake
rake	stake
hire	slice
bake	scrape

rip	chop
dip	stop
dig	scrub
tug	snap
pop	knot
wrap	trap

_____

_____

_____

_____

_____

_____

_____

_____

_____

_____

_____

_____

_____

_____

Plurals: -S and -ES

Name _____

A word that stands for one of something is a singular word. A word that stands for two or more of something is a plural word. Most plurals are formed by adding **-s** to a singular word. When a word ends in **s, ss, sh, ch,** or **x,** add **-es** to form its plural. When a word ends in a consonant followed by **y,** change the **y** to **i** and add **-es.**

Read each sentence below. Complete the sentence by writing the plural form of the word shown below each blank.

1. People have been interested in _____birds_____ almost since the beginning of
   (bird)
   time.

2. All birds have feathers and wings, though not all birds are _____.
   (flyer)

3. _____, for example, are the fastest birds on land, but they cannot fly.
   (Ostrich)

4. Penguins, which have short, solid _____, use their wings like
   (body)
   _____.
   (flipper)

5. Many birds construct nests on the ground, in tree _____, or in
   (branch)
   _____.
   (bush)

6. Their nests may be made of mud, twigs, leaves, or different kinds of _____.
   (grass)

7. The nest of the smallest bird in the world, the bee hummingbird, is less than two
   _____ high.
   (inch)

8. In some species, the _____ of the male bird are more brightly colored
   (feather)
   than those of the female.

9. In a few, _____ are brighter; in others, both sexes look alike.
   (female)

10. Many pet birds, such as _____ and _____, are
    (finch)   (canary)
    valued for their beautiful singing voices.

Forming plurals in context: -s, -es

Plurals: Changing *F* to *V*

Name _____

To form the plural of most words that end in **f** or **fe,** change the **f** or **fe** to **v** and add **-es.**

calf   cal**ves**   knife   kni**ves**

Read the newspaper headlines below. Using the rule above, complete each headline by writing the plural form of the word shown below the blank.

1. City Cleaning Crews to Pick up _____Leaves_____ Next Week
    (Leaf)

2. Twin Brothers' _____ Saved in Daring Rescue
    (Life)

3. Judge Gets Tough on Shoplifters and _____
    (Thief)

4. Children Attend Holiday Party Dressed as _____
    (Elf)

5. Workers Demand Insurance for Husbands and _____
    (Wife)

6. Farmers Feeding Laboratory-Grown Grain to _____
    (Calf)

7. Knights-Chargers Game Scoreless in Both _____
    (Half)

8. Audiences Amazed by Daring Performer Who Juggles _____
    (Knife)

9. Bakery Donates 1,000 _____ to Food Pantry
    (Loaf)

10. Neighbors Form Lookout Group to Protect Property, _____
    (Self)

11. New Library to Include Revolving _____, Computerized Catalogs
    (Shelf)

12. Fairgrounds Pavement Causes Injury to Horses' _____
    (Hoof)

13. Firefighters Collect Used Coats, Boots, _____ for Needy
    (Scarf)

Plurals: Words That End in O

Name _____

Words that end in a vowel and **o** form their plurals by adding **-s**.

radio**s**   rodeo**s**   kangaroo**s**   igloo**s**   shampoo**s**

Some words that end in a consonant and **o** form their plurals by adding **-s**. Others add **-es**.

photo**s**	soprano**s**	hero**es**
auto**s**	piano**s**	potato**es**
pro**s**	burro**s**	tomato**es**
solo**s**	Eskimo**s**	

Read each clue and the list of words. Find the word in the list whose plural matches the clue. Write the plural form of the word next to the clue.

1. pack animals that look like small donkeys _____burros_____   rodeo

2. jumping animals that carry their young in pouches _____   igloo

3. musical instruments with black and white keys _____   shampoo

4. pictures taken with a camera _____   kangaroo

5. vegetables from which spaghetti sauce is made _____   photo

6. people who show great courage or do brave things _____   piano

7. vegetables that grow underground _____   burro

8. soaps used to clean hair _____   hero

9. contests in which people ride horses and rope cattle _____   potato

10. dome-shaped houses made of snow blocks _____   tomato

Read the list of words below. Then read the sentences that follow. Write the plural form of a word from the list to complete each sentence.

Eskimo   radio   auto   solo   soprano   pro

1. Marta's mother has a job selling televisions, tape players, and _____radios_____.

2. Our school chorus needs two _____ to sing _____.

3. Sled dogs are often used by _____ to travel over ice in the far north.

4. I like to watch college football games, but Jan would rather watch the _____.

5. As a hobby, my brother likes repairing the engines of old _____.

Forming plurals of nouns ending in *o* from definitions and in context

Irregular Plurals

Name _____

The plurals of some words are formed by changing the spellings of their singular forms.

tooth - teeth	child - children	woman - women	goose - geese
mouse - mice	man - men	foot - feet	ox - oxen

The plural forms of some words can be the same as their singular forms.

deer   sheep   fish   moose

Write the plural form of each word or phrase below.

1. eyetooth _____eyeteeth_____

2. cold foot _____

3. goldfish _____

4. grandchild _____

5. reindeer _____

6. ox _____

In each blank below, write the plural form of the word shown in parentheses. Then use the words you have written to complete the titles of magazine articles that follow.

_____sheep_____   _____   _____
(sheep)   (tooth)   (mouse)

_____   _____   _____
(fish)   (moose)   (foot)

_____   _____   _____
(woman)   (goose)   (man)

_____   _____
(deer)   (child)

1. "Do _____Mice_____ Really Like Cheese?"

2. "_____ Are Back in Lake Ontario"

3. "Grow Your Own Wooly Sweaters: How to Raise _____ "

4. "A Birdwatcher's Guide to Wild Ducks and _____ "

5. "Your Body's Chopping, Slicing, Dicing Tools: Your _____ "

6. "Mammals with Antlers: Elk, _____, Caribou, and _____ "

7. "Heroes of Science: _____ and _____ Who Changed the World"

8. "Stay on Your Toes by Taking Good Care of Your _____ "

9. "Checkers, Marbles, and Other Favorite _____'s Games"

Name _____

Read the list of words below. Notice that each word can be made plural by adding **-s** or **-es,** by changing letters, or by changing a letter and adding **-es.** Then read the story that follows. In each blank, write the plural form of the list word that best completes the sentence.

hero	pitch	loss	photo	fly	foot	handkerchief
team	Bobcat	bench	inning	fan	base	story

After eight _____ innings _____ of play, the two softball _____

were tied. On the scoreboard, each team had a row of zeros. The Tigers were up to bat, but

they were feeling gloomy. Earlier, Rita, their best hitter, had hit two grounders and two pop

_____. Helene, the pitcher for the _____, had a record of

ten wins and only two _____. Rita now faced Helene again, and her

confidence was low. Helene's first two _____ to Rita had been strikes.

Helene wound up for the third pitch and hurled the ball toward home plate. Rita eyed the ball

carefully and then belted it into a row of wooden _____ three hundred

_____ away. The Tiger _____ cheered and waved

_____ as Rita circled all three _____. She had regained

her playing ability and become one of their _____. The next day, the

newspaper carried several _____ about the game and half a page of color

_____.

Review of plurals

Review and Apply: Composition

Name _____

There are seventeen errors in the paragraph below. Proofread the paragraph. Draw a line through each error and write the correction above it.

Grand Canyon National Park, in Arizona, welcomes about 2½ million man, woman, and childrens a year. Most park visitor view the canyon, which is a mile deep in some place, by driving autoes along roads that go around the canyon from above. Some familys take a two-day hike through the canyon. Since the walk is over 20 miles, other visitores save their foot by riding mule into the canyon. The most adventurous visitors enter the canyon on the Colorado River, which flows through it. They ride in a large rubber raft or flat-bottom boat called a dory. The park has a wide variety of animals, including fishs, bighorn sheeps, mule deeres, and wild burroes. Evergreens and aspens, trees whose leafs flutter with the gentlest of breezes, grow along the canyon rim. No matter how they see the park, visitors to the Grand Canyon should take cameras and plenty of film. The scenery and wildlife offer hundreds of opportunitys to take breathtaking photoes.

Review of plurals

Singular and Plural Possessives

Name _____

To make most words show ownership, add an apostrophe (') and **s.** To make a plural word that ends in **s** show ownership, add just an apostrophe.

Read each sentence below. Complete the sentence by adding ' or **'s** to the word shown below the blank.

1. The _____morning's_____ thunderstorm threatened to close the sidewalk art fair.
   (morning)

2. The _____ sudden downpour sent people scurrying for shelter.
   (storm)

3. A few _____ exhibits were damaged by high winds and water.
   (artists)

4. All the _____ brightly colored covers were soaked and heavy with puddles.
   (tents)

5. The flowering _____ branches were stripped of their petals.
   (bushes)

6. The _____ face-painting exhibit
   (youngsters)
   became a stream of swirling colors as the paint washed over the sidewalk.

7. In less than an _____ time, the
   (hour)
   angry storm was over.

8. The _____ rays poked through the
   (sun)
   clouds and seemed to push them away.

9. The _____ tall steeples could be
   (churches)
   seen from far away.

10. Relief shone on the _____ faces as
    (exhibitors)
    they returned to their stands.

Forming singular and plural possessives in context

Irregular Plural Possessives

<u>Name</u> _____

To make a plural word that does not end in **s** show ownership or belonging, add an apostrophe (') and **s.**

Read the lines from bulletin board postings below. Rewrite each group of words, using **'s** to form words that show ownership or belonging.

1. Attention: Basketball Team of Women

    <u>Attention: Women's Basketball Team</u>

2. Breakfast Club of Men to meet Friday

    _____

3. Story Hour of the Children cancelled this week

    _____

4. class project of the Freshmen needs volunteers

    _____

5. Remember the birthdays of your grandchildren with this reminder.

    _____

Read the list of words below. Then read the sentences that follow. In each blank, write the **'s** form of the list word that best completes the sentence.

feet   oxen   women   geese   teeth   children   mice

1. Not including their tails, _____<u>mice's</u>_____ bodies are between two and four inches long.

2. It is your _____ hard outer layer of enamel that protects them from decay and from breaking easily.

3. _____ large, heavy bodies make them able to pull heavy loads.

4. Your _____ comfort depends on shoes that fit well.

5. Except for their legs and feet, _____ bodies are covered almost entirely with feathers.

6. Many _____ books have large, colorful pictures and few words.

7. The department store is having a special week-long sale on _____ dresses.

Review and Apply: Comprehension

Name _____

Read the list of words below. Then read the sentence clues that follow. Fill in the crossword puzzle by adding **'s, s',** or **es'** to the list word that best completes the clue. For two of the list words, you will need to make spelling changes.

wife   piano   canary   child   sheep   box
bus   brush   coach   pilot   fish   ax   watch

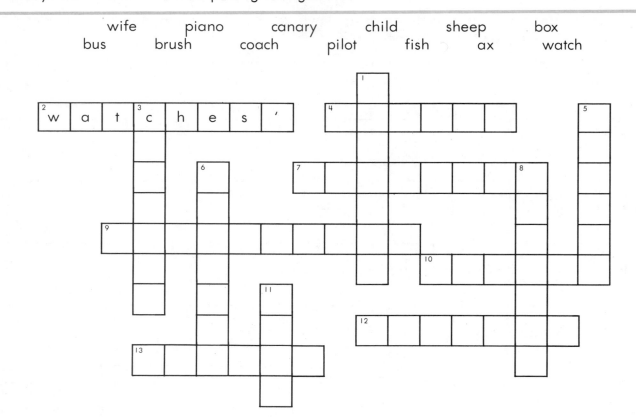

ACROSS

2. None of the _____ bands in the jewelry display fit my little sister's wrist.
4. Of the four couples, three of the _____ husbands had grown up in the same community.
7. My _____ name is Sunshine because its feathers are brilliant yellow.
9. The teacher learned all the _____ names in less than a day.
10. Two of the cardboard _____ lids were torn and did not fit tightly.
12. Because the _____ handle was cracked, the painter threw it away.
13. Most of the goldfish looked alike, but one _____ tail was black.

DOWN

1. This _____ keys are made of plastic instead of ivory.
3. The swimming _____ daughter did not make the championship team this year.
5. Twelve of the school _____ tires are being replaced with snow tires.
6. To work for an airlines, a _____ vision must be excellent.
8. That _____ wool will be sheared by the farmer tomorrow.
11. Which _____ blade needs to be sharpened?

Review of singular and plural possessives

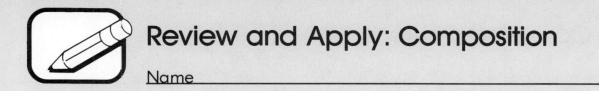

You and Grogan, your space partner, have just returned to your home planet of Urch after visiting the planet Earth. All your Urchin friends have gathered to welcome you and hear about your trip. Grogan has drawn a picture to show the Urchins some of Earth's animal life. Grogan's memory is not very good, though, and there are some mistakes in the drawing. Look at the picture and read the words that follow. Then, using the possessive form of each word, write a paragraph telling Grogan how to correct the picture.

| pony | moose | ostrich | foxes | cat | mice |
| geese | kangaroo | wolves | bushes | pigs | calf |

_____

_____

_____

_____

_____

_____

_____

_____

Compound Words

Name _____

A compound word is formed by joining two smaller words together: **rain** + **bow** = **rainbow**

Read the groups of words below. Then read the clues that follow. For each clue, join a word from Group A with a word from Group B to form a compound word that matches the clue. Write the word next to the clue. You will use each word in Group A twice.

Group A	bill	book	head	sea	water
Group B	sickness	ache	proof	store	fold
	line	shore	melon	mark	board

1. large bold type printed above a newspaper article _____headline_____

2. place to buy books, magazines, and newspapers _____

3. pain in the head _____

4. land beside an ocean _____

5. paper or thin card used to hold one's place in a book _____

6. water-filled fruit that is green outside and pink inside _____

7. large sign used for advertising _____

8. not letting water get through _____

9. wallet for paper money _____

10. illness caused by the movement of sailing on an ocean _____

Read the rows of words below. Then read the sentences that follow. Complete each sentence by joining a word from Group A with a word from Group B to form a compound word. Use each word only once.

Group A	flash	pass	straw	eye	suit
Group B	sight	light	port	case	berries

1. I took so many clothes on our trip, I had to sit on my _____suitcase_____ to shut it.

2. The miner's _____ shone dimly because it needed new batteries.

3. In the summer, many people eat _____ they have grown in their gardens.

4. Before taking a trip to a foreign country, you must have a _____.

5. My brother's new glasses have improved his _____ greatly.

Forming compound words from definitions and in context

Compound Words

Read the list of compound words below. Then read the incomplete book titles and descriptions that follow. In each description, circle two compound words. Then write the best compound word from the list to complete the book title.

Handbook	Baseball	Upside
Wildlife	Houseplants	Cookbook	Shortcuts

1. ***Favorite Brand Name Recipe*** _____**Cookbook**_____ An illustrated collection of popular recipes that have appeared on food packages for ages. (Everything) from a simple family snack to an elegant meal. 416 pages, (hardcover) book. $15.95.

2. ***The New 35MM Photographer's*** _____ 400 photos in color and black and white. This guide is easy to read and gives all the tips you need for successful picture taking, indoors or out. 1987 copyright, 240 pages. $14.95.

3. ***The New Complete Book of Collectible*** _____ ***Cards*** Fascinating, fun, and overflowing with facts about this great sport. Find out why these cards are such a hot item, why they bring high prices, what makes a card rare, and more. Price guide plus information on buying, selling, and trading. Book Warehouse special price $14.98.

4. ***How a Fly Walks*** _____ ***Down and Other Curious Facts*** Why is the sky blue? What are freckles? Is quicksand really dangerous? These and dozens of other questions are answered in this interesting and entertaining book. 256 softbound pages. $6.95.

5. ***The Encyclopedia of North American*** _____ A treasure for anyone interested in animal life. Alphabetically arranged listings cover hundreds of animals, answering questions about habits, breeding, size, diet, and history. Originally sold for $35.00, now selling for closeout price of $14.98.

6. ***Quilting*** _____ Now you can make your own beautiful quilts and bedspreads in less time than you ever dreamed possible! A wealth of ideas that save time for the beginning or advanced quilter. Includes photos, drawings, patterns, and patchwork designs. 8½ x 11 inches, $9.95.

7. ***Illustrated Guide to Popular*** _____ Provides all the details you need to know for growing plants at home or in your greenhouse. Covers many kinds of cacti, plus other flowering and non-flowering plants. Full of pictures, this guide includes color photos and artwork. $9.98.

Contractions

Name _____

A contraction is a short way to write two words. It is written by putting two words together and leaving out a letter or letters. An apostrophe (') takes the place of the letters that are left out. **Won't** is a special contraction made from the words **will** and **not.**

was + not = wasn't   I + have = I've   will + not = won't

Below are some people's comments about movies they have seen. Read each comment and the pair of words shown below each blank. Complete the comment by writing the contraction that stands for each word pair.

1. "If you _____ don't _____ love *Animal Sense,* you _____ got any."
          (do not)   (have not)

2. "For all those adults who think _____ outgrown fairy tales, *Puppy*
                                          (they have)
    Longstocking will be a real pleasure."

3. "*Space Train* is out of this world. _____ got to see it."
                                                (You have)

4. "*A Chorus Lion* is the funniest movie _____ seen in a long time.
                                                  (we have)
    _____ roar with laughter."
          (You will)

5. "*The Umpire Strikes Out* may be the best comedy _____ see all year.
                                                            (we will)
    The script-writers _____ been batty."
                              (must have)

6. "I _____ expect to be so enthusiastic about a race-car movie. But *The*
          (did not)
    Brake Fast Club will be a winner, _____ sure."
                                              (I am)

7. "You _____ miss *Smokey and the Band.* You _____
              (should not)   (will not)
    see a better musical this year."

8. "See *Toastbusters.* _____ far from crummy."
                                (It is)

9. " _____ seen lots of boxing films, and _____ tell you
          (I have)   (I will)
    Eddie and the Bruisers is bound to be a hit."

82   Forming contractions in context

Contractions

Name _____

Read the word pairs below. Then read the sentences that follow. Complete each sentence by forming a contraction from one of the word pairs. For sentences 1 through 8, choose word pairs from Group A. For sentences 9 through 15, choose words from Group B.

Group A				
would not	she is	could not	what is	can not
did not	I am	there is	she will	have not	must have

Group B				
could not	I am	she had	let us	
it is	that is	I have	I will	who is

1. Last week, when I _____couldn't_____ find Rascal, I was really worried.

2. She is usually well-behaved, and _____ no dog more loyal.

3. It _____ been while Mom was taking out the trash that she left the door open and Rascal slipped out.

4. We _____ discover until two hours later that she had disappeared. I was especially anxious because Rascal was due to have puppies any day.

5. "_____ the matter?" Sam Fenton asked as I ran up the street desperately calling Rascal's name.

6. "Rascal has escaped and I _____ find her," I explained.

7. "_____ sorry, but I _____ seen her," Sam replied.

8. "I _____ worry," he went on. "_____ reappear like magic when _____ hungry."

9. Then Mrs. Lynch, _____ Sam's neighbor, came out and suggested that we drive around town to look for Rascal.

10. "_____ take the pick-up truck," she said. "_____ parked in the garage. You get in it, and _____ get the keys."

11. I hurried into Mrs. Lynch's garage, and _____ when I knew my worries were over.

12. Somehow, Rascal had managed to get into the back of the truck. _____ snuggled down into a pile of old rags and blankets.

13. Nestled beside her were three newborn pups—the most adorable ones _____ ever seen.

14. Rascal looked up at me as if to say, "_____ glad to be found."

15. I, of course, _____ have been happier.

Review and Apply: Comprehension

Name _____

Read the article below. Complete each unfinished sentence by writing the contraction that stands for the two words shown below each blank. Then reread the article and circle all the compound words. There are thirteen compound words.

_____Who's_____ the wealthiest person in the world, and _____
(Who is)   (what is)
his or her income? _____ the tallest flagpole or the oldest lighthouse?
                    (Where is)
_____ find the answers to these and other interesting questions in the
(You will)
Guinness Book of World Records. While glancing through this paperback,

_____ sure to find some odd achievements. For example, Jay Gwaltney's
(you are)

record for eating trees _____ been broken since he set it in Chicago in 1980.
                        (has not)
Deciding he must be the $10,000 prizewinner in a contest, he ate an 11-foot birch tree.

Gwaltney finished the meal in 89 hours and commented that its taste _____
                                                                      (was not)
bad.

If _____ thinking Gwaltney is somewhat crazy, _____
   (you are)   (you will)
really be astonished by Michel Lotito of France. Lotito, also known as "Mr. Eat Anything,"

_____ eat things as tasty or tender as trees. Since 1966, _____
(does not)   (he has)
eaten 10 bicycles, a supermarket cart, 7 television sets, 6 chandeliers, and a small passenger

airplane. As if that _____ enough, he has also eaten a coffin! As one
                     (were not)

newspaper writer points out, _____ hope nobody was inside at the time.
                             (let us)
The Guinness book doesn't say why Lotito does such strange things.

If _____ like to earn a place in the Guinness book by beating Lotito's
   (you would)
record, don't try it. Its editors write that _____ published this unusual stunt
                                             (they have)
only since _____ unlikely to be challenged. They _____
           (it is)   (will not)
list records for eating anything else that could be dangerous.

Review of compound words and contractions

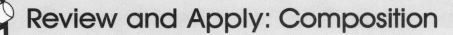

Review and Apply: Composition

Name _____

The paragraph below could appear in the *Guinness Book of World Records.* Read it and notice that it contains three compound words that have been underlined. Then read the list of words that follows. Notice that each word can be joined with at least one other list word to form a compound word. Choose words from the list to form at least ten compound words. Use the ten compound words in two short paragraphs of your own that could appear in the *Guinness Book of World Records.* Underline the compound words you write.

    In 1980, Jerry Mercer and Arden Chapman stood at opposite ends of the <u>Northeast</u> Louisiana University <u>football</u> field. Twenty times, Mercer threw a grape at Chapman. On the twentieth throw, Chapman caught the grape <u>inside</u> his mouth. It was a distance of 319 feet, 8 inches.

breath	back	paint	apple	down	tub
earth	cat	ship	pop	fish	corn
jelly	gold	skate	board	fall	worm
basket	tooth	snow	quake	ball	cycle
bare	grand	touch	fall	foot	wreck
bath	motor	water	taking	sauce	brush

_____

_____

_____

_____

_____

_____

_____

_____

_____

_____

_____

_____

_____

_____

Prefixes, Suffixes, and Roots

Name _____

Many words can be divided into small parts that have meaning. Understanding the meaning of word parts can help you understand the meaning of whole words.

A prefix is a letter or group of letters that can be added to the beginning of a word. Write the prefix of each word below.

1. unfair _____un-_____
2. rebuild _____
3. prepay _____
4. mistreat _____

5. dislike _____
6. imperfect _____
7. nonliving _____
8. incomplete _____

A suffix is a letter or group of letters that can be added to the end of a word. Write the suffix of each word below.

1. useless _____-less_____
2. loudly _____
3. rusty _____
4. breakable _____

5. restful _____
6. childish _____
7. illness _____
8. enjoyment _____

A root is a word part to which a prefix, suffix, or another root can be added. The root of *transportation* is **port.** Complete each sentence below by writing the root of the given word.

1. The root of *reporter* is _____port_____.
   (re-, port, -er)

2. The root of *prediction* is _____.
   (pre-, dict, -ion)

3. The root of *geography* is _____.
   (geo-, graph, -y)

4. The root of *introduction* is _____.
   (intro-, duct, -ion)

5. The root of *projector* is _____.
   (pro-, ject, -or)

Identifying prefixes, suffixes, and roots

Prefixes: *UN-*, *MIS-*, and *PRE-*

Name _____

A prefix is a letter or group of letters that can be added to the beginning of a word.

Prefix	Meaning	Example
un-	not, opposite of	**un**tied (not tied)
mis-	badly, wrongly	**mis**treat (to treat badly)
pre-	before	**pre**pay (to pay before)

Read the clues below. Add **un-, mis-,** or **pre-** to each underlined word to form a word that matches the clue. Write the new word in the blank.

1. not <u>expected</u> _____ unexpected _____

2. <u>understand</u> wrongly _____

3. <u>arrange</u> before _____

4. <u>pronounce</u> wrongly _____

5. not <u>aware</u> _____

6. bad <u>behavior</u> _____

7. <u>test</u> before _____

8. bad <u>fortune</u> _____

9. not <u>common</u> _____

10. <u>view</u> before _____

Read the sentences below. Complete each unfinished word by writing **un-, mis-,** or **pre-** in the blank.

1. It is not easy to buy food or pay bills if you are _____un_employed.

2. Finding a word in a dictionary is a good way to avoid _____spelling it.

3. While boating, it is a good idea to take the _____caution of wearing a life jacket.

4. Many toddlers attend _____school before going to kindergarten.

5. Fortunately, the driver of the automobile was _____hurt in the accident.

6. Because I do not speak French, I'm afraid I may have _____pronounced the girl's name.

7. Maria was late for school because she _____placed her umbrella and was looking for it.

Prefixes: *NON-, RE-,* and *FORE-*

Name _____

A prefix is a letter or group of letters that can be added to the beginning of a word.

Prefix	Meaning	Example
non-	not, opposite of	**non**living (not living)
re-	back, again	**re**write (to write again)
fore-	in front, before	**fore**warn (to warn before)

Read the groups of words below. Then read the sentences that follow. Write the word that best completes each sentence. For sentences 1 through 5, choose words from Group A. For sentences 6 through 10, choose words from Group B.

Group A	foretold	nonsense	forecasts	foretells	respin
Group B	readjust	nonscientific	foretell	rebuilding	reconsider

1. Long ago, people did not have the aid of up-to-date weather _____forecasts_____ on radio or television.

2. By watching nature's patterns, though, people were able to predict the weather. These patterns were often described in poems that _____ the weather.

3. One poem, for example, _____ the coming of good weather after bad: "When spiders weave their webs by noon, fine weather is coming soon."

4. It may sound like _____, but there is some truth to this old saying.

5. Because damp air absorbed by spider webs makes their silk threads shorten and snap, spiders must _____ their damaged webs during a damp day.

_____

6. As drier air comes near, the webs break less, are easier to spin, and do not need repeated _____.

7. Swallows adjust their flying height depending on the air pressure. When changing weather causes air-pressure changes, swallows _____ their flying height.

8. So, this poem to _____ weather came into being: "Swallows fly high; clear blue sky. Swallows fly low; rain we shall know."

9. Of course, predicting weather by _____ ways is not always reliable. But then, scientific methods aren't always failproof, either.

10. So the next time you see a beautiful morning sky as you head out the door with no umbrella, think about this: "Red sky at night; sailors' delight. Red sky at morning; sailors take warning." You may want to _____ taking the umbrella.

Using words with prefixes in context: *non-, re-, fore-*

Prefixes: *IR-*, *INTER-*, and *SEMI-*

Name _____

A prefix is a letter or group of letters that can be added to the beginning of a word.

Prefix	Meaning	Example
ir-	not, opposite of	**ir**responsible (not responsible)
inter-	between, among	**inter**national (between nations)
semi-	half, partly	**semi**circle (half circle)

Read the list of words below. Then read the sentences that follow. Add **ir-, inter-,** or **semi-** to a list word to form a word that best completes each sentence.

gloss	mission	resistible	circle	national
view	responsible	regular	annually	conscious

1. A person who cannot be depended on or be trusted with important matters is an

   _____irresponsible_____ person.

2. A paper that is cut in the shape of half a circle is a _____.

3. Something that is not average or not as it should be is _____.

4. News that tells about happenings that have taken place between or among countries is

   _____ news.

5. A hospital patient who is only partly alert, awake, and aware of what is happening is

   _____.

6. Paint that is only half as shiny as paint with a full gloss, or shine, is

   _____ paint.

7. If you make trips to your dentist's office every six months, you visit him or her

   _____.

8. If you have an overwhelming desire to eat lemons every night at midnight, you have an

   _____ urge to eat sour foods.

9. A break between two parts of a concert, play, or other performance is an

   _____.

10. A meeting between people in which one person asks for information from the other is an

   _____.

Prefixes: *DIS-*, *EN-*, and *POST-*

Name _____

A prefix is a letter or group of letters that can be added to the beginning of a word.

Prefix	Meaning	Example
dis-	not, opposite of	**dis**like (not like)
en-	in, into	**en**trust (trust in)
post-	after, later, behind	**post**war (after war)

Read each clue and the list of words. Write the word from the list that matches the clue.

1. the opposite of "put something together" _____disassemble_____   postwar

2. to place in an unsafe situation _____   enclose

3. a note added to the end of a friendly letter _____   discontented

4. to close in, surround _____   disassemble

5. not happy _____   postscript

6. involve _____   disappear

7. after a war _____   entangle

8. become invisible or unable to be seen _____   endanger

Read the base words below and notice that **dis-** or **en-** can be added to each one. Then read the paragraphs that follow. Complete the sentences in each paragraph by writing the same base word in both blanks and correctly adding **dis-** or **en-** to each word.

able   closed   courage

1.   After a witness _____disclosed_____ information about the crime, police went to

the scene. An officer dusted for fingerprints and _____ the evidence in
a large bag.

2.   Although Dad tried to _____ me from playing football, he let me

decide about joining the team. He still fears I may be hurt, but he does _____
me to play my best.

3.   Polio can _____ a person by destroying nerves and causing muscles

to become paralyzed. Fortunately, a vaccine will _____ a person to
develop antibodies that fight against and prevent polio.

Prefixes: *IN-*, *SUB-*, and *BI-*

Name _____

A prefix is a letter or group of letters that can be added to the beginning of a word.

Prefix	Meaning	Example
in-	not, opposite of	**in**complete (not complete)
sub-	under, below	**sub**marine (under water)
bi-	two	**bi**cycle (two wheels)

Read the list of words below. Then read the lines from advertisements that follow. Add **in-**, **sub-**, or **bi-** to a list word to form a word that completes each sentence. The new word should have the same meaning as the words shown below the blank.

standard	freezing	digestion	expensive
focal	cycle	visible	weekly

1. Dr. Ken C. Better will fit you with contacts, a pair of reading glasses, or

    _____ bifocal _____ glasses quick as a wink!
    (for seeing
    both near and far)

2. Just two teaspoons of Yummy Tummy will cure your _____ faster than
    you can say "oink."   (stomachache)

3. Buy Armor Auto Shine today. It's like putting an _____ screen of
    protection on your car.   (unable to be seen)

4. Best of all, a telephone from Wright Connections is so _____ you'll want
    to buy two of them!   (not costly)

5. When you buy windows from The Glass House, you get the best! If you buy windows

    anywhere else, you may be accepting a _____ product.
                                          (below average)

6. Believe it or not, this _____ from Wheely Small, Inc. folds to a small
                            (two-wheeled vehicle)
    carrying size in less than twenty seconds.

7. *Hollywood Happenings* will arrive in your mailbox _____. You'll have
                                                       (every fourteen days)
    time to read each copy from cover to cover before a new one arrives.

8. A wool-lined coat from Cloaks for Waggers will keep your fuzzy friend warm even in

    _____ temperatures.
    (below 32° F.)

Prefixes: *IM-, OVER-,* and *TRI-*

Name _____

A prefix is a letter or group of letters that can be added to the beginning of a word.

Prefix	Meaning	Example
im-	not, opposite of	**im**perfect (not perfect)
over-	too much	**over**eat (eat too much)
tri-	three	**tri**angle (three angles)

Read the sentences below. Complete each unfinished word by writing **im-, over-,** or **tri-** in the blank.

1. I entered Jansen's Department Store and headed through the narrow, ____over____crowded aisles toward the toy department.

2. "I bought this _____cycle here yesterday," I said to the department manager. "However, there are some things wrong with it."

3. "When I put the parts together," I went on, "the _____angular seat did not fit."

4. "Besides that, the box shows _____color streamers hanging from the ends of the handlebars. But there weren't any in the box."

5. "Anything else?" the manager snapped rather _____patiently.

6. "Yes," I continued, feeling slightly annoyed. "I believe I was also _____charged."

7. For a moment, the manager looked as though she might leap over the counter at me. Then

   she took a deep breath and said, "I'm sorry, ma'am. I didn't mean to be _____polite."

8. "It's been an _____possible day," she quickly explained. "First I _____slept and was late for work."

9. "At lunchtime my car _____heated, and I had to walk two miles to a service station."

10. "When I finally got back to work, my head sales clerk went home ill. Now the other clerk

    is saying that she's _____worked."

11. "I guess an _____perfect tricycle doesn't make your day any better," I said.

12. "No, but it's _____proper to take my troubles out on you," she said with an apologizing smile. "Wait here, and I'll get another tricycle from the back room."

13. When she returned with a fully assembled tricycle, my face brightened. "I don't look

    forward to customer complaints," she said. "But the _____joyed look on your face has changed my day from bad to better."

Forming words with prefixes in context: *im-, over-, tri-*

Prefixes: *IN-*, *CO-*, and *MID-*

Name _____

A prefix is a letter or group of letters that can be added to the beginning of a word.

Prefix	Meaning	Example
in-	in, into	**in**take (take in)
co-	with, together	**co**pilot (pilot together)
mid-	middle	**mid**night (middle of night)

Read the list of words below. Then read the sentences that follow. In each blank, write the word from the list that best completes the sentence. You should use one word twice.

coauthors	in	June	Wednesday
July	into	with	middle
incoming	live	noon	look

1. If you live at the midpoint of a city block, you live at or near the _____middle_____ of the block.

2. When you pick up the receiver of a ringing telephone, you are answering an _____ phone call.

3. If you have a midyear birthday, your birthday is in _____ or _____.

4. To cooperate with someone means to work or get along _____ him or her.

5. If you have arranged to see a doctor at midday, you should be at the doctor's office by _____.

6. To exist means to "live," so the word *coexist* means to "_____ _____."

7. To indent the first line of a paragraph means to set it _____ from the left side.

8. Two people who write a book together are _____.

9. If you belong to a club that meets midweek, the club meetings are held on _____.

10. *Spect* is a word part that means "look," so the word *inspect* means to "_____ _____."

Review and Apply: Comprehension

Name _____

The newspaper headlines below have words with prefixes. Read the headlines. Then answer the questions that follow.

Subfreezing Temperatures Endanger Bicyclists; Midwinter Race Postponed

Two Coworkers Discover Impurities in Milk; 3,000 Gallons Recalled

Nonprofit Cancer-Research Organization Holds Semiannual Fund-Raising Carnival

Misprinted Forecast Calls for 10 Feet of Snow in Miami

Association of International Scientists Hopes to Uncover Mystery of Bermuda Triangle

Illinois Workers' Income Up This Year; Unemployment Down

Overweight Postoperative Patients Develop Irregular Heartbeats

Homeowners Take Precautions Against Invisible Radon Gas

1. Did heart trouble appear in certain people before or after surgery? _____

   What might such people do to avoid the trouble? _____

2. What Florida city had an odd weather prediction? _____ Why was it

   odd? _____

3. To what group might an African chemist, a European geologist, and an Asian biologist all

   belong? _____

   What area of the world will this group be studying? _____

4. The weather caused what sporting event to be moved to a later date? _____

   _____ Why? _____

5. Were most people in Chicago richer or poorer this year than last? _____

6. What group is holding a twice-yearly event? _____

   What is the purpose of the event? _____

7. What is radon? _____ Is it dangerous to people?

   _____ Where might radon be found? _____

8. What problem occurred at a dairy? _____

   Who found the problem? _____ What did the dairy do about the

   problem? _____

9. Which prefix has two different meanings and appears twice in the headlines? _____

Review of words with prefixes

Review and Apply: Composition

Name _____

Members of the school board in your town are thinking of making school days shorter by making the school year longer. Instead of going to school from 9:00 A.M. to 3:30 P.M., September through mid-June, you would go from 8:30 A.M. to 12:00 noon, all year round. The school board has agreed to listen to students' opinions on the matter. Your class is against the idea. They have elected you to be their spokesperson. Write a paragraph or more telling the school board why the school year should not be changed. Use at least eight of the words below or eight words of your own that have prefixes.

nonsense	reconsider	ineffective	substandard	unfair
misjudge	foresee	disagree	encourage	impossible
overworked	irresponsible	cooperate	indoors midyear	predict

_____

_____

_____

_____

_____

_____

_____

_____

_____

_____

_____

_____

_____

_____

_____

_____

_____

_____

Review of words with prefixes

Suffixes: -ENCE, -IVE, and -FUL

Name _____

A suffix is a letter or group of letters that can be added to the end of a word.

Suffix	Meaning	Example
-ence	state or condition of being	sil**ence** (state or condition of being silent)
-ive	having, tending to	expens**ive** (having expense)
-ful	full of	rest**ful** (full of rest)

Read each clue and the list of words. Write the word from the list that matches the clue.

1. state of being unlike others _____difference_____   frightful

2. full of hurt and aching _____   attractive

3. tending to cost a great deal _____   interference

4. having the power to draw attention _____   difference

5. full of terror _____   painful

6. the condition of getting in the way of something _____   adhesive

7. state of waiting calmly _____   forgetful

8. having the ability to adhere or be sticky _____   expensive

9. act of carrying out someone's orders _____   patience

10. full of not remembering _____   obedience

Read the list of words below. Then read the sentences that follow. Write the word from the list that best completes each sentence.

intelligence	reflective	careful	absence	powerful

1. Although I still suffered from a cold, I returned to school after an _____absence_____ of three days.

2. Coyotes, wolves, and foxes have _____ jaws that can close on their prey like a steel trap.

3. Eva wrapped her bicycle with _____ tape so it would be easy to see when she carried newspapers after dark.

4. Chimpanzees, known for their _____, are able to learn a few words and signs that allow them to "talk" with people.

5. Dad warned the movers to be _____ when they packed the antique china.

Suffixes: -Y, -ER, and -HOOD

Name _____

A suffix is a letter or group of letters that can be added to the end of a word.

Suffix	Meaning	Example
-y	tending to, having	rust**y** (tending to or having rust)
-er	person who, thing that	teach**er** (person who teaches)
-hood	state or condition of being	child**hood** (state of being a child)

Read the newspaper headlines below. Complete each unfinished word by writing **-y, -er,** or **-hood** in the blank.

1. Chilly_____, Frost_____ Weather Damages Fruit Farm_____s' Trees

2. Court Finds Bank_____ Guilt_____ of Dishonest_____

3. Box_____ Remembers Boy_____ Dream of Becoming a Prize-fight_____

4. New Computer Print_____ Makes Letter-Writing Speed_____

5. Factory Says New Toast_____ May Have Fault_____ Heat_____ Wires

6. Island_____s Upset About Dumping of Garbage, Dirt_____-Tasting Water

7. Children's Theater Perform_____s Make Child_____ Stories Come Alive

8. Truck_____ Enjoys Life on the Road as Well as Mother_____

9. Teach_____ Saves Camp_____s from Storm_____ Mountain Weather

10. Research_____ Links Child_____ Sickness to Salt_____ Foods

11. Men, Women over 25 Feel Better Prepared for Duties of Parent_____

12. Neighbor_____ Holds Garage Sale to Aid Little League Play_____s

Suffixes: -ATION, -AL, and -ISH

Name _____

A suffix is a letter or group of letters that can be added to the end of a word.

Suffix	Meaning	Example
-ation	state of condition of being	transport**ation** (state of being transported)
-al	relating to	natur**al** (relating to nature)
-ish	like	child**ish** (childlike)

Read the list of words below. Then read the sentences that follow. Write the word from the list that best completes each sentence.

continual	reddish	information	explanation	comical
combination	reservation	musical	selfish	stylish

1. Before handing out our homework, Mrs. Ludington gave the class an

   _____explanation_____ of how to multiply numbers.

2. I really enjoy singing in the school chorus even though I have never had any

   _____ training.

3. The setting sun gave the cloudy sky a _____ appearance.

4. In order to be sure that we would have a room at the hotel, Mom made a

   _____ before we arrived.

5. The _____ washing of waves against the shore caused land around the lake to slowly wear away.

6. Because Jeff thought mostly of himself and rarely offered to help others, his classmates

   thought of him as a _____ person.

7. Because my mother likes pepperoni and I like mushrooms, we ordered a pizza with a

   _____ of the two toppings.

8. Clothing and fashion are important to Mr. Weber, so he always wears very

   _____ clothes.

9. We laughed at the actor's _____ part in which he acted like a hound dog in a veterinarian's office.

10. At the library, Wren found books, two magazines, and a tape that gave her

    _____ for her report on penguins.

Using words with suffixes in context: -ation, -al, -ish

Suffixes: -EN, -LESS, and -MENT

Name _____

A suffix is a letter or group of letters that can be added to the end of a word.

Suffix	Meaning	Example
-en	made of; to make or become	wool**en** (made of wool); bright**en** (to make bright)
-less	without	use**less** (without use)
-ment	state or condition of being	enjoy**ment** (state or condition of enjoying)

Read the clues below. Add **-en, -less,** or **-ment** to each underlined word to form a word that matches the clue. For three of the underlined words, you will need to drop the letters **ed** or **d** before adding a suffix.

1. made of <u>silk</u> _____ silken _____

2. state of being <u>punished</u> _____

3. without <u>taste</u> _____

4. state of being <u>excited</u> _____

5. make <u>dark</u> _____

6. made of <u>gold</u> _____

7. without <u>sleep</u> _____

8. state of being <u>amused</u> _____

9. make one feel <u>fright</u> _____

10. without <u>hope</u> _____

Read the sentences below. Complete each unfinished word by writing **-en, -less,** or **-ment** in the blank.

1. Pablo used a soft cloth to polish the wood_____ en _____ body of his violin.

2. Landing an astronaut on the moon was a great achieve_____ in the history of space flight.

3. I could tell from the thin, bony body that the home_____ dog hadn't eaten or been cared for in a long time.

4. New curtains and a fresh coat of paint will bright_____ the dull living room.

5. You can imagine my astonish_____ when I opened the closet door and my friends jumped out, yelling, "Surprise!"

Suffixes: *-ION*, *-TION*, *-ITY*, and *-IBLE*

Name _____

A suffix is a letter or group of letters that can be added to the end of a word.

Suffix	Meaning	Example
-ion, -tion	state or condition of being	act**ion** (state or condition of acting)
-ity	quality of being	visibil**ity** (quality of being visible)
-ible	able	revers**ible** (able to be reversed)

Read the list of words below. Then read the sentences that follow. Write the word from the list that best completes each sentence.

ability	infection	flexible	collapsible	introduction
necessity	description	generosity	collection	invisible

1. It is important to keep a cut or open wound clean in order to prevent _____infection_____.

2. Although the sun's most damaging rays are _____, they can cause skin to burn badly.

3. Training can improve a runner's _____ to race long distances.

4. Before the football game began, there was an _____ of the coaches and players.

5. At the end of the summer, Mom folds up our _____ lawn chairs and stores them in the garage.

6. Ramon has a large _____ of postage stamps from countries around the world.

7. Thanks to the _____ of many people, enough money was gathered to add a new surgery wing to the hospital.

8. Because he does gymnastic drills daily, the dancer's body is strong and _____.

9. When our neighbors' cat was missing, they posted signs with Tabby's picture and _____.

10. For a deep-sea diver, a full tank of oxygen is a _____.

Using words with suffixes in context: *-ion, -tion, -ity, -ible*

Suffixes: -SION, -NESS, and -ABLE

Name _____

A suffix is a letter or group of letters that can be added to the end of a word.

Suffix	Meaning	Example
-sion	state or condition of being	divi**sion** (state of being divided)
-ness	state or condition of being	ill**ness** (state or condition of being ill)
-able	able to be, can be	break**able** (can be broken)

Read the list of words below. Then read the sentences that follow. Write the word from the list that best completes each sentence.

extension	sadness	comfortable	collision
weakness	unbelievable	valuable	rudeness
decision	forgetfulness	enjoyable	nervousness

1. When you make up your mind about something, you are making a _____decision_____.

2. If your ankles are not strong enough to hold you up while ice skating, you have a _____ in your ankles.

3. When one automobile hits another, a _____ has taken place.

4. If you are often not able to remember things, you have a habit of _____.

5. If you take pleasure in taking pictures with a camera, photography is a hobby that is _____ for you.

6. An electric cord that makes another electric cord longer by plugging into it is an _____ cord.

7. A person who is not polite to others may be disliked for his or her _____.

8. The things that you own and are of great worth to you are your _____ possessions.

9. A sofa with soft cushions on which you are able to take it easy and fall asleep is a _____ sofa.

10. A person who feels ill or nervous about going on stage before a large group is suffering from a kind of _____ called stage fright.

11. A story that you find hard to accept as true is an _____ story.

12. A person who cries in sorrow is feeling _____.

Suffixes: -ANCE, -IST, and -OUS

Name _____

A suffix is a letter or group of letters that can be added to the end of a word.

Suffix	Meaning	Example
-ance	state or condition of being	appear**ance** (state of appearing)
-ist	person or thing that makes or does	art**ist** (person that makes art)
-ous	full of, having	joy**ous** (full of joy)

Below are people's notes about a jazz concert. Read each sentence and the word shown below the blank. Complete the word by adding **-ance, -ist,** or **-ous.** If a word has a line through the last letter, drop the letter before adding the suffix.

1. "I enjoyed last night's _____performance_____ by Razzmatazz Jazz more than any other
   (perform)
   music show I've ever attended."

2. "They may not be world-_____, but they certainly put on a first-class,
   (famé)
   entertaining show."

3. "For such a well-known artist, I thought Robin Earl seemed more than a little bit

   _____ in front of her fans."
   (nervé)

4. "I really liked the way the _____ played the strings and came up with a
   (guitar)
   ringing sound."

5. "Razzmatazz Jazz is the finest team of jazz _____s this city has hosted
   (art)
   in five years."

6. "I saw Razzmatazz Jazz in their first live _____ five years ago. They
   (appear)
   were good then, but they're really great now!"

7. "I wish the _____ could have played another piece or two."
   (pianó)

8. "They're as much fun to watch as they are to listen to. Their jokes and silly dances are

   quite _____."
   (humor)

9. "Gary Lotilla's skill with the strings and bow makes me wish I'd stuck with music lessons

   and become a _____."
   (violin)

Forming words with suffixes in context: -ance, -ist, -ous

Suffixes: -LY, -OR, and -SHIP

Name _____

A suffix is a letter or group of letters that can be added to the end of a word.

Suffix	Meaning	Example
-ly	in a way that is like; every	loud**ly** (in a loud way); year**ly** (every year)
-or	person who, thing that	sail**or** (person who sails)
-ship	state or condition of being	friend**ship** (state of being a friend)

Read the sentences below. Complete each one by adding **-ly, -or,** or **-ship** to each word shown in parentheses.

1. An (act) _____actor_____ from the college theater spoke to us about ways to raise

   the (member) _____ of our drama club.

2. A favorite character in *The Wizard of Oz* is the (coward) _____ lion who,
   at the end of a frightening journey, discovers he really does have courage after all.

3. The band (conduct) _____ raised her baton (slow) _____,

   and the band began playing (soft) _____.

4. Lee Ying, a well-known (sculpt) _____, will be an

   (exhibit) _____ at the stone-carvers' fair.

5. One of the rights and duties of (citizen) _____ is to be a responsible

   (elect) _____ at voting time.

6. The swim team has been in training four times (week) _____ in hope of

   winning the city (champion) _____.

Words With More Than One Suffix

Name _____

A suffix is a letter or group of letters that can be added to the end of a word. Some words have more than one suffix.

hope + **ful** + **ness** = hope**fulness**   act + **ive** + **ly** = act**ively**

Read the suffixes below. Then read the items that follow. Follow the item directions, using the suffixes to form new words.

-al   -less   -ness   -ive   -ful   -ly   -ish   -ous

1. Form a new word by adding two suffixes to the word *music*. _____musically_____

2. Form two new words by adding two suffixes each to the word *fool*.

    _____   _____

3. Form two new words by adding two suffixes each to the word *attract*.

    _____   _____

4. Form two new words by adding two suffixes each to the word *nerve*. Before adding the suffixes, drop the final **e** from *nerve*. _____   _____

5. Form four new words by adding two suffixes each to the word *care*. _____
    _____   _____   _____

Use the words you wrote above to complete the sentences below.

1. Some _____musically_____ talented youngsters have begun learning to play the piano as young as two years of age.

2. The _____ of the store's window case caused people walking by to stop and look at the goods.

3. Shaking hands and a cracking voice were signs of my _____ while giving a report to the class.

4. The police officer taught the children to look _____ in all directions before crossing the street.

5. Before the invention of the airplane, most people thought the idea of a flying machine was pure _____.

6. Clothes, papers, and books were _____ scattered across the teenager's bedroom.

Forming words with more than one suffix in isolation; Using words with more than one suffix in context

Words With More Than One Suffix

Name _____

Read the suffixes below. Then read the sentences that follow. Complete each sentence by adding two suffixes to the word shown below the blank.

-al   -ly   -ous   -ful   -ish   -less   -ness

1. I knew how to answer the questions on the math test, but my _____carelessness_____ caused me to score lower than I should have. (care)

2. The circus acrobat swung from a trapeze, dropped to a trampoline below, and

   _____ landed on his toes. (grace)

3. I have no lunch money today because I _____ spent my last dollar yesterday. (fool)

4. The firefighter was honored for her _____ in the daring rescue. (courage)

5. The puppy's wide eyes, floppy ears, and friendly _____ made me want to take it home. (play)

6. The weather this spring has been _____ warm and dry. (exception)

7. Thinking mostly of yourself and caring very little about other people are known as

   _____. (self)

8. A great flash of lightning came _____ close to hitting the hundred-year-old oak tree. (danger)

9. I felt a sense of wonder and reward as I _____ dashed toward the finish line of the ten-mile footrace. (breath)

Solve the word puzzles below by writing a word or suffix in each blank to form new words.

1. fear + ful + ly = _____fearfully_____ – ful + less = _____fearlessly_____

2. childishness – _____ = childish + ly = _____

3. joy + ous + ly = _____ – ous + ful = _____

4. hopelessness – _____ + ful = hopefulness – ness + ly = _____

5. help + _____ + _____ = helpfully – ful + less – ly + ness = _____

Review and Apply: Comprehension

Read the words and suffixes below. Then read the story. In each blank, write the word or suffix that makes sense. For paragraph 1, choose words and suffixes from Group A. For paragraph 2, choose from Group B. For paragraph 3, choose from Group C.

Group A	companions	possibility	aviation	-er	-al	-ly	-ful	-ment	-hood
Group B	happiness	scientists	creative	immeasurable	-y	-en	-or	-ish	-ous
Group C	influence	visible	-ance	-ship	-less	-ment			

1 You've likely heard of the Wright brothers and their contribution to

_____aviation_____. But did you know there was a Wright sister? Katherine Wright was

one of Wilbur and Orville's most faith_____ believers. The three had become close

_____ after their mother died during Katherine's late child_____. Later,

Katherine's brothers, who had always been interested in mechanic_____ things, became

serious_____ interested in the _____ of flying. Katherine, eager to lend

encourage_____ and be a help_____, stitched cloth covers for the wings of gliders.

2 Though many folks laughed at the Wright brothers' fool_____ ideas, Katherine was

proud of their courage_____ efforts and _____ ideas. She talked her

invent_____ brothers into attending a meeting where they could share ideas with other

_____. Later, as flight experiments failed, one after another, it was

Katherine's cheer_____ spirit that helped bright_____ Wilbur and Orville's days. Finally,

in 1903, when the brothers sent home a wire from Kitty Hawk, saying, "Success/ four flights/

engine power alone," Katherine's _____ was _____.

3 As the brothers carried on their work, Katherine kept up her involve_____. She became

Orville's nurse after he crashed in a test flight, and journeyed with both brothers through

Europe. Though her place in history has not been as _____ as her brothers',

history might have been different had it not been for Katherine Wright's

_____. Without her friend_____ and assist_____, her brothers might

have become hope_____ during their early days of failure. It seems that Katherine was

indeed the "Wright" sister for Wilbur and Orville—in more ways than one!

Review and Apply: Composition

Name _____

You've just returned from a trip to Jupiter. You unexpectedly landed in the middle of a neighborhood of creatures called Jupes. Now that you've returned to Earth, a reporter is interviewing you about the trip. Answer the reporter's questions, using at least one word that has a suffix for each answer. You may want to use some of the words listed below.

achievement	weightless	famous	scientist	ability	protection
incredible	exploration	television	darkness	portable	friendship
neighborhood	fearful	ticklish	frighten	active	natural
talker	survivor	carefully	furry	difference	assistance

1. After landing, what was the first thing you saw from your spaceship? _____
   _____

2. What did the Jupes look like? _____
   _____

3. What did you think when you saw the Jupes coming toward your ship? _____
   _____

4. What did the Jupes do when you got out of your spaceship? _____
   _____

5. How did the Jupes seem to feel about your landing in the middle of their neighborhood?
   _____

6. How did you communicate with the Jupes? _____
   _____

7. What do Jupes do all day? _____
   _____

8. What is the most amazing thing about Jupes? _____
   _____

9. What unusual habit or custom did you observe among the Jupes? _____
   _____

10. In what way are Jupes like human beings? _____
    _____

Roots

Name_____

A root is a word part to which a prefix, suffix, or other root can be added to form a new word.

Root	Meaning	Example
port	carry	trans**port**
spect	look, watch, see	in**spect**
duct	take, lead	con**duct**

Read the roots and their meanings below. Then read the sentences that follow. Complete the unfinished word in each sentence by writing the correct root.

scribe - write   **mit** - send   **cede** - go
pel - drive, push   **spect** - see, look, watch   **duct** -lead, take
pos - put, place   **ject** - throw, force   **port** - carry

1. Pro- means "forward," so *to push forward* is *to* pro*pel*_____. *To throw forward is to*

   pro_____. *To look forward is to* pro_____.

2. Trans- means "across," so *to send across* is *to* trans_____. *To carry across is to*
   trans_____.

3. De- means "away from," so *to take away from* is *to* de_____. *De- can also mean*

   down, so to write down is to de_____.

4. In- means "into," so *to look into* is *to* in_____. *To write into is to* in_____.

   To force into is to in_____.

5. Re- means "back," so *to throw back* is *to* re_____. *To push back is to*

   re_____. *To go back is to* re_____.

6. Com- means "together," so *to put together* is *to* com_____e.

7. Pre- means "before," so *to go before* is *to* pre_____. *To write before is to*

   pre_____.

In each sentence below, circle the word that correctly completes the sentence.

1. This coupon allows a customer to (describe, deduct) 25¢ from the cost of a bar of soap.
2. Friday is the day that (precedes, prescribes) Saturday.
3. A bug bomb is used to (repel, report) flies, bees, and other insects.
4. A songwriter's job is to (reject, compose) music.
5. To write your name on the inside cover of a book is to (inscribe, inject) the book.

       Forming words with roots in isolation; Using words with roots in context

Roots

Name

A root is a word part to which a prefix, suffix, or other root can be added to form a new word.

Read the roots and their meanings below. Then read the sentences that follow. Using the underlined word as a clue, complete the unfinished word in each sentence by writing the correct root. In one sentence, the root will form a word by itself.

aud - hear, listen   **dict** - say, declare   **puls** - drive, push

miss - send   **spec** - see, look, watch   **script** - write

1. To <u>say</u> words aloud so that another person may write them down is to _____dictate.

2. A powerful ruler who <u>declares</u> laws and gives orders is a _____ator.

3. <u>Diction</u> is the way in which a person uses words, so a book that tells how words can be

   used is a _____ionary.

4. If something is loud enough to be <u>heard</u>, it is _____ible.

5. A group of people who gather to <u>hear</u> something, such as a speech, is an _____ience.

6. A room in which a crowd gathers to <u>hear</u> something is an _____itorium.

7. <u>Handwriting</u>, or a kind of print that looks like handwriting, is called _____.

8. An object that is <u>sent</u> through the air with force is a _____ile.

9. A duty or task that a person is <u>sent</u> elsewhere to attend to is a _____ion.

10. The beating of blood vessels as blood <u>pushes</u> through them is a _____e.

11. Glass or plastic lenses that help a person <u>see</u> better are _____tacles.

12. Something that is wonderful to <u>look</u> at is _____tacular.

13. People who <u>watch</u> something, such as a sports game, are _____tators.

Roots

Name _____

A root is a word part to which a prefix, suffix, or other root can be added to form a word.

Read the roots and their meanings below. Then read each sentence and the words below the blank. Write the word choice that correctly completes each sentence.

spect - see, look, watch	**ject** - throw, force	**pos** - put, place
scribe, script - write	**duct** - lead, take	**mit** - send
dict - say, declare	**pel** - drive, push	**port** - carry

1. A machine that "throws" an image, or picture, onto a screen is a _____projector_____.
    (projector, prospector)

2. A person who puts notes of music together to make a song is a _____.
    (composer, conductor)

3. Equipment that sends out radio or television waves is a _____.
    (transmitter, transporter)

4. A name, date, or words written on a coin is an _____.
    (inscription, injection)

5. On an engine, a fanlike blade that pushes a vehicle forward is a _____.
    (prospector, propeller)

6. A person who finds out what is happening and carries the news back to other people is a

    _____.
    (reporter, subscriber)

7. A person who says what the weather will be like before it takes place is a weather

    _____.
    (predictor, conductor)

8. A person who checks something by looking at it closely is an _____.
    (importer, inspector)

9. Someone who leads a band or chorus during a music show is a

    _____.
    (conductor, composer)

10. A liquid form of medicine that is forced into the body, such as a shot of penicillin, is an

    _____.
    (injection, inspection)

Using words with roots in context

Roots

Name _____

A root is a word part to which a prefix, suffix, or other root can be added to form a word.

Read the roots and their meanings below. Then read the sentences that follow. Form a word to complete each sentence by combining a root from Group A with a root from Group B, in that order.

Group A   **tele** - far   **phono** - sound, voice   **micro** - small

Group B   **phone** - sound, voice   **scope** - look at   **graph** -write   **gram** - something written

---

1. A tool for <u>looking</u> at things that are <u>far</u> away is a _____telescope_____.

2. A tool for <u>looking</u> at things that are very <u>small</u> is a _____.

3. A tool that makes "<u>small</u>" <u>sounds</u> "bigger" or louder is a _____.

4. A machine that plays <u>sounds</u> that are "<u>written</u>" into the grooves of a record is a

   _____.

5. An instrument for hearing a <u>voice</u> that is <u>far</u> away is a _____.

6. A machine used to <u>write</u> a message to someone <u>far</u> away is a _____.

7. A <u>written</u> message sent by wire to someone <u>far</u> away is a _____.

Read the sentences below. Use what you know about roots to write a word, word part, or phrase that completes each sentence.

1. *Kaleido* comes from two roots meaning *pretty shape*, so a *kaleidoscope* is a toy used to

   <u>look at pretty shapes</u> _____.

2. Film is used for making photographs. Microfilm is a kind of film that is used to make very

   _____ pictures of book, magazine, and newspaper pages.

3. *Calli* comes from a root meaning *beauty*, so *calligraphy* is hand_____
   that is beautiful.

4. Vision is being able to see. A machine that makes it possible to see a show that is

   happening far away is a _____.

5. Adolphe Sax made something that plays a musical sound. It is a saxo_____.

Review and Apply: Comprehension

Name _____

Read the index for the yellow pages of a phone book below. Notice that many of the words contain roots. Use the index to answer the questions that follow.

Audio Equipment		**Eyeglasses**	250	**Pharmacies**	334	**Telegrams,**	
Dealers	123	**Garage Door**		**Phonographs**		**Novelty**	359
Parts & Repair	125	**Operating**		see Audio		**Telegraph**	
Automobile		**Devices**	259	Equipment		**Services**	362
Dealers	159	**Imported**		**Photography**		**Telephones**	
Inspections	168	**Products**	270	Equipment	345	Answering	
Service	175	**Lawn Mowers**		Studios	349	Machines	367
Bookstores	206	Riding	287	**Prescriptions**		Equipment	370
Calligraphers	239	Self-Propelled	288	see Pharmacies		Service & Repair	376
Dictating		**Magazine**		**Projectors**	351	**Telescopes**	381
Machine		**Subscription**		**School Supplies**	354	**Televisions**	
Transcribing	245	**Agents**	295	**Spectacles** - see		Cable Service	384
Dictating		**Microphones**	299	Eyeglasses		Dealers	387
Machines	247	**Microscopes**	301			Parts & Supplies	391
		Office Supplies	329			Repair	396

1. On what page of the phone book would you look if you wanted to find a store that sells portable televisions? _____

2. You need a dictionary for school. Under what index listing would you look for the name of a place to buy one? _____

3. What two kinds of lawn mowers are listed? _____

4. What kind of services are listed on page 362? _____

5. Your doctor has written you a prescription for penicillin. Under what listing will you find the name of a place to get it filled? _____

6. You need a new tablet of composition paper for school. Name two listings under which you could find a store that sells composition paper. _____

7. The transmitter for your garage-door opener is broken. On what page of the phone book will you find the name of a company that sells new transmitters? _____

8. What listings come directly before and after the listing for microphones? _____

_____

9. The needle for your record player needs to be replaced. On what page will you find the name of a place to buy a new one? _____

Review of words with roots

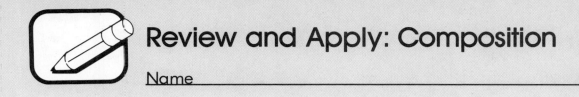

Review and Apply: Composition

Name _____

Ward Root, an inventor, invented each of the things pictured below. However, Ward did not name any of his inventions, and now he has forgotten what they do. Your job is to figure out what each thing does and to give it a name that uses at least two word roots. You may add letters such as **a, i, o, er,** or **or.** After you decide on a name for each invention, write it beside the picture. Then tell what the invention does.

port - carry	**micro** - small	**aud** - hear, listen	**script** - write	**tele** - far
dict - say	**spect** - see	**phone** - voice, sound	**scope** - look at	**graph** -write
mit - send	**ject** - throw	**duct** - take	**pos** - put	**pel** - drive, push

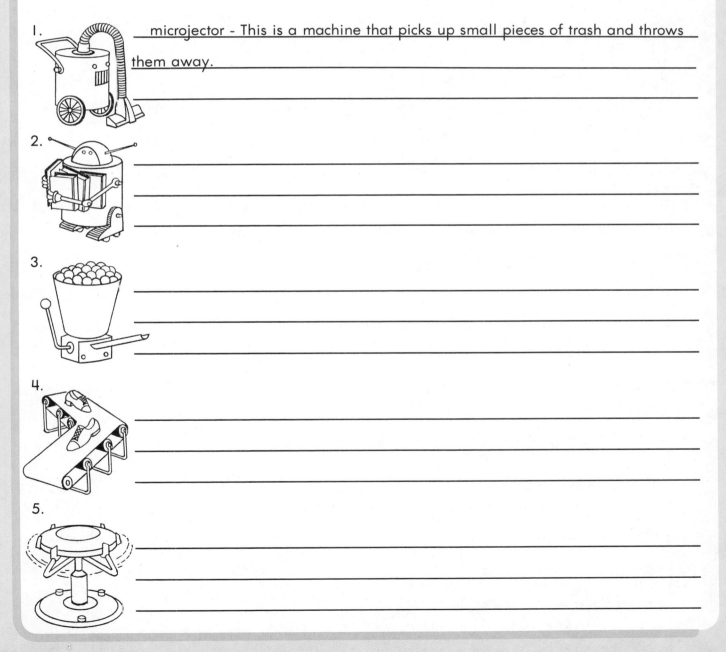

1. microjector - This is a machine that picks up small pieces of trash and throws them away. _____

_____

2. _____

_____

_____

3. _____

_____

_____

4. _____

_____

_____

5. _____

_____

_____

Syllables

Name _____

Words are made of small parts called syllables. Each syllable has one vowel sound, so a word has as many syllables as it has vowel sounds.

> stone - 1 syllable   raincoat - 2 syllables   butterfly - 3 syllables

Name the pictures. Write the number of syllables you hear in each picture name.

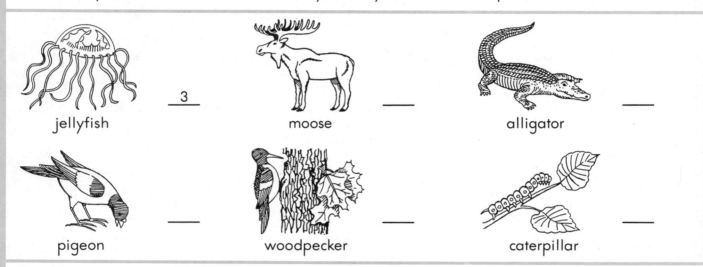

jellyfish   3   moose   ___   alligator   ___

pigeon   ___   woodpecker   ___   caterpillar   ___

A compound word should be divided into syllables between the words that make it compound.

Read the list of words below. Divide each word into syllables by drawing a line between the syllables. Then read the sentences and write the list word that best completes each one.

| star/fish | catfish | bluebird |
| sheepdog | greyhound | stinkbug |

1. Many animals, such as the _____starfish_____, which has five arms, take their names from the shapes of their bodies.

2. Others, such as the _____ and _____, have been named because of their body color.

3. Some animals, such as the _____, with its whiskerlike feelers, have a name that is a combination of two animal names.

4. The _____ also has a combination of two animal names, but the reason is different. This animal is known for guarding and herding flocks of sheep.

5. A few animals are named for their more unpleasant qualities. The _____, as you can guess, is one of these.

Syllables

Name _____

A word that has a prefix or suffix can be divided into syllables between the prefix or suffix and the base word.

re/pay   un/tie   cheer/ful   dark/ness

Read the words below. Then write each word and draw a line between its syllables.

1. nonsense _____non/sense_____
2. sleepy _____
3. disease _____
4. wooden _____
5. impure _____

6. forecast _____
7. artist _____
8. lovely _____
9. homeless _____
10. poorly _____

Read the sentences below. Choose the best word from those you wrote above to complete each sentence.

1. Because stream water may be _____impure_____, people who camp and must use it for drinking should boil it thoroughly.

2. Grandma Moses was a well-known _____ who did not begin painting until she was seventy-six years old.

3. We took Wags to the veterinarian because she was eating _____ and was always _____.

4. Eating foods low in fats and watching how much you weigh are two ways to lower your chances of developing heart _____.

5. Mrs. Richards grows roses in her yard. She gave our family a _____ bunch of flowers last week.

6. Today's weather _____ calls for several inches of snow.

7. *Huckleberry Finn* is a book about a _____ boy and an escaped slave who float down the Mississippi River on a _____ raft.

8. Children learn to talk by repeating the sounds they hear, even though their talk may sound like nothing more than _____ to us.

Syllables

Name _____

Some words have two consonants between two vowels. These words can usually be divided between the two consonants.

but/ter	mon/key	c i r/cus
vc/cv	vc/cv	vc/cv

Read the sentences and the words shown below each blank. In each blank, write the word that has the VC/CV pattern.

1. If you ever think some of your parents' rules are silly, you may feel _____ better _____
   (thankful, better)

   after reading some very old city laws that _____ children.
   (concern, relate to)

2. Although they may have been reasonable when they were _____, today
   they make no sense at all.   (written, created)

3. For example, in Janesville, Wisconsin, it is illegal for a child to pull a

   _____ tooth. Parents who _____ such behavior can
   (baby, dentist's)   (approve of, permit)
   be sent to jail.

4. If you hate to take baths, move to Pickens, Oklahoma. It's against the law to take a bath in

   that town during the _____ months.
   (autumn, winter)

5. A law in Columbia, Pennsylvania, _____ an adult from tickling a child
   (keeps, forbids)

   _____ the chin with a feather in _____ to get the
   (under, beside)   (order, trying)
   child's attention.

6. If you visit Wakefield, Rhode Island, do not _____ a movie theater
   (enter, exit)

   sooner than four hours after eating _____, or you'll be breaking the law.
   (onions, garlic)

7. By all means, watch your eating habits while in Halstead, _____. It is
   (Kansas, Texas)

   a violation for a child to eat ice cream with a fork in a _____
   (public, quiet)

   place. _____ it would be more sensible to use a knife!
   (Perhaps, Surely)

Identifying words with the VC/CV syllable-division pattern and using them in context

Syllables

Name _____

Words that have one consonant between two vowels can be divided into syllables in two ways. When you see such a word, say it. If the first vowel sound is long, divide the word after the first vowel. If the first vowel sound is short, divide the word after the consonant that follows the vowel.

1	ē/ven	pā/per	2	vĭs/it	mĕt/al
	v/cv	v/cv		vc/v	vc/v

Listed below are some things that Tracy and Robert need to buy at the grocery store. One word in each item contains the V/CV or VC/V pattern. Divide the shopping list into two parts by writing the items with a V/CV-pattern word under Tracy's name. Write the items with a VC/V-pattern word under Robert's name.

Grandma's Gravy Mix
Wagon Wheel Dog Food
Chef's Salad Dressing
Redman Radish Dip
Sur-Cheap Tuna

Good Flavor Orange Juice
Ame's Silver Polish
Never-Fail Pie Crusts
Chelsea Paper Plates
World-Famous Pea Soup

Magic Dusting Spray
Farm Time Bacon
Petal-Soft Tissues
Citril Lemon Juice
Fiber-Rich Bread

Tracy (V/CV)

Grandma's Gravy Mix
_____
_____
_____
_____
_____
_____

Robert (VC/V)

_____
_____
_____
_____
_____
_____
_____

Review and Apply: Comprehension

Name _____

Below is a key that shows five patterns for dividing words into syllables. Study the key and read the story that follows. In each blank, write the word whose syllable pattern matches the pattern shown by the key number. Then draw a line to divide the word into syllables.

1 = prefix or suffix   2 = compound word   3 = VC/CV   4 = V/CV   5 = VC/V

A few years ago, Richard Dean lost his job. To make ends meet, he made and sold

_____bas/kets_____. One day he met a _____ who had planted
3 - (jewelry, baskets)   1 - (lady, farmer)

willow trees just a foot apart. Because the _____ grew straight, Richard
                                             3 - (saplings, branches)

could make fine baskets from them. The farmer gave Richard some plans for making a chair

from the willow saplings. Learning by trial and error, Richard _____ his
                                                     5 - (finished, painted)

chair and took it to the _____ Gallery, a small shop in Columbus, Ohio.
                              2 - (Benchworks, Nature)

When the chair sold almost immediately, Mr. Dean decided to go _____ the
                                                         2 - (study, into)

business of furniture making. Working in a barn near Johnstown, Ohio, Richard makes

beautiful furniture from bent _____ and twigs. Richard spends about five
                                      3 - (branches, willows)

hours making a simple piece of furniture such as a chair or _____. He
                                                       2 - (nightstand, table)

makes chairs, _____, and swings in different sizes—all from willow
                       2 - (headboards, sofas)

saplings. Using _____ green wood, he gently bends saplings to form the
                     3 - (only, mostly)

_____ curving arcs and spokes that give the pieces their special look. From
   1 - (special, graceful)

Alaska to the _____, Richard's _____ of furniture
                2 - (desert, Southeast)   4 - (items, anthems)

add interest to kitchens, patios, and courtyards throughout the country.

Review of identifying syllable-division patterns of words in context

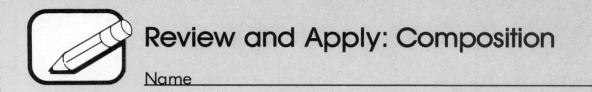

Name _____

Each word puzzle below stands for a familiar phrase. For example, puzzle 1 stands for the words *monkey around.* Look at each puzzle. Then read the words that follow. Notice that the words have different syllable patterns. Using the syllable patterns as clues, figure out the meaning of each puzzle and write the missing word in the correct blank.

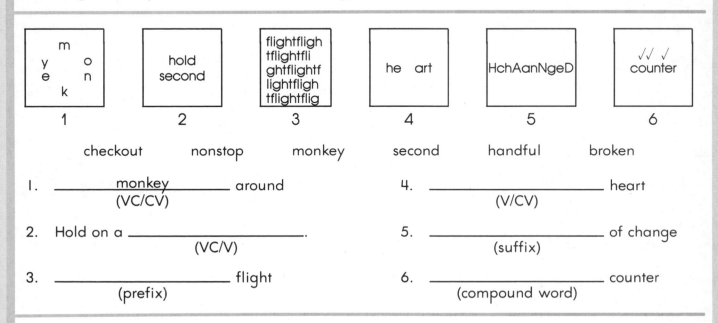

m y o e n k	hold second	flightfligh tflightfli ghtflightf lightfligh tflightflig	he art	HchAanNgeD	√√ √ counter
1	2	3	4	5	6

checkout   nonstop   monkey   second   handful   broken

1. _____monkey_____ around
   (VC/CV)

2. Hold on a _____.
   (VC/V)

3. _____ flight
   (prefix)

4. _____ heart
   (V/CV)

5. _____ of change
   (suffix)

6. _____ counter
   (compound word)

Now try making some puzzles yourself. The phrases are given below the boxes. Fill in each box to match its phrase by arranging the words in a special way.

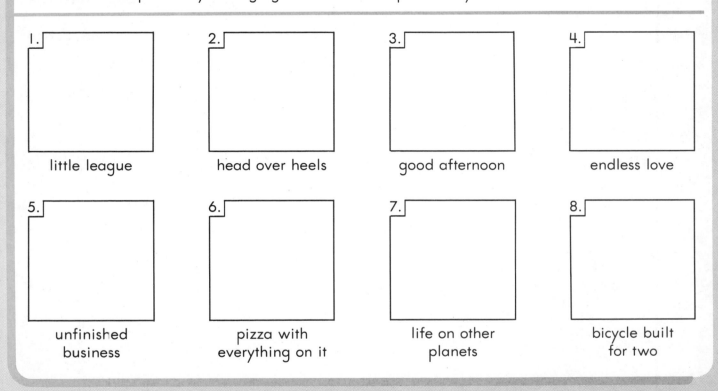

1. little league

2. head over heels

3. good afternoon

4. endless love

5. unfinished business

6. pizza with everything on it

7. life on other planets

8. bicycle built for two

Review of identifying syllable-division patterns of words

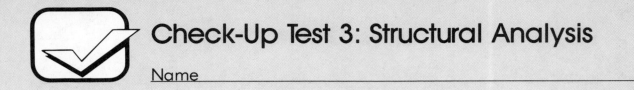

Check-Up Test 3: Structural Analysis

Name _____

There are seventeen errors in the story below. Proofread the story. Draw a line through each error and write the correction above it. Then follow the directions below the story.

1   Have you ever wondered how actors and actress make movies without geting hurt in the dangerous scenes? Well, the truth is, they dont act in those scenes themselfs. Men and woman called stunt people play those parts instead. Stunt people fall from windows, roofs, and bridges. They drive auto that end up in crash. They play the parts of thiefs, fighters, or other people who may get hurt while filming.

2   Being a stunt person isnt an easy way to make a liveing. These people spend hours practiceing their tricks. They must be able to roll, fall, jump, and land without hurting their bodys. Each trick must be carefully planed and done in the safe way possible. At the same time, the trick must be convince enough for an audience to believe.

3   No matter how well a stunt has been planned, theres always a chance that something can go wrong. Just one incorrect move or one misjudged distance can cause an accident. An air bag that a stunt person is to fall on may break. A car seat that is supposed to collapse during a crash may get stuck. An unexpected breeze may throw a falling actor off course. Even though other jobs are safer and easyer, most stunt people love what they do. The danger is just part of the job. Besides, a difficult stunt pays off in two ways. The harder the stunt, the more the person gets paid. It also pays off by giving the person something to be proud of.

1. Circle the three words in paragraph 1 that have a suffix. Write **1** above each word.

2. Circle the word in paragraph 2 that has two suffixes. Write **2** above the word.

3. Divide the compound word in paragraph 2 into syllables. Write **3** above the word.

4. Circle the word in paragraph 2 that has a root meaning "hear." Write **4** above the word.

5. Circle the three words in paragraph 3 that have a prefix. Write **5** above each word.

Assessment of structural analysis skills

Check-Up Test 4: Structural Analysis

Name _____

Read and follow each set of directions below.

1. Write the base word of each of these words.   advising _____

   marries _____   confided _____

2. Add **-ed** to these words.   wrap _____   ignore _____

3. Add **-ing** to these words.   soothe _____   obey _____

4. Add **-er** to these words.   clear _____   dizzy _____

5. Add **-est** to these words.   dreary _____   cute _____

6. Write the plural forms of these words.   potato _____

   life _____   goose _____   nursery _____

7. Rewrite each group of words below to show ownership.

   the dishes of the restaurant _____

   the customers of the merchants _____

   books of children _____

8. Circle the words that are compound words: combine   strawberry   prevent   throughout

9. Write the contractions for these words.   they are _____

   there is _____   will not _____

10. Add one of these prefixes or suffixes to each underlined word to form a word that matches
    each clue.   **im-   over-   pre-   -ish   -ist   -less**

    one who makes <u>art</u> _____   not <u>proper</u> _____

    without <u>worth</u> _____   <u>sleep</u> too much _____

    <u>pay</u> before _____   like a <u>fool</u> _____

11. Write one of these words to match each clue.   **repel   spectators   report   audience**

    people who listen _____   to push back _____

    to carry back _____   people who watch _____

12. Draw a line to divide each of these words into syllables.

    widow   textile   wooden   rifle   rebuild   snowstorm

READING

Friendship

Adapted from *The Wind in the Willows* by Kenneth Grahame

This story tells about four friends who live in the country. Here, two of the friends talk over a problem.

The Mole had long wanted to make friends with the Badger. He seemed, by all accounts, to be an important person, though rarely visible. Still, his unseen nearness was felt by everybody about the place. But whenever the Mole mentioned his wish to the Water Rat, he always found himself put off. "It's all right," the Rat would say. "Badger will turn up some day or other—he's always turning up—and then I'll introduce you. The best of fellows! But you must not only take him *as* you find him, but *when* you find him."

"Couldn't you ask him here—dinner or something?" said the Mole.

"He wouldn't come," replied the Rat simply. "Badger hates company, and invitations, and dinner, and all that sort of thing."

"Well, then, supposing we go and call on *him?*" suggested the Mole.

"Oh, I'm sure he wouldn't like that at *all,*" said the Rat, quite alarmed. "He's so very shy, he'd be sure to have his feelings hurt. I've never even dared to call on him at his home myself, though I know him so well. Besides, we can't. It's quite out of the question, because he lives in the very middle of the Wild Wood."

"Well, supposing he does," said the Mole. "You told me the Wild Wood was all right, you know."

"Oh, I know, I know, so it is," replied the Rat, avoiding the Mole's concern. "But I think we won't go there just now. Not *just* yet. It's a long way, and he wouldn't be at home at this time of year anyhow, and he'll be coming along some day, if you'll wait quietly."

The Mole had to be content with this. But the Badger never came along, and it was not till summer was long over, and cold and frost and muddy roads kept them much indoors, and the swollen river raced past their windows with a speed that mocked at boating of any sort or kind, that he found his thoughts dwelling again on the lone gray Badger, who lived his own life by himself, in his hole in the middle of the Wild Wood.

Application of reading skills in a literature context

Literature

Name _____

A. Under each word, write the name of the story animal that it best describes.

friendly   cautious   shy

_____   _____   _____

B. In each group, check the sentence or sentences that are true.

1. _____ The Mole wants to meet the Badger.

_____ The Badger wants to meet the Rat.

_____ The Rat wants to meet the Mole.

2. _____ The Badger lives in the Wild Wood.

_____ The Badger lives in a hole.

_____ The Mole and the Rat live in the city.

C. What reasons does the Rat give for not inviting the Badger to dinner?

_____

_____

_____

D. Draw a line to connect each word on the left with its meaning on the right.

1. introduce   a. hardly ever
2. mentioned   b. swelled up
3. replied   c. interest
4. visible   d. put off
5. concern   e. spoke of
6. rarely   f. able to be seen
7. avoiding   g. answered
8. swollen   h. meet
9. delay   i. keeping away from

Reading and Writing Wrap-Up

Name _____

A. Check each reason that might explain why the Rat puts off introducing the Mole to the Badger.

   1. _____ The Rat does not like to eat dinner with his friends.

   2. _____ The Rat wants to keep the Mole as a friend for himself alone.

   3. _____ The Rat wants to keep the Badger as a friend for himself alone.

   4. _____ The Rat does not know the Badger as well as he says he does.

   5. _____ The Rat does not want the Mole and the Badger to become friends.

   6. _____ The Rat is afraid of going into the Wild Wood to find the Badger.

   7. _____ The Rat does not know where the Badger lives.

   8. _____ The Rat is afraid the Mole and the Badger will become friends and he will be left out.

B. Check the answer that tells how much time passes during the story. Then write the words from the story that prove your answer is true.

   _____ a few days   _____ many months   _____ several years

   _____

   _____

C. A summary is a brief statement that gives the main points of a story. It tells only the important parts of the story. In your own words, write a summary of the story on page 122.

   _____

   _____

   _____

   _____

   _____

   _____

   _____

Application of thinking skills in a literature context

Name _____

WRITING

Choose one of the following writing suggestions.

What Is a Friend?

Describe your best friend by telling what it is about this person that you especially like. You might write an advertisement praising your friend. Or you might retell a particular incident that shows why this person is a good friend to you. Or you might write a poem describing the qualities you like in your friend.

Mole Meets Badger

Write a conclusion for the story on page 122. You might begin with the following sentence if you need help getting started.

One cold winter afternoon while the Rat was dozing in his armchair before the fire, the Mole decided to go out by himself and explore the Wild Wood in the hope of at last meeting the Badger.

_____

_____

_____

_____

_____

_____

_____

_____

_____

_____

_____

_____

_____

_____

_____

_____

Antonyms

Name _____

An antonym is a word that has the opposite meaning of another word.   wet - dry

Read each row of words below. In the first blank beside the row, write the word that is shown in dark print. In the second blank, write the antonym of the word in dark print.

1.	**create:**	make, destroy, creature	create	destroy
2.	**flood:**	drought, rain, desert	_____	_____
3.	**clumsy:**	awkward, fool, graceful	_____	_____
4.	**alert:**	awake, delighted, drowsy	_____	_____
5.	**poverty:**	dollar, wealth, poor	_____	_____
6.	**severe:**	bad, mild, miserable	_____	_____
7.	**thaw:**	freeze, snow, ice	_____	_____
8.	**victory:**	win, game, defeat	_____	_____
9.	**purchase:**	buy, sell, merchandise	_____	_____
10.	**imaginary:**	make-believe, dream, real	_____	_____

Read the list of words below. Then read the sentences that follow. Write the word from the list that is an antonym for the underlined word in each sentence.

gradually   precious   obedient   nervous   swelling   dreadfully

1. We had to postpone our Saturday picnic plans because the weather was <u>delightfully</u> cold and rainy.   dreadfully

2. Although Carmen said she was <u>calm</u> about her piano performance, she played remarkably well.   _____

3. As rain continued to fall, the river <u>immediately</u> rose until it overflowed its banks.   _____

4. It took several months of patience and training to teach Muttsy to be <u>naughty</u>.   _____

5. Melinda found a shiny glasslike stone that turned out to be a <u>worthless</u> gem.   _____

6. Pain, redness, and <u>shrinkage</u> are indications that a wound has become infected.   _____

Identifying antonyms in isolation and in context

Synonyms

Name _____

A synonym is a word that has the same or nearly the same meaning as another word.

big - large   bright - shiny   small - little

Read the list of words below. Then read the sentences that follow. Write the word from the list that is a synonym for the underlined word in each sentence.

journeys	trade	simple	enjoy	major	performers
demands	marry	hard	twirl	remain	

1. Circus <u>actors</u> and stagehands lead lives very different from most of us.

    _____performers_____

2. A circus group <u>travels</u> from town to town for ten months of every year.

    _____

3. While traveling across the country, the circus stops in almost every <u>important</u> city.

    _____

4. The journey is <u>difficult</u>, but the circus people get used to it.

    _____

5. Many of them would not like to <u>stay</u> in one town for long.

    _____

6. They <u>like</u> seeing different parts of the country.

    _____

7. Most circus members grow up in the circus and <u>wed</u> other circus people.

    _____

8. Many circus tricks look <u>easy</u>, but the performers are highly skilled athletes.

    _____

9. Trapeze artists, for example, must be exact in every move as they hang, swing, flip, and <u>spin</u>.

    _____

10. The <u>duties</u> of circus life leave the members little time for outside friends or entertainment.

    _____

11. The circus is a way of life for these people, though, and most of them wouldn't <u>exchange</u> it for any other.

    _____

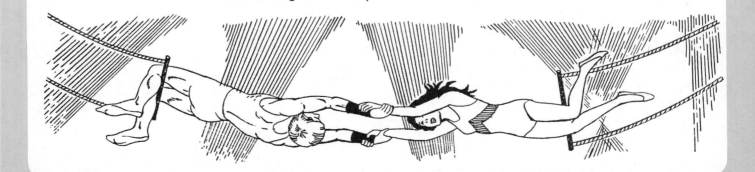

Identifying synonyms in context

127

Synonyms

Read the groups of words below. Then read the story that follows. For each underlined word, choose a list word that is a synonym. For paragraph 1, choose words from Group A. For paragraph 2, choose from Group B. For paragraph 3, choose from Group C. Write the synonym in the blank whose number matches the number of the underlined word.

Group A	caverns	stream	winds	pools	point	experience	trip
Group B	clinging	pitched	fall	enjoyed	chilly	swiftly	struggled
Group C	immediately	survived	crew	realizes	crouched	attempted	ledge

1   In June, 1985, Roman Lazowski and Michael Hall planned a (1) <u>journey</u> through the (2) <u>caves</u> of Spring Mill State Park. Both men had made the trip before, and Michael had a good deal of (3) <u>practice</u> exploring caves. The underground tunnel closely follows a narrow, deep (4) <u>brook</u>. At one (5) <u>spot</u>, the cave ceiling drops to four feet. After a distance, the passageway (6) <u>turns</u> through chest-deep (7) <u>puddles</u> of water.

2   At first, the two cavers (8) <u>liked</u> wading through the (9) <u>cool</u> water, but then rain began to (10) <u>descend</u> outside. Soon the water in the cave stream was running deep and (11) <u>fast</u>. The strong current (12) <u>tossed</u> the two men from wall to wall as they desperately (13) <u>fought</u> to get through the cave. Somehow they managed to pull themselves from the water. (14) <u>Grabbing</u> onto the tunnel wall, they thought the water would soon go down.

3   Unfortunately, Roman fell backward into the rushing water. After hitting a wall of rock, he blindly felt around and found a three-foot-long (15) <u>shelf</u>. (16) <u>Stooped</u> on the ledge, Roman watched the stream steadily rise. Michael bravely (17) <u>tried</u> to reach Roman, but the current quickly carried him a hundred yards downstream to daylight. Michael was rushed to a hospital (18) <u>instantly</u>. Two days later, a (19) <u>team</u> of rescuers reached Roman and pulled him to safety. Roman (20) <u>understands</u> he is fortunate to have (21) <u>lived</u>. Now every day seems especially meaningful to him.

1. _____trip_____
2. _____
3. _____
4. _____
5. _____
6. _____
7. _____
8. _____
9. _____
10. _____
11. _____
12. _____
13. _____
14. _____
15. _____
16. _____
17. _____
18. _____
19. _____
20. _____
21. _____

Identifying synonyms in context

Synonyms

Name _____

Read the list of words below. Then read the sentences that follow. In each blank, write the list word that is a synonym of the word shown below the blank.

recordings	survive	ocean	headed	coast	creature
commotion	encourage	beat	dangerous	spectators	attempted
environment	toward	course	strayed	professors	promptly

1. In October, 1985, a whale stirred up quite a ____commotion____ near the
(disturbance)
_____ of California.
(shore)

2. The whale, a _____ so large that its home is the Pacific Ocean, swam
(animal)
under the Golden Gate Bridge and _____ up the Sacramento River.
(went)

3. Humphrey, as _____ named the whale, was in a _____
(watchers)
situation.
(unsafe)

4. A shallow river is too small for a forty-ton whale. Besides that, whales, like other
_____ animals, need salt water.
(sea)

5. In an _____ of fresh water, a whale cannot _____
(surrounding)
(live)
more than a few weeks.

6. Scientists, _____, and fishing guides _____ to get
(teachers)
(tried)
Humphrey to turn around.

7. They _____ on pipes, played sound _____ of other
(banged)
(tapes)
whales, and used tugboats to _____ him to swim back to the Pacific.
(urge)

8. After more than three weeks, Humphrey finally reversed his _____ and
(direction)
swam back _____ the ocean.
(to)

9. A few days later, another whale _____ into the same area.
(wandered)

10. This one _____ headed out, though. Perhaps Humphrey had given it a
(quickly)
warning!

Review and Apply: Comprehension

Name _____

Read the groups of words below. Then read the story that follows. In each blank, write the list word that is either a synonym (S) or antonym (A) of the word shown below the blank. For synonyms, choose words from Group 1. For antonyms, choose from Group 2.

Group 1: Synonyms	kinds ideas	road device	helpful because	perhaps	folks pedestrian	student created	prize lid

Group 2: Antonyms	straight problem	won	enjoy bottom	dark young	rainy could

Young _____folks_____ _____ entering contests of all
          (people-S)   (dislike-A)

_____. In a contest held for _____ inventors, about
  (types-S)   (elderly-A)

80,000 ideas were mailed in. A five-year-old _____ _____
                                    (pupil-S)   (lost-A)

a $250 _____ for making an umbrella with a flashlight attached to it.
     (award-S)

Using the umbrella, a _____ _____ easily see and be
               (walker-S)   (couldn't-A)

seen on _____, _____ days. A second-grade child
     (bright-A)   (sunny-A)

thought of a _____ to help keep a class of children in a
     (thing-S)

_____ line while walking along a _____. One
  (crooked-A)   (street-S)

eighth-grade pupil _____ a peanut butter jar that has a
           (made-S)

_____ on both ends. That way, there's no _____
  (cover-S)   (solution-A)

reaching the peanut butter at the _____ of the jar, _____
               (top-A)   (since-S)

the jar has no bottom. Young people have a lot of good _____ for
                                   (thoughts-S)

_____ inventions. _____ you have an idea or two of
  (useful-S)   (Maybe-S)

your own!

                                          Review of antonyms and synonyms

Review and Apply: Composition

Name _____

Read the words below. Then read the paragraph that follows. The underlined words in it are vague or overused. They could be replaced with synonyms that are more descriptive. Using the word list and any words of your own, rewrite the paragraph, replacing the underlined words with synonyms.

continued	major	illness	officials	prevented	challenge
crippling	task	illnesses	vaccinate	efforts	poverty-stricken
youngsters	plenty	disease	nations	diseases	accomplishing
funding	deadly	achieved	scarred	action	realize

     Workers at the World Health Organization (WHO) have a <u>hard problem</u>. They <u>know</u> that far too many of the world's children die from sicknesses that could be <u>stopped</u>. For example, there has been <u>a lot</u> of polio vaccine in the United States for over thirty years. But many <u>children</u> in <u>poor</u> <u>countries</u> have not been protected from this <u>bad</u>, <u>killing</u> <u>sickness</u>. One of WHO's jobs is to <u>protect</u> all the world's children against preventable <u>sicknesses</u>. One of the <u>big</u> problems in <u>doing</u> this <u>job</u> is <u>money</u>. Much has been <u>done</u> since WHO began stepping up its <u>work</u> in 1974. Smallpox, for example, a <u>sickness</u> that <u>marked</u>, blinded, or often killed its victims, was completely wiped out in the late 1970's, thanks to the <u>work</u> of WHO. With <u>lasting</u> work, WHO <u>workers</u> hope that all preventable <u>sicknesses</u> may one day be sicknesses of the past.

_____

_____

_____

_____

_____

_____

_____

_____

_____

_____

_____

_____

_____

Review of antonyms and synonyms

Homophones

Name _____

Homophones are words that sound the same but have different spellings and different meanings.

would - wood   right - write   flour - flower

Read the sentences below. In the blanks, write the pair of homophones from each sentence.

1. Talking aloud in the library is not allowed because it disturbs others.

    _____aloud_____   _____allowed_____

2. If you bury these seeds, in two months a berry bush will sprout.

    _____   _____

3. There is a ten percent discount on these boots if you buy them by the end of the week.

    _____   _____

4. Please hang these clothes in the bedroom closet and then close the door.

    _____   _____

5. Three crews of sailors went with us on our tropical ocean cruise.

    _____   _____

6. Do you remember what day these library books are due?

    _____   _____

7. If the police find your car illegally parked, you will be given a ticket and fined.

    _____   _____

8. Next year, the company will hire new workers at salary levels higher than this year's.

    _____   _____

9. Because heavy fog and mist slowed the airport traffic, we missed our flight to Boston.

    _____   _____

10. Mom planted two rows of tulips in the garden near a pink rose.

    _____   _____

11. I felt tired, weak, and feverish because I had the flu last week.

    _____   _____

Identifying homophones in context

Homophones

Name _____

Read the list of homophones and their meanings below. Then read the sentences that follow. In each blank, write the homophone that correctly completes the sentence.

aisle - pathway   **isle** - island
coarse - rough   **course** - class
find - locate   **fined** - charged money as punishment
passed - went by   **past** - history
presence - nearness, being there **presents** - gifts
principal - head of a school **principle** - rule or truth
their - belonging to them **there** - in that place   **they're** - they are
threw - tossed   **through** - between
to - toward   **too** - also   **two** - a number
wood - what trees are made of **would** - past tense form of *will*

1. Mrs. Lin walked down the supermarket _____aisle_____.
    (aisle, isle)

2. She _____ the grapefruit display because she couldn't decide between
    (past, passed)
    pink grapefruit and the regular kind.

3. _____ were _____ kinds of cherries.
    (There, Their, They're)   (two, to, too)

4. Next she wondered where she might

    _____ the salad dressings.
    (find, fined)

5. Noticing the _____ of a stock clerk,
    (presence, presents)

    Mrs. Lin asked her in what _____ she
    should look.   (aisle, isle)

6. After finding the dressings, she _____
    (through, threw)
    a coin in the air to determine her choice of French
    dressing.

7. She wondered if one of the schools in town offered a

    _____ on the _____
    (course, coarse)   (principals, principles)
    of grocery shopping.

Using homophones in context

Homographs

Name _____

Homographs are words that have the same spelling but different meanings. Sometimes they are pronounced differently.

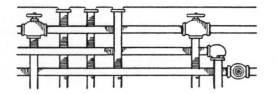

The building's old pipes are made of **lead.**

Ms. Garvey will **lead** the children down the hall.

Read each pair of sentences and circle the homographs. Then draw a line from each sentence to the picture it tells about.

Jessica sat on a park bench and fed a (dove.)

Valerie (dove) into the water headfirst.

A small band on the pigeon's leg identified its owner.

The band played three songs during the football game.

In the spring, the farmer sows new seed in the field.

The farmer fed the sows and their piglets.

Do not waken the children from their rest.

You may have the rest of the salad.

The wind blew the kite into a tree.

Wind the kite string in a ball.

Identifying and determining meanings of homographs

Homographs

Name _____

Read the list of homographs below. Then read each pair of meanings that follow. Write the homograph from the list that matches both meanings.

bill	tire	bow	wind	bank
close	ring	yard	tear	row

1. a. place to save money   b. land beside a river   _____bank_____

2. a. jewelry for a finger   b. bell-like sound   _____

3. a. strong breeze   b. to twist   _____

4. a. knotted ribbon on a gift   b. to bend in greeting   _____

5. a. near   b. to shut   _____

6. a. rubber around a wheel   b. become weary   _____

7. a. move a boat with oars   b. straight line   _____

8. a. paper telling how much to pay   b. bird's beak   _____

9. a. drop of water from the eye   b. to rip   _____

10. a. grassy area around a house   b. thirty-six inches   _____

Read the homographs and their meanings below. Then read the sentences that follow. In each sentence, decide the meaning of the underlined homograph. Write the letter of the correct meaning in the blank.

coast - a. seashore   b. to ride or slide without power
light - a. not heavy   b. not dark
palm - a. tree that grows in warm climates   b. flat side of a hand
present - a. opposite of absent   b. to give something to another person
pupil - a. student   b. part of the eye
spoke - a. wire that supports a bicycle wheel   b. did speak

1. Hundreds of people take winter vacations on the Atlantic <u>coast</u>. __a__

2. Last year, I was a <u>pupil</u> in Mrs. Yee's class. ____

3. The <u>palm</u> offered the sunbathers very little shade. ____

4. We plan to <u>present</u> our teacher with a surprise for her birthday. ____

5. The author <u>spoke</u> to the audience about her trip to South America. ____

6. It was not yet <u>light</u> when I got out of bed yesterday morning. ____

Review and Apply: Comprehension

Name _____

Read the list of homophones and their meanings below. Then read the story that follows. In each blank, write the homophone that correctly completes the sentence.

feat - daring act	**feet** - part of the body for walking
hall - long, narrow room	**haul** - carry
heard - listened	**herd** - group of animals
hole - opening	**whole** - entire
night - opposite of day	**knight** - king or queen's servant
our - belonging to us	**hour** - sixty minutes
peak - top of a mountain	**peek** - look
stairs - steps	**stares** - fixed looks

We were relaxing in the living room while watching a television mystery (last)

_____ night _____. Suddenly Nikki sprang to her _____ and
(night, knight)   (feat, feet)

whispered, "What's that noise?" Mom grabbed a bat from the corner of the room and crept

down the _____ toward the kitchen. By this time, my sister had scurried up
(hall, haul)

the _____ to hide in her bedroom closet. Meanwhile, I stayed in the
(stairs, stares)

living room and hid my face in my arms. Every once in a while, I looked up briefly to take a

_____ at anything that might be happening. Soon I _____
(peek, peak)   (heard, herd)

laughter coming from the kitchen. Coming into the living room, Mom explained, "Lucky

jumped to the window ledge and climbed through a _____ in the screen!"
(hole, whole)

After showing _____ neighbors' cat to the front door, Mom and I sat back
(hour, our)

down to watch the news. Nikki, in the meantime, fell asleep on her closet floor.

Read the homographs and their meanings below. Then find each of the listed homographs in the story above and circle them. Decide the meaning of each homograph as it is used in the story. Write the letter of the correct meaning in the blank beside the homograph below.

1. last   _a_   a. the one just past   b. go on and on; continue; endure
2. bat   ____   a. a flying mammal   b. piece of baseball equipment
3. hide   ____   a. stay out of sight   b. animal skin
4. arms   ____   a. part of the body   b. weapons

Review of homophones and homographs

Read the list of homophones and their meanings below. Then read the story that follows. In some sentences, the wrong homophone has been used. Circle those homophones. Write the correct homophones above them. You should find twelve errors.

aisles - pathways
be - exist
by - near, beside
for - in order to do something
hall - long, narrow room
in - within
new - not old
not - meaning *no*
oar - long paddle used to row a boat
one - single
their - belonging to them
to - toward
way - direction

isles - islands
bee - buzzing insect
bye - good-bye
four - number after three
haul - carry
inn - hotel
knew - did know
knot - tangled string
or - word that gives a choice
won - did win
there - in that place
too - also
weigh - find the heaviness of something

Both Sarah and Delia had trouble with there lockers on the first day of school. Sarah thought and thought, but she could not remember her locker combination. She new the first number was either twelve oar twenty-one, but she could not remember which. She tried over a dozen combinations, but knot won of them worked. Angry and late, she raced down the haul to class. Upon reaching room 1206, she suddenly remembered the combination—twelve, zero, six!

Delia knew her combination, but she walked up and down the isles looking four her locker. She knew it was at the end of a row, but she couldn't find the row. It could bee near the gym, or it could be bye the side entrance. She decided to try her combination on the first and last locker inn every row. Delia not only found her locker, but she also found her weigh around the school.

Multiple Meanings

Name _____

Many words have more than one meaning. Most dictionaries show the different meanings of a word by placing a number before each meaning.

Read the dictionary entries below. Then read the sentences. Use the entries to decide the meaning of each underlined word. In the blank, write the number of the correct meaning.

camp er /kam′pər/ *n* **1** a person who lives outdoors in a tent or other temporary shelter **2** a vehicle designed for camping that is either self-propelled or pulled by an automobile

cast /kast/ *n* **1** the act of throwing or tossing: *The sea workers made a cast of the fishing net.* **2** a mold into which a hot liquid substance, such as wax, can be poured so that when it hardens, the substance takes the shape of the mold **3** a group of actors in a play **4** a hard bandage made of plaster of paris put on a part of the body to keep it still while healing

faint /fānt/ *adj* **1** weak, dizzy feeling of the body: *The crowded room was so hot, I felt faint.* **2** not strong or distinct; pale: *The handwriting in the old book was very faint.*

tis sue /tish′ ü/ *n* **1** the substance that forms the parts of animals and plants **2** a paper handkerchief

vol ume /vol′ yəm/ *n* **1** one of a series of books forming a collection **2** amount of sound: *Please turn down the volume on your radio.* **3** the amount of space taken up by something: *This trunk has a volume of three cubic feet.*

1. Use this <u>tissue</u> to wipe the glue off your hands. __2__

2. Our family rented a <u>camper</u> for our trip to the Smoky Mountains. ____

3. Because I had a fever, I felt <u>faint</u> and unsteady on my feet. ____

4. Our class is collecting orange juice cans to use as <u>casts</u> for candle making. ____

5. The third <u>volume</u> of the library's encyclopedia set is missing. ____

6. Although Mom is a <u>camper</u>, Dad would rather stay in a hotel while on a trip. ____

7. After the show, the members of the <u>cast</u> gave their acting teacher a dozen roses. ____

8. If you stay in the sun too long without being protected, the <u>tissue</u> that forms the surface of the skin will burn. ____

9. Our new refrigerator has greater <u>volume</u> than our old one, so it holds more food. ____

10. The voice on the other end of the telephone was so <u>faint</u> I could hardly hear it. ____

11. Dee wasn't able to go swimming last summer because her arm was in a <u>cast</u>. ____

12. The band's <u>volume</u> increased as it neared the end of the song. ____

13. That artist is known for the <u>faint</u> pink and purple skies in her paintings. ____

14. The worm flew off my fishing line when I made a quick <u>cast</u>. ____

15. The homesick <u>camper</u> felt better after she received a letter from her parents. ____

Identifying meanings of words that have multiple meanings in context

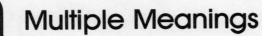

Multiple Meanings

Name _____

Read the dictionary entries below. Then read the sentences. Complete each sentence by writing the correct entry word. You will use some words more than once. In the blank that follows the sentence, write the number of the word's correct meaning.

---

land /land/ *n* **1** soil; earth: *Mrs. Smith grows wheat on her land.* **2** a country: *He comes from a land far away.*

odd /od/ *adj* **1** unusual; STRANGE: *Aunt Gert told us an odd story about Mars.* **2** only one from a pair or set: *There is an odd glove in the closet.* **3** not even; having one left over when divided by two

or ange /ȯr inj, är′ inj/ *n* **1** a round, sweet, juicy fruit: *I will eat an orange for lunch.* **2** the color made by mixing red and yellow: *That shade of orange is really bright.*

pitch er /pich′ ər/ *n* **1** a jug or container used to hold and pour liquids: *The pitcher of milk fell to the floor.* **2** a baseball player who throws the ball to the batter: *Li is our team's pitcher.*

quar ter /kwȯrt′ ər/ *n* **1** an American or Canadian coin worth twenty-five cents **2** one of four equal parts: *One quarter of eight is two.*

show er /shour, shou′ ər/ *n* **1** a brief rainfall **2** a party given by friends who bring gifts for a particular occasion **3** a bath in which water pours down on a person from an overhead nozzle

---

1. Pedro will like this jogging suit because his favorite color is _____orange_____. __2__

2. A _____ of the students in our class are absent with the flu. ____

3. An anteater is an _____-looking creature that catches ants with its long, sticky tongue. ____

4. The waiter filled our glasses with water from a metal _____. ____

5. Our neighbor took a _____ at our house because his hot water heater had broken. ____

6. We dug up a small area of _____ in the backyard to be used as a vegetable garden. ____

7. Because there was an _____ number of players, one team had seven members, and the other had eight. ____

8. We had a _____ for Mr. and Mrs. Wilson before their baby arrived. ____

9. I prefer to cut rather than peel an _____ because I don't like getting the sticky juice on my hands. ____

10. The neighborhood children held a carnival and charged a _____ for admission. ____

Review and Apply: Comprehension

Read the dictionary entries below. Notice that each word has more than one meaning. Then read the story. Complete each unfinished sentence by writing the correct entry word in the blank. In the parentheses at the end of the blank, write the number of the word's meaning.

ap pear /ə pir′/ *v* **1** to come into sight: *The stars appear at night.* **2** seem: *You appear to be ill.* **3** to come out in print; be published: *The book will appear in bookstores next month.*

ar ti cle /ärt′ i kəl/ *n* **1** a nonfiction piece of writing in a magazine or newspaper **2** a thing: *A scarf is an article of clothing.* **3** a word such as *a, an,* or *the* used before a noun to limit its meaning

cer tain /surt′ ən/ *adj* **1** sure: *Are you certain you locked the door?* **2** specific but not named: *Carlita can repair the engine after she buys a certain part.*

char ac ter /kar′ ik tər/ *n* **1** the qualities that make up a person: *Jeremy has a gentle character.* **2** a strange or odd person: *Gus was quite a character.* **3** a person in a story: *An outlaw is the main character in the movie.*

film /film/ *n* **1** a roll or strip of plastic material used in a camera for taking photographs **2** a motion picture; movie

scout /skout/ *n* **1** one sent ahead to get information **2** one sent to search for talent: *He is a basketball scout.* **3** boy scout **4** girl scout

ti tle /tīt′ əl/ *n* **1** a legal right to something, such as property: *Who has title to that land?* **2** a paper showing ownership: *Juan keeps the title to his car in the glove box.* **3** the name of a book or film **4** a name that shows a person's condition, rank, or occupation, such as *Ms., Doctor,* or *Uncle*

Gone With the Wind, the most widely read novel in history, is a love-and-war story set in the South during the Civil War. The author, Margaret Mitchell, had never written a novel before writing *Gone With the Wind.* She had become a skilled writer some years earlier as a writer of _____ s ( ) for the *Atlanta Journal.* After writing the book, Mitchell was not _____ ( ) of her writing talent. She called the book "lousy" and did not try to sell it. However, a talent _____ ( ) from the Macmillan Company talked Mitchell into sending him her unfinished book and offered to buy the publishing rights. The book had to go through some changes before it could _____ ( ) in stores. For example, the original _____ ( ) had been *Tomorrow Is Another Day.* A main _____ ( ), Scarlett O'Hara, was named Pansy until just a few weeks before the book was published in 1936. In 1939, the story was made into a _____ ( ) that is still popular today.

Review of words with multiple meanings

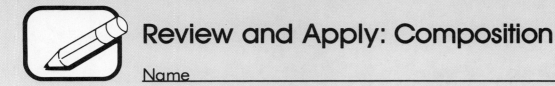

Review and Apply: Composition

Name _____

Read the list of words and their meanings below. For each word, write one sentence that uses both meanings of the word.

patient	a. person under medical care	b. willing to wait
pitcher	a. container for pouring liquid	b. baseball player
bowl	a. play a game with pins and a ball	b. rounded dish
husky	a. sled dog	b. big and strong
loaf	a. to be lazy	b. shaped mass of bread
palm	a. inside of the hand	b. kind of tree
racket	a. something used to hit a tennis ball	b. loud noise

1. A doctor's patient must sometimes be patient while waiting to be seen.

_____

_____

_____

_____

_____

_____

_____

_____

_____

_____

_____

_____

_____

_____

_____

_____

_____

_____

Review of words with multiple meanings

Idioms

Name _____

An idiom is a phrase or expression that cannot be understood by the meaning of its separate words. For example, **run into** is an idiom. To run into a friend has nothing to do with running into or with hitting a person. It means "to meet."

Read the words and phrases below. Then read the sentences that follow. Complete each sentence by writing a word or phrase that has the same meaning as the idiom shown below the blank.

fly	reject	found	visit
not laugh	became angry	rest	went to bed
stop	waited near		

1. After the football game, the news people _____waited near_____ the locker room to talk to the players.   (hung around)

2. Mrs. Bilington _____ when, by accident, I slammed a baseball
                  (blew a fuse)
through her front picture window.

3. The lifeguard blew her whistle at the two girls and told them to _____
the splashing.   (cut out)

4. Luis was awake past midnight last night, so he _____ early tonight.
                  (hit the sack)

5. A comedian who can _____ while telling a joke usually gets laughs by
              (keep a straight face)
surprising an audience.

6. I _____ this old photograph while cleaning out my bedroom closet.
        (ran across)

7. While on vacation, Dina plans to swim, read books, and _____.
              (take it easy)

8. Our neighbors are moving out of town, but they've invited us to _____
whenever we're near their new home.   (drop in)

9. I had to _____ Sue Lee's party invitation because I'd already made
           (turn down)
plans to attend a concert.

10. The quickest way to get from Indianapolis to St. Louis is to _____.
              (catch a plane)

Determining meanings of idioms in context

Figures of Speech

Name _____

A figure of speech is a phrase that compares two things that are not really alike but are similar in at least one way. A figure of speech may use the words *like* or *as* to tell how one thing is like another. For example, a person's hair may be described as *black as night* or *like silk*. A figure of speech may compare two things by saying that one thing *is* another. For example, in describing what your hair looks like when you get out of bed, you might say *My hair is a mop.*

Read the figures of speech below. Then read the sentences that follow. Complete each sentence by writing the figure of speech that has the same meaning as the words shown below the blank.

is a clown	like two cents	is a snail
hard as a rock	is a walking encyclopedia	as smooth as glass
like a bull in a china shop	is a chicken	am a real bear

1. My little brother _____is a chicken_____ when it comes to going to sleep in a darkened
   (is afraid)
   room all by himself.

2. Because the cornbread had not been tightly sealed in its wrapper, after a week it was
   _____.
   (stale)

3. There was not even a breeze, and the lake water was _____.
   (calm)

4. If I don't get enough sleep at night, I _____ when I have to get up the
   next morning.   (am grumpy)

5. Uncle Fred causes lots of accidents because he's _____.
   (clumsy)

6. I was so embarrassed at forgetting my neighbor's name, I felt _____.
   (almost worthless)

7. Whenever her bedroom needs cleaning, Marlena _____ about getting it
   done.   (is slow)

8. Because my friend Harold _____, the teacher sometimes has to speak
   sternly to him.   (is silly)

9. My mother always knows the answers to quiz game questions because she
   _____.
   (is smart)

Review and Apply: Comprehension

Name _____

Read the words and phrases below. Then read the story and notice the idiom or figure of speech below each blank. In each blank, write the word or phrase that has the same meaning as the words below the blank. You will use one word twice.

waiting	first thing	get angry	saw	calm
hurry	finally	quickly	reach	stuck

Today has really been horrible. ____First thing____ this morning, I broke my
(Right off the bat)

mother's expensive necklace, and she gave me a scolding. Then I moved

_____ to get downstairs for breakfast and tore the hem of my pants. After
(like mad)

putting on another pair, I _____ myself in a mirror and noticed they had
(caught sight of)

shrunk from many washings. By this time, I knew I'd have to _____, or I'd
(step on it)

be late for school. I dashed up the street toward the bus stop, but looking ahead, I saw the bus

had left me behind. I was ready to _____, but instead I sat down on the
(throw a fit)

curb to _____ myself. Before long, Mom drove by on her way to work.
(get a hold of)

"Maybe the bus is hung up in traffic," I said. "Let's follow its usual route and see if we can

_____ it." Sure enough, we found the bus a mile away,
(catch up with)

_____. Mom dropped me off at the intersection, and I ran down the
(caught like a bug in a web)

sidewalk _____ and motioned to the bus driver. _____
(like greased lightning)   (At last)

seated on the bus, I began to feel sick as I rode to school. I realized I had forgotten my math

homework. "What a great way to start a Monday," I thought, quietly laughing at myself. "I

can't imagine what else today has _____ for me!"
(in store)

Review of idioms and figures of speech

Review and Apply: Composition

Name _____

Imagine that you're spending the week at summer camp. Using at least six of the idioms and figures of speech below, write a letter to a friend. Tell about your adventures. You may also use your own idioms and figures of speech.

drives me buggy	as hungry as a bear	hang in there
like cats and dogs	take care	is a blast
is a doll	is a ball of energy	like a refrigerator
got carried away	as cold as ice	broke out
as hard as a rock	got the hang of	hit it off
is a riot	drop a line	as dry as a bone
let off steam	looks like a tornado struck	threw a party
worked like a horse	like a bottomless pit	is a sport

_____
_____
_____

Dear _____

_____
_____
_____
_____
_____
_____
_____
_____
_____
_____
_____

_____
_____

Analogies

Name _____

An analogy is a way to compare two things. It shows their relationship. The relationship between the first pair of words is the same as the relationship between the second pair of words. Analogies can be stated in two ways.

Finger is to *hand* as *toe* is to *foot*.   *Big* is to *little* as *cold* is to *hot*.
finger : hand : : toe : foot   big : little : : cold : hot

Read the list of words below. Then read the sentences that follow. Complete each sentence by writing the list word that completes the analogy.

sour   cow   calendar   gas   night   car

1. *Sun* is to *day* as *moon* is to _____night_____.

2. *Sugar* is to *sweet* as *lemon* is to _____.

3. *Lamp* is to *electricity* as *car* is to _____.

4. *Ride* is to *bike* as *drive* is to _____.

5. *Time* is to *clock* as *date* is to _____.

6. *Egg* is to *hen* as *milk* is to _____.

Read each analogy below. Figure out the relationship between the first pair of words. Then complete the second pair by writing the word from parentheses that has the same relationship.

1. cold : cool : : hot : _____warm_____ (weather, snow, warm, oven)

2. painter : picture : : author : _____ (book, pencil, paint, read)

3. chair : sit : : bed : _____ (table, television, stand, sleep)

4. mother : daughter : : father : _____ (sister, son, family, man)

5. fish : swim : : rabbit : _____ (bunny, hop, ears, water)

6. stop : go : : in : _____ (out, over, above, around)

7. basketball : court : : baseball : _____ (bat, diamond, play, football)

8. mud : dirty : : soap : _____ (clean, wash, bathtub, dishes)

9. spider : web : : bird : _____ (leaves, fly, branches, nest)

10. horse : colt : : cow : _____ (barn, calf, farm, pony)

Analogies

Name _____

Read the sentences below. Complete each one by writing the word from parentheses that completes the analogy.

1. *Butterfly* is to *fly* as *fish* is to _____swim_____. (cocoon, swim, moth, water)

2. *Smile* is to *frown* as *happy* is to _____. (sad, mouth, glad, face)

3. *Leaf* is to *tree* as *bloom* is to _____. (garden, branch, soil, flower)

4. *Dime* is to *ten* as *nickel* is to _____. (money, fifteen, one, five)

5. *Lend* is to *borrow* as *beautiful* is to _____. (steal, ugly, pretty, give)

6. *Carrot* is to *bean* as *apple* is to _____. (food, fruit, orange, peel)

7. *Crayon* is to *color* as *violin* is to _____. (guitar, music, paint, drum)

8. *Orchard* is to *trees* as *garden* is to _____. (flowers, dig, grass, pick)

9. *Bill* is to *William* as *Bob* is to _____. (Robert, boy, Smith, John)

10. *Oar* is to *row* as *scissors* is to _____. (paper, sharp, boat, cut)

Read the list of words below. Then read the analogies that follow. Complete each one by writing the correct list word.

| neck | arm | fire | wheel | win |
| girl | see | nation | whale | string |

1. shirt : button : : shoe : _____string_____

2. door : knob : : car : _____

3. desert : camel : : ocean : _____

4. glacier : ice : : sun : _____

5. lungs : breathe : : eyes : _____

6. collar : neck : : sleeve : _____

7. gift : present : : country : _____

8. ring : necklace : : finger : _____

9. brother : boy : : sister : _____

10. defeat : loss : : victory : _____

Review and Apply: Comprehension

Name _____

Look at each pair of pictures below. Think about the ways in which the picture parts are alike. Then write an analogy to show the comparison. If you wish, you may use some of the following words in your analogies.

canvas	curtains	antler	rain	bird	feather	cloud
wing	pour	vase	pond	tusk	picture	glass
window	trunk	cage	milk	bloom	leaf	elephant
pitcher	flower	fall	nose	bowl	frame	deer

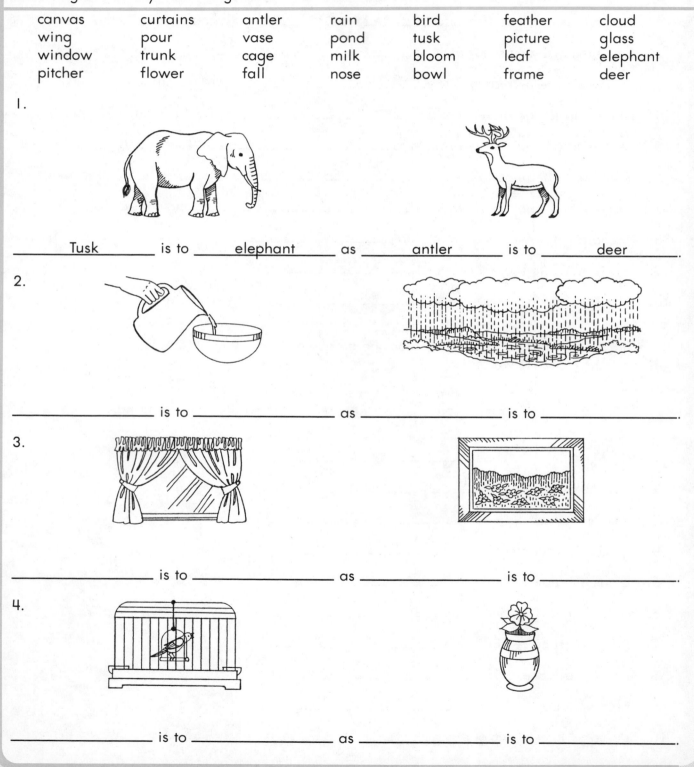

1.

_____Tusk_____ is to _____elephant_____ as _____antler_____ is to _____deer_____.

2.

_____ is to _____ as _____ is to _____.

3.

_____ is to _____ as _____ is to _____.

4.

_____ is to _____ as _____ is to _____.

Review of analogies

Review and Apply: Composition

Name _____

Questions, questions, questions! Your four-year-old cousin, for whom you are babysitting, is always asking questions. Below are some of your cousin's questions. Answer each one and then write an analogy that illustrates your answer.

1. How is a toothbrush like a broom? __Both a toothbrush and a broom__ ____

    __are used for cleaning.__ ____

    ___Toothbrush___ is to _____teeth_____ as _____broom_____ is to _____floor_____.

2. How is a house like a fish bowl? _____

    _____

    _____ is to _____ as _____ is to _____.

3. How is a violin like a drum? _____

    _____

    _____ is to _____ as _____ is to _____.

4. How is a door like a zipper? _____

    _____

    _____ is to _____ as _____ is to _____.

5. How is baseball like hockey? _____

    _____

    _____ is to _____ as _____ is to _____.

6. How is a button like a shoestring? _____

    _____

    _____ is to _____ as _____ is to _____.

7. How is a refrigerator like a silo? _____

    _____

    _____ is to _____ as _____ is to _____.

Review of analogies

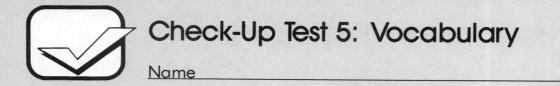

Check-Up Test 5: Vocabulary

Name _____

Read the story. Then, using the underlined story words, follow the directions below.

When a baby kangaroo is born, it is <u>as big as your thumb</u>. The baby, which is called a joey, cannot see, hear, walk, or jump. It crawls into a <u>pouch</u> on its mother's stomach and <u>remains</u> there about eight months. During that time, its body grows and develops more fully.

A full-grown kangaroo is 6 to 7 <u>feet</u> tall and <u>weighs</u> 100 to 150 <u>pounds</u>. Its hind legs are much larger than the front ones because they are used for jumping. A long, muscular <u>tail</u> helps the kangaroo keep its balance when it stands, walks, and jumps. The kangaroo has a small head, similar to a deer's, with a pointed nose. Its large ears stand upright on top of its head. They can turn from front to back, allowing the kangaroo to <u>pick up sounds like radar</u>.

The kangaroo <u>is the pogo stick of the animal world</u>. It can <u>cover</u> short distances at speeds up to 40 miles an <u>hour</u> and <u>leap</u> over trees and bushes that are 6 feet tall. About this animal that <u>begins</u> life the size of a thumb but later jumps higher than even the <u>finest</u> basketball player, one thing is <u>certain</u>: The kangaroo is surely an animal that grows by leaps and bounds!

Follow each of the directions below. Use the underlined words from the story above.

1. Write the words that are synonyms for these words.   stays _____

    jump _____   sack _____

2. Write the words that are antonyms for these words.   worst _____

    ends _____   uncertain _____

3. Write the words that are homophones for these words.   ways _____

    tale _____   our _____

4. Write the phrases that have these meanings.   small _____

    jumps well _____

    hear well _____

5. Write the words that can have either of these two meanings.

    (a) parts of the body used for walking   (b) units of 12 inches _____

    (a) go over; travel   (b) blanket _____

6. Complete the sentence by writing the same word in both blanks.

    The worker _____ the heavy metal stakes into the ground with a sledge

    hammer that weighs five _____.

Check-Up Test 6: Vocabulary

Name _____

Read the words below. Use them to answer the questions that follow.

content	time	orange	solution	seller	guard	find
finger	week	seal	humorous	weave	backward	fair
left	decide	loaf	leave	unhappy	towed	

1. Write the antonyms of these words.   forward _____

    problem _____   arrive _____

2. Write the synonyms of these words.   protect _____

    funny _____   miserable _____

3. Write the homophones of these words.   we've _____

    toad _____   cellar _____

4. Complete each sentence below by writing the same homograph in both blanks.

    After three weeks of work, Jim was _____ with the _____
    of his history report.

    Peter _____ the room, walked down the hall, and turned _____.

    To keep the contest _____, there were five judges at our

    county-_____ tractor pull.

5. Write the words that can have either of these meanings.

    (a) to be lazy   (b) a large shape of baked bread _____

    (a) sea mammal   (b) to close or fasten tightly _____

    (a) reddish-yellow color   (b) a citrus fruit _____

6. Write the word that has the same meaning as each underlined phrase below.

    If you <u>run across</u> my old photograph album, please let me know. _____

    I can't <u>make up my mind</u> about what color to paint the room. _____

7. Complete each analogy below.

    Date is to *calendar* as _____ is to *watch*.

    December is to *year* as *Saturday* is to _____.

    Belt is to *waist* as *ring* is to _____.

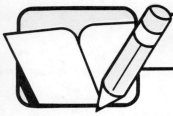

READING

Exercise and Health

Exercise comes from a Latin word that means "to keep busy." Keeping busy is a way of keeping healthy. You need exercise for your mind, your body, and your personality.

Exercising Your Mind

Exercise helps improve your mind. It keeps your mind working well. Everyone should do some mental exercises every day. These kinds of exercises help you think clearly. They help you solve problems quickly and easily. They help you understand your feelings better. They help you study and learn new things to make life more interesting.

You can do mental exercises by yourself or with other people. Reading and thinking are two kinds of exercises for your mind that you can do by yourself. You can write a poem or do arithmetic. You can put together a puzzle with a friend or play a thinking game with your family.

Exercising Your Body

Exercise helps keep your body healthy. You must use your muscles to keep your body in good shape. When you exercise your body, your muscles become strong. A healthy body helps you sleep well and work well. Physical exercise helps control your weight, improves your blood flow, and makes you look and feel fit and healthy.

Some kinds of physical exercise are good for your whole body. These include walking, running, jumping rope, and swimming. You can also work on different parts of your body. You can stretch and bend and lift weights. Playing sports is still another way to keep your body in good shape. It exercises your mind, too.

Exercising Your Social Skills

Exercise helps you improve your social skills, or the ways you behave with other people. Social exercises help you learn to make and keep friends. They also help you to become a good neighbor and a good citizen.

Working and playing with others are two ways to improve your social skills. Playing a game of volleyball or working with classmates to prepare a health report helps you learn cooperation. When you cooperate, you want to do your best for the team or the group — and for yourself. Then you feel good. Games and other kinds of teamwork help you learn to play fair and to lose gracefully. The more you work at improving your skills, the more successful you'll be.

Application of reading skills in a health context

Name _____

A. Answer the following questions.
    1. What does the word *exercise* mean?

    _____

    2. What three kinds of exercise does everyone need?

    _____   _____   _____

B. List three ways that mental exercise helps you.

    1. _____

    2. _____

    3. _____

C. List three ways that physical exercise helps you.

    1. _____

    2. _____

    3. _____

D. List three ways that social exercise helps you.

    1. _____

    2. _____

    3. _____

E. Read each sentence below. Check the answers that correctly complete the sentence.

    1. You can improve your social skills by _____ with others.

        _____ playing   _____ fighting   _____ working

    2. You cooperate with others when you _____.

        _____ follow the rules   _____ play fair   _____ have to win

Reading and Writing Wrap-Up

Name _____

A. Draw a line to match each word on the left with its meaning on the right.

    1. mental   a. having to do with the personality

    2. physical   b. having to do with the body

    3. social   c. working with others for the good of all

    4. cooperation   d. having to do with the mind

B. Read each phrase below. Write *mental, physical,* or *social* to tell what kind of exercise is described. Some phrases may describe more than one kind of exercise. Write all the answers that fit each description. The first one has been done for you.

    1.   mental, physical, social   marching in the band

    2. _____ jumping rope

    3. _____ riding a bicycle

    4. _____ washing cars with your scout group to raise money

    5. _____ reading the front page of the newspaper

    6. _____ introducing a new student to your classmates

    7. _____ working math problems

    8. _____ playing basketball

    9. _____ doing a crossword puzzle

C. Choose one of the numbered items in Part B and tell why you gave the answer or answers you did. Tell exactly how the exercise would improve a person's mind, body, or social skills.

_____

_____

_____

_____

_____

Name _____

WRITING

My Exercise Journal

Every day for a week, write down the exercises you do for your mind, your body, and your personality. Try to do each kind of exercise every day.

SUNDAY *Mental* _____

Physical _____

Social _____

MONDAY *Mental* _____

Physical _____

Social _____

TUESDAY *Mental* _____

Physical _____

Social _____

WEDNESDAY *Mental* _____

Physical _____

Social _____

THURSDAY *Mental* _____

Physical _____

Social _____

FRIDAY *Mental* _____

Physical _____

Social _____

SATURDAY *Mental* _____

Physical _____

Social _____

Guide Words

Name _____

The two words at the top of a dictionary page are called guide words. The first guide word is the same as the first word listed on the page. The second guide word is the same as the last word listed on the page. To find a word in the dictionary, decide if it comes in alphabetical order between the guide words on a page. If it does, you will find the word on that page. For example, the word **home** falls between the guide words **hollow** and **hop.**

Read each pair of guide words and the words that are listed below them. Circle the words in each list that could be found on a page that has that pair of guide words.

bass / bobcat	**burro / cobra**	**caterpillar / crow**	**dog / elephant**
(beaver)	copperhead	catfish	dinosaur
baboon	cow	cricket	dove
boxer	bulldog	cuckoo	dragonfly
bat	buzzard	cardinal	deer
bobwhite	cat	crocodile	eagle
bluegill	camel	collie	dolphin
beagle	canary	chipmunk	elk
bluebird	buffalo	chimpanzee	duck

Read the words below. Then look at the guide words above. For each word below, write the guide words between which the word would be found in a dictionary.

1. butterfly _____ burro _____ / _____ cobra _____

2. eel _____ / _____

3. coyote _____ / _____

4. bloodhound _____ / _____

5. donkey _____ / _____

6. bear _____ / _____

7. bobcat _____ / _____

8. button _____ / _____

9. chickadee _____ / _____

Using guide words

Guide Words

Name _____

Read the six pairs of guide words and their dictionary page numbers. Then read the list of words that follow. Write the page number on which each list word would be found in the dictionary.

damage / **disease** - p. 130   **doubt** / **faucet** - p. 152   **flavor** / **hotel** - p. 188
human / **jealous** - p. 234   **jingle** / **lantern** - p. 257   **leather** / **lodge** - p. 270

1. giraffe _____p. 188_____

2. locomotive _____

3. design _____

4. language _____

5. envelope _____

6. invention _____

7. jungle _____

8. lemon _____

9. hesitate _____

10. instrument _____

11. dinosaur _____

12. electricity _____

Read the sentences and word choices below. Using the guide words above, complete each sentence by writing the word that would be found on the dictionary page whose number is shown beside the word choices.

1. It is _____dangerous_____ to dive into a shallow pond.
     (p. 130 - unsafe, dangerous)

2. Grandma taught me how to play a folk song on the _____.
                                                     (p. 188 - guitar, banjo)

3. Spot is afraid of _____, so he hides under my bed during a storm.
          (p. 270 - lightning, thunder)

4. It was fortunate that no lives were lost during the _____.
                                                    (p. 234 - hurricane, tornado)

5. Two people paddled down the river in a _____.
                                      (p. 257 - kayak, canoe)

6. I bought this _____ on sale at Kale's Department Store.
          (p. 234 - jewelry, jacket)

7. Miguel plans to be a _____ after he graduates from college.
          (p. 130 - doctor, dentist)

8. There were _____ people at the holiday party.
          (p. 188 - forty, fifty)

Guide Words

Name _____

Read the list of words below. Then read the guide words that follow. Write each word or phrase below the correct pair of guide words. Then number each list of words to show how they would be listed in alphabetical order.

respiration	saliva	blood	appendix	artery	vitamin
biceps	tissue	pupil	stomach	cell	breath
pulse	bladder	reflex	capillary	vein	
cartilage	aorta	cerebrum	tendon	calcium	
blood vessel	cerebellum	spine	bacteria	breathe	
taste	red blood cell	skeleton	ventricle	retina	

1. **abdomen / bone**

_____aorta_____ ___1___

_____ _____

_____ _____

_____ _____

_____ _____

_____ _____

_____ _____

_____ _____

2. **brain / cornea**

_____ _____

_____ _____

_____ _____

_____ _____

_____ _____

_____ _____

_____ _____

_____ _____

3. **plasma / skin**

_____ _____

_____ _____

_____ _____

_____ _____

_____ _____

_____ _____

_____ _____

4. **skull / vocal cord**

_____ _____

_____ _____

_____ _____

_____ _____

_____ _____

_____ _____

_____ _____

_____ _____

Using guide words

Entry Words

Name _____

The word you look up in a dictionary is called an entry word. An entry word shows the spelling of the word and its syllables. Entry words are printed in dark type at the left of each column on the dictionary page. An entry word together with its meanings is called an entry.

cit y /sit′ ē/ *n, pl* **cit ies 1** a large town: *Chicago is a large city.* **2** the people of a city: *The city elected a new mayor in this year's election.*

drea ry /drir′ ē/ *adj* **drea ri er; drea ri est 1** gloomy: *The room looked dreary without any windows.* **2** causing feelings of sadness: *The rainy weather put me in a dreary mood.* —**drea ri ly** *adv* —**drea ri ness** *n*

When you look for a word in a dictionary, look for the base word. For example, if you want to find **cities,** look for **city.** If you want to find **drearily,** look for **dreary.** Any spelling changes for different forms of the entry word are usually listed at the beginning or end of the entry.

An abbreviation for an entry word's part of speech is usually listed at the beginning or end of the entry. In the first example above, **n** means that **city** is a noun. Abbreviations for other forms of the entry word are usually listed beside those forms. In the second example, **adv** means that **drearily** is an adverb.

Read each word below. In the first blank, write the entry word you would look for to find the word in a dictionary. Then look up the entry word in a dictionary. In the second blank, write the dictionary abbreviation for the entry word's part of speech.

1. starved _____starve_____ ___v___
2. politely _____ _____
3. simplest _____ _____
4. improves _____ _____
5. punishing _____ _____
6. orchards _____ _____
7. uglier _____ _____
8. victories _____ _____
9. defenseless _____ _____
10. admired _____ _____
11. territories _____ _____
12. shaggiest _____ _____

13. radishes _____ _____
14. multiplied _____ _____
15. preparing _____ _____
16. sadder _____ _____
17. speeches _____ _____
18. sombreros _____ _____
19. irrigated _____ _____
20. amazing _____ _____
21. gratefulness _____ _____
22. scarcely _____ _____
23. marshes _____ _____
24. shallowest _____ _____

Entry Words and Dictionary Meanings

Name _____

Read the dictionary entries below. Then read the sentences that follow. Complete each sentence by writing the correct entry word. You will use some entry words more than once. In the blank that follows the sentence, write the number of the word's correct meaning.

bulb /bulb/ *n* **1** the underground resting stage of a plant, consisting of a short stem base enclosed in thick leaves **2** a round glass object that glows when put into the socket of an electric light

calf /kaf/ *n, pl* **calves 1** a baby cow **2** the back of the leg between the knee and the ankle

free /frē/ *adj* **1** having liberty **2** without cost

iron /īrn, ī′ ərn/ *n* **1** metal used in making a large number of building materials, tools, and machinery: *The rail is made of iron.* **2** an electrical hand tool used for pressing or smoothing cloth

key /kē/ *n* **1** a tool made to open locks **2** a lever on a musical instrument or machine that is pushed down by the fingers: *This piano key plays a C note.* **3** something that helps with finding the answer: *We found the key to the problem.*

lace /lās/ *n* **1** a decoration used on clothing **2** a string used for bringing two edges together, such as a lace for tying a shoe

nail /nāl/ *n* **1** a thin, pointed piece of metal used to hold pieces of wood together **2** something that grows on a finger or toe: *The nail on Kay's little finger is broken.*

1. Rosa wore a red velvet dress with _____lace_____ around the collar. __1__

2. The fish I caught wasn't big enough to eat, so I set it _____. ____

3. Mr. Wise had to break a window to get into his apartment because he locked his _____ inside. ____

4. Plant this _____ in the fall, and in the spring you'll have a beautiful red tulip. ____

5. Terry broke the _____ on her big toe when she stubbed it. ____

6. By pouring water into an _____, you can use steam to press the wrinkles out of your clothes. ____

7. The runner had to drop out of the race because she had a painful cramp in the _____ of her left leg. ____

8. One _____ on the typewriter is stuck. ____

9. That lamp doesn't work because the _____ is burned out. ____

10. The department store is giving _____ theater tickets to each customer who buys twenty-five dollars' worth of goods. ____

11. Cindy tied her ice skate with twine because the _____ broke. ____

Using entry words in context; Determining word meaning from context

Dictionary Meanings and Word Histories

Name _____

Many words in the English language have been borrowed from other languages. Some have come from the names of people or places. A few are made of letters from two or more words. Most dictionaries list a word history, or etymology, for some entry words. A word history tells what language the entry word comes from. It shows how the word is spelled in that language and what it means. Usually, a word history is shown before or after the meaning.

al li ga tor /al′ ə gāt′ ər/ n [from Spanish *el lagarto*, meaning "the lizard"] a large animal that lives in rivers and has a long body, short legs, thick skin, and a long tail

chop su ey /chop sü′ ē/ n [from Chinese *tsap sui*, meaning "odds and ends"] a food made from bamboo shoots, bean sprouts, onions, mushrooms, and meat or fish cut up, cooked in a sauce, and often served over rice or fried noodles

Fer ris wheel /fer′ əs hwēl/ n [named after George Ferris, the American engineer who invented it] an amusement park ride made of a large revolving wheel that has seats hanging from it

jum bo /jum′ bō/ adj. [from *Jumbo*, the name of a large elephant in P.T. Barnum's circus] very big

ra dar /rā′ där/ n [from the beginning letters of *radio detecting and ranging*] an electronic detector that sends out a powerful beam that reflects off a distant object to show its position and direction of movement

tu lip /tü′ lip, tyü′ lip/ n [from Turkish *tülbend*, meaning "turban"] a plant with a thick stem, long narrow leaves, and a cup-shaped flower

Answer each question by using the sample entries above.

1. From what language does the word *alligator* come? _____Spanish_____ What do the words from which *alligator* comes mean? _____

2. After whom was the Ferris wheel named? _____

3. The word *radar* comes from a combination of what four words? _____
   _____

4. From what language do the words *chop suey* come? _____ What do the words mean? _____

5. After what was the word *jumbo* named? _____

6. What is the Turkish word from which *tulip* comes? _____ What is the meaning of this word? _____ Was the tulip probably named for the shape of the stem, the leaves, or the flower? _____

7. Which three entry words began as English words? _____
   _____

Review and Apply: Comprehension

Name _____

Read the dictionary entries below. Use them to answer the questions that follow.

¹**inch** /inch/ *n, pl* **inch es** [from Old English *ynce*, which came from Latin *uncia*, meaning "one twelfth"] one of twelve equal parts of a foot (about 2.5 cm): *The baby's finger is an inch long.*
²**inch** *v* to move very slowly, a little at a time: *The line of people waiting to purchase theater tickets inched toward the ticket booth.*

rul er /rü′ lər/ *n* **1** one who governs or rules: *Queen Elizabeth is the ruler of Great Britain.* **2** a marked strip of wood or metal for drawing lines or measuring
spa ghet ti /spə get′ ē/ *n, pl* [from Italian, from the plural of *spaghetto*, meaning "little strings"] a food made of wheat dough that is formed into long, thin strands and boiled in water before eating

1. Circle the pair of words that would be guide words for each dictionary entry shown in dark print below.

   a. **inch**   instead / invisible   inactive / income   idea / imagine

   b. **ruler**   rust / saddle   royal / rug   ruin / rush

   c. **spaghetti** slipper / spacecraft   sparrow / squirt   sour / statue

2. Which entry word can be used as either a noun or a verb? _____

3. From what two languages did the word *inch* come? _____

4. Which entry word is the plural form of an Italian word? _____ What

   was the Italian meaning of this word? _____

5. What was the meaning of the word from which the word *inch* came? _____

6. Look at the underlined word in each sentence below. Write the number of the word's meaning.

   a. Before buying a picture frame, Rachael measured the length and width of the picture

      with a <u>ruler</u>. ____

   b. From 1862 to 1908, Tz'u-hsi, one of the most powerful women in history, was the <u>ruler</u>

      of China. ____

7. Look at the underlined word in each sentence below. Write the dictionary abbreviation for the word's part of speech.

   a. An <u>inch</u> of snow fell while we were sleeping last night. ____

   b. Antonio watched a caterpillar <u>inch</u> its way across a tree limb. ____

8. What other form of the word *inch* is listed in the entry for *inch*? _____

Review of guide words, entry words, part-of-speech labels, dictionary meanings, and word origins

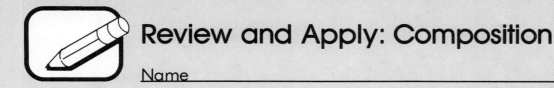

Review and Apply: Composition

Name _____

This is your chance to invent the wackiest word in the English language. No one else knows the word, so it's your job to write a dictionary entry for it. Follow the directions below.

1. Think of a wacky word and write it here. _____

2. Write two guide words (real words) between which your word would fall.

    _____

3. Write the meaning of your wacky word. _____

    _____

4. As what part of speech would your word be used? Use one of these abbreviations to name

    its part of speech: *n, v, adj, adv, conj, prep, pron, int.* _____

5. Think of a second meaning for your word. It should have the same part of speech as the

    first meaning. _____

    _____

6. For each meaning, write a sentence using the word. _____

    _____

7. Did you form your wacky word from another word or words? Tell how it got its name.

    _____

8. Does your word have an unusual plural or an **-ed, -ing, -er,** or **-est** form? Write any

    forms of your word. _____

9. Using the examples below, write a complete dictionary entry for your wacky word.

anchor   **astronaut**   _____

ar rive *v* **ar rived; ar riv ing** [from Latin *arripare,*   _____
meaning "to come to shore"] **1** to reach a place to
which one is going: *Ricardo will arrive in New York*   _____
today. **2** to come: *I can't wait for my birthday to*
arrive.   _____

as sem bly *n, pl* **as sem blies 1** a group of people   _____
meeting together for some purpose: *Our mayor*
talked to us at the assembly today. **2** a collection   _____
of parts that make up a unit: *The airplane had lost*
its tail assembly.   _____

Pronunciation Key and Respellings

Name _____

A dictionary can show you how words are pronounced. An entry word is followed by a respelling. The respelling is made up of letters and special symbols. The words in the dictionary's pronunciation key show you how to pronounce each letter or symbol. By combining the sounds for each symbol and letter, you can pronounce the word.

Pronunciation Key

/a/ = apple, tap	/k/ = kick, can	/th/ = thing, both
/ā/ = ate, say	/l/ = laugh, pail	/u/ = up, cut
/är/ = car, heart	/m/ = mouse, ham	/ü/ = soon, rule
/ãr/ = hair, care	/n/ = nice, ran	/u̇/ = look, put
/b/ = bat, cab	/ng/ = ring, song	/v/ = vine, live
/ch/ = chain, chair	/o/ = father, hot	/w/ = wet, away
/d/ = door, sad	/ō/ = old, so	/y/ = yes, you
/e/ = get, egg	/o̊/ = ball, dog	/yü/ = use, cute
/ē/ = even, bee	/oi/ = boy, oil	/yu̇/ = cure, pure
/f/ = fan, off	/ou/ = house, cow	/z/ = zoo, zero
/g/ = goat, big	/p/ = pan, nap	/zh/ = pleasure, beige
/h/ = her, happy	/r/ = ran, race	/ə/ = a (around)
/hw/ = wheel, why	/s/ = sun, mess	e (better)
/i/ = is, fit	/sh/ = she, rush	i (rabbit)
/ī/ = ice, tie	/t/ = toy, mat	o (doctor)
/j/ = jump, gentle	/Ŧh/ = they, smooth	u (upon)

Use the pronunciation key above to pronounce each respelling below. Then read the words in the row. Circle the word that matches the respelling.

1.	/ə pēl'/	apple	uphill	(appeal)	appear
2.	/dēd/	deed	did	dead	deep
3.	/gaj' ət/	engage	jagged	garage	gadget
4.	/ring' kəl/	ring	wrinkle	wriggle	ringlet
5.	/kə nü'/	canoe	can	kennel	canyon
6.	/bam bü'/	bandage	banana	balloon	bamboo
7.	/feŦh' ər/	father	feather	future	farther
8.	/haz' ənt/	haze	hesitate	hasn't	has
9.	/hüm/	whom	hum	who	humid
10.	/nōn/	none	noon	known	noun
11.	/jē og' rə fē/	jogging	jealousy	geography	geology
12.	/shan' də lir'/	sandier	champion	shabby	chandelier

Using a pronunciation key; Reading dictionary respellings

Pronunciation Key and Respellings

Name _____

In most dictionaries, a short form of the pronunciation key can be found on each page.

Pronunciation Key

/a/ = apple, tap; /ā/ = ate, say; /är/ = car, heart; /ãr/ = hair, care; /ch/ = chain, chair; /e/ = get, egg; /ē/ = even, bee; /hw/ = wheel, why; /i/ = is, fit; /ī/ = ice, tie; /ng/ = ring, song; /o/ = father, hot; /ō/ = old, so; /ȯ/ = ball, dog; /oi/ = boy, oil; /ou/ = house, cow; /sh/ = she, rush; /ᵫh/ = they, smooth; /th/ = thing, both; /u/ = up, cut; /ü/ = soon, rule; /ù/ = look, put; /yü/ = use, cute; /yù/ = cure, pure; /zh/ = pleasure, beige; /ə/ = a (around), e (better), i (rabbit), o (doctor), u (upon)

Read the first word in each row below. Then read the respellings in the row. Use the key to pronounce the respellings. Circle the one that matches the word.

1.	launch	(/lȯnch/)	/lənch/	/lach/
2.	petal	/ped' əl/	/pet' əl/	/pȯrt' ə bəl/
3.	house	/hȯrs/	/hüz/	/hous/
4.	quiet	/kwī' ət/	/kwit/	/kwīt/
5.	cherries	/cher' ish/	/cher' ēz/	/chēz/
6.	swarm	/swȯmp/	/swam/	/swȯrm/
7.	delicate	/del' i kət/	/del' i gāt/	/ded' i kāt/

Read each respelling below. Then read the sentence and the words shown in parentheses. Complete the sentence by writing the word that matches the respelling.

1. /rā' zər/ My brother bought a new _____razor_____ because he lost his old one.
(eraser, razor)

2. /sik' əl/ The garden hose is hanging in the garage near Mom's _____.
(sickle, cycle)

3. /sēd' ər/ One of the things I like most is the smell of _____.
(cedar, cider)

4. /bi nēth'/ Scamper's favorite place to sleep is _____ my bed.
(beside, beneath)

5. /ri sēt'/ The woman wasn't able to read the _____ without her glasses.
(receipt, recipe)

6. /kus' təmz/ Rita's report was about the _____ of other countries.
(costumes, customs)

Accent Marks

Name _____

Dictionary respellings of words that have two or more syllables show the syllables by putting a space or mark between them. When a word has more than one syllable, one syllable is usually said with more stress than the others. In the respelling /fin′ ish/, the accent mark after the first syllable shows that **fin** is said with more stress than **ish.** In some words, the syllables in the entry word are not the same as the ones in the respelling.

Use the key to pronounce each respelling in List A. Then read the words in List B. Write the word from List B that matches each respelling. Leave a space between its syllables. Then put an accent mark after the syllable that is said with more stress.

Pronunciation Key

/a/ = apple, tap; /ā/ = ate, say; /är/ = car, heart; /ãr/ = hair, care; /ch/ = chain, chair; /e/ = get, egg; /ē/ = even, bee; /hw/ = wheel, why; /i/ = is, fit; /ī/ = ice, tie; /ng/ = ring, song; /o/ = father, hot; /ō/ = old, so; /ò/ = ball, dog; /oi/ = boy, oil; /ou/ = house, cow; /sh/ = she, rush; /ᵺh/ = they, smooth; /th/ = thing, both; /u/ = up, cut; /ü/ = soon, rule; /ů/ = look, put; /yü/ = use, cute; /yů/ = cure, pure; /zh/ = pleasure, beige; /ə/ = a (around), e (better), i (rabbit), o (doctor), u (upon)

List A		List B
1. /fē es′ tə/	_____fi es′ ta_____	ma roon
2. /bā′ ləf/	_____	pa ren the sis
3. /kar′ ik tər/	_____	e mo tion
4. /i mō′ shən/	_____	ci der
5. /sīd′ ər/	_____	fi es ta
6. /mə rün′/	_____	ki mo no
7. /kə mō′ nə/	_____	bai liff
8. /pə ren′ thə səs/	_____	char ac ter

The words below have been divided into syllables. Say each word and listen for the stressed syllable. Put an accent mark after the stressed syllable in each word.

1. bliz′zard	5. beau ti ful	9. car pen ter
2. dis turb	6. a wake	10. par rot
3. vol ca no	7. cal en dar	11. ge og ra phy
4. si ren	8. fu ri ous	12. gov ern ment

Recognizing accented syllables

Accent Marks

Name _____

Two-syllable words that are spelled alike may have different respellings. They may be pronounced with the stress on different syllables. Read the dictionary entries below. Use the accent marks to say each word and listen for the stressed syllable.

¹**con tent** /kən tent′/ *adj* pleased; satisfied: *Mrs. Meyers is content with her son's grades in school.*

²**con tent** /kon′ tent/ *n* **1** something that is contained—often used in the plural, **contents:** *The contents of the box fell out on the floor.* **2** the subject matter treated: *The content of her speech made everyone unhappy.* **3** amount held: *These jars have a content of one gallon each.*

¹**des ert** /dez′ ərt/ *n* a hot, sandy area with few trees and little water: *We were thirsty and hot in the desert.*

²**de sert** /di zərt′/ *v* **de sert ed; de sert ing** to leave or abandon a person or thing that one should stay with

¹**min ute** /min′ ət/ *n* one of sixty equal units of time in an hour: *Let the water boil for one minute.*

²**mi nute** /mī nüt′/ *adj* **1** very small; tiny

¹**re fuse** /ri fyüz′/ *v* **re fused; re fus ing 1** to say no to: *She tried to refuse my offer of help.* **2** to decline to do: *The horse might refuse to jump.*

²**ref use** /ref′ yüs, ref′ yüz/ *n* something to be thrown away; trash

Read each sentence below. Write the underlined word, leaving a space between its syllables. Put an accent mark after the stressed syllable in each word. Use the entries to help you.

1. On cold winter days, Luis is <u>content</u> to stay indoors and read. _____con tent′_____

2. Some insects are so <u>minute</u>, they can't be seen by the naked eye. _____

3. Although it would have been easy, Michael did not <u>desert</u> his old friends after he became a well-known singer. _____

4. It is hard to <u>refuse</u> one's favorite foods while dieting. _____

5. Our team scored a touchdown in the last <u>minute</u> of the game. _____

6. Once a week, city workers on a truck take away the <u>refuse</u> from the bins behind our apartment building. _____

7. The teacher liked the <u>content</u> of my report but said that the handwriting could be improved. _____

8. A cactus can survive in the <u>desert</u> because it needs little water. _____

9. A soldier who chooses to <u>desert</u> the army will be punished. _____

10. Our new aquarium has a larger <u>content</u> than the one that broke. _____

11. The Sahara, in Africa, is the largest <u>desert</u> in the world. _____

Recognizing accented syllables of homographs in context

Name _____

Read the list of words below. Then read the paragraph and the respellings shown below the blanks. Use the pronunciation key to pronounce the respellings. In each blank, write the list word that matches the respelling. You will use only twelve of the list words.

libraries	native	capsule	carriage	stroll	variety	tutors	Hobby
wouldn't	Acquire	capital	vanity	courses	horseback	Happy	wooden
lawbreakers	nature	Aquarium	stroke	garage	tourists	houseboat	coarse

Pronunciation Key

/a/ = apple, tap; /ā/ = ate, say; /är/ = car, heart; /ãr/ = hair, care; /ch/ = chain, chair; /e/ = get, egg; /ē/ = even, bee; /hw/ = wheel, why; /i/ = is, fit; /ī/ = ice, tie; /ng/ = ring, song; /o/ = father, hot; /ō/ = old, so; /ò/ = ball, dog; /oi/ = boy, oil; /ou/ = house, cow; /sh/ = she, rush; /ŦH/ = they, smooth; /th/ = thing, both; /u/ = up, cut; /ü/ = soon, rule; /ù/ = look, put; /yü/ = use, cute; /yù/ = cure, pure; /zh/ = pleasure, beige; /ə/ = a (around), e (better), i (rabbit), o (doctor), u (upon)

Bermuda is a tiny island in the Atlantic Ocean. The east side of the island is well known

for its historic sights. In the town of St. George's, heavy _____wooden_____ frames
/wùd' ən/

that were once used to hold _____ are on display. Outside St. George's,
/lò' brāk ərz/

_____ lovers enjoy visiting the Bermuda _____, where
/nā' chər/   /ə kwer' ē əm/

they can see 150 kinds of sea life. In the _____ city, Hamilton, visitors can
/kap' ət əl/

ride around town in a _____ drawn by horses. Or they may
/kar' ij/

_____ through the beautiful Par-la Ville Gardens. The west side of
/strōl/

Bermuda, with its famous pink, sandy beaches, attracts sports lovers. Besides swimming and

diving, visitors can choose from a wide

_____ of sports. They
/və rī' ət ē/

may play golf on the finest

_____ or play tennis on
/kōrs' əz/

all-weather courts. They take a morning

_____ ride along the
/hòrs' bak/

beach before breakfast. No wonder so many

_____ have agreed with
/tùr' əsts/

Mark Twain, who called Bermuda "The

_____ Island."
/hap' ē/

Review and Apply: Composition

Name _____

Use the pronunciation key to pronounce each respelling below. In the first blank, write the word that matches the respelling. In the blanks that follow, write a riddle that uses the word for an answer. If you need to, you may change the spelling of your answer to better fit the riddle, as has been done in the example.

Pronunciation Key

/a/ = apple, tap; /ā/ = ate, say; /är/ = car, heart; /ār/ = hair, care; /ch/ = chain, chair; /e/ = get, egg; /ē/ = even, bee; /hw/ = wheel, why; /i/ = is, fit; /ī/ = ice, tie; /ng/ = ring, song; /o/ = father, hot; /ō/ = old, so; /ȯ/ = ball, dog; /oi/ = boy, oil; /ou/ = house, cow; /sh/ = she, rush; /ŦH/ = they, smooth; /th/ = thing, both; /u/ = up, cut; /ü/ = soon, rule; /u̇/ = look, put; /yü/ = use, cute; /yu̇/ = cure, pure; /zh/ = pleasure, beige; /ə/ = a (around), e (better), i (rabbit), o (doctor), u (upon)

1. /mü′ vē/ _____movie_____   Where do cows take their dates on Saturday nights?

    ___Answer: To the drive-in MOOOOOOOOvies!_____

2. /ā′ kȯrn/ _____   _____

    _____

3. /krak′ ərz/ _____   _____

    _____

4. /gō′ fər/ _____   _____

    _____

5. /ə las′ kə/ _____   _____

    _____

6. /bat′ ə rēz/ _____   _____

    _____

7. /nā′ bər hu̇d/ _____   _____

    _____

8. /tə bog′ ən/ _____   _____

    _____

9. /fur′ ni chər/ _____   _____

    _____

Check-Up Test 7: Dictionary Skills

Name _____

Read the sample dictionary entries below. Use them to answer the questions that follow.

plum /plum/ n **1** a round, purple juicy fruit that grows on a tree **2** a dark bluish-purple color

¹**pres ent** /prez′ ənt/ n something given; a gift

²**pre sent** /pri zent′/ v **1** to hand over; give: *We will present the prize today.* **2** to bring before the public: *Our class will present a play next month.*

rest /rest/ v **1** to lie down **2** to stop work or activity

sand wich /san′ wich, san′ dwich/ n, pl **sand wich es** [named for the fourth Earl of Sandwich, a British official who invented it so he could continue to play a card game without stopping for a meal] two pieces of bread with meat, cheese, jam, or another filling between them

um brel la /um′ brel′ ə/ n [from Italian *ombrella*, meaning "parasol," from Latin *umbra*, meaning "shade"] a folding frame covered with cloth or plastic, used for protection against weather

1. Circle the pair of words that would be guide words for the dictionary entries above.

     pledge/unusual   parrot/ugly   plural/under

2. Which entry word is listed as both a noun and a verb? _____

3. What is the plural form of *sandwich*? _____

4. Name the two languages and words from which *umbrella* came.

     _____

5. What were the meanings of the two words from which *umbrella* came?

     _____

6. Look at the underlined word in each sentence below. In the blank, write the word, leaving a space between its syllables. Put an accent mark after the stressed syllable.

     Our club will <u>present</u> a slide show of our trip to the Grand Canyon. _____

     I made a brass letter opener as a birthday <u>present</u> for Dad. _____

     The committee will <u>present</u> a silver medal to the athlete. _____

7. Look at the underlined word in each sentence below. In the blank, write the number of the word's meaning.

     After digging the hole for the fence post, Gina sat down to <u>rest</u>. ____

     Noise from the nearby midnight train made it hard for me to <u>rest</u> last night. ____

     Mom wants to decorate the room in lavender, but I prefer <u>plum</u>. ____

     I have a bologna sandwich, carrot sticks, and a <u>plum</u> for lunch. ____

Assessment of dictionary skills

Look at the pronunciation key and read the list of words that follow. Use the pronunciation key to pronounce each respelling. Write the word the respelling stands for.

Pronunciation Key

/a/ = apple, tap; /ā/ = ate, say; /är/ = car, heart; /ãr/ = hair, care; /ch/ = chain, chair; /e/ = get, egg; /ē/ = even, bee; /hw/ = wheel, why; /i/ = is, fit; /ī/ = ice, tie; /ng/ = ring, song; /o/ = father, hot; /ō/ = old, so; /ȯ/ = ball, dog; /oi/ = boy, oil; /ou/ = house, cow; /sh/ = she, rush; /ᵗh/ = they, smooth; /th/ = thing, both; /u/ = up, cut; /ü/ = soon, rule; /u̇/ = look, put; /yü/ = use, cute; /yu̇/ = cure, pure; /zh/ = pleasure, beige; /ə/ = a (around), e (better), i (rabbit), o (doctor), u (upon)

graceful   employment   cushion   aisle   shower   education   cautious   saucer

1. /sȯ′ sər/ _____

2. /shou′ ər/ _____

3. /im ploi′ mənt/ _____

4. /ej′ ə kā′ shən/ _____

5. /grās′ fəl/ _____

6. /kȯ′ shəs/ _____

7. /ku̇sh′ ən/ _____

8. /īl/ _____

Use the dictionary entries below to answer the questions that follow.

crust /krust/ *n* **1** the hard, dark surface of a piece of bread **2** the pastry portion of a pie **3** the outer part of the earth

ga rage /gə rozh′, gə roj′/ *n* **1** a building where cars are kept **2** a repair shop for cars

wade /wād/ *v* **wad ed; wad ing 1** to step through water, mud, or sand **2** to make progress, but with great difficulty

Write the number of the meaning of the underlined word in each sentence.

1. Mom took the car to the garage so a mechanic could change the engine oil. ____

2. After the thunderstorm, the workers had to wade through puddles in the parking lot. ____

3. Chun cut the crusts off the sandwiches and cut them into small pieces. ____

4. The lawyers will wade through the list of questions in order to find some answers. ____

5. Molly finished mowing the lawn and then stored the lawn mower in the garage. ____

6. Scientists found rare fossils buried within the crust of the earth. ____

7. What other forms of the word *wade* are listed in the entry for *wade*?

   _____ _____

8. What part of speech is the word *garage*? Write the dictionary abbreviation. ____

Name _____

Three Kinds of Rocks

Do all rocks look alike to you? They aren't. Rocks are different in the way they are formed and in how they look. Take a close look at the next rock you see.

Igneous Rocks

How Igneous Rocks Are Formed Deep inside the earth's crust is a hot liquid called magma. When magma cools, it becomes rock. Some magma cools very slowly while it is still deep inside the earth. Magma that rises to the surface of the earth cools more quickly. All rocks formed from magma—whether they cool slowly or quickly—are called igneous rocks. *Igneous* means "fiery."

Kinds of Igneous Rocks Magma that cools slowly forms a rock called granite. Granite is used in making buildings and monuments. Lava is magma that comes from volcanoes. It cools quickly. The Hawaiian Islands are largely made up of this kind of rock. Obsidian is another kind of rock formed from lava. It looks like black glass and is often used in making rings, pins, and other kinds of jewelry.

Sedimentary Rocks

How Sedimentary Rocks Are Formed Some rocks are formed from other rocks that have broken up into pieces of gravel or sand. These pieces of gravel and sand are called sediment. In the bottoms of lakes and rivers, many deposits of sediment are squeezed together to form sedimentary rocks.

Kinds of Sedimentary Rocks Rocks that have been ground into sand may be squeezed together to form sandstone. When you look at sandstone, you can see the tiny grains of sand that have formed the rock.

When mud and clay are mixed with water and pressed together, a rock called shale is formed. Shale appears to be made up of very thin slabs.

Animal bones and shells crushed into fine pieces by heavy ocean water may form a rock called limestone. Much of this rock is found in Ohio and Kentucky.

Metamorphic Rocks

How Metamorphic Rocks Are Formed Metamorphic rocks are rocks that have been changed in some way. Heat and pressure can act on both igneous and sedimentary rocks to change them into metamorphic rocks. You can see bands of light and dark color in some metamorphic rocks but not in others.

Kinds of Metamorphic Rocks Heat and pressure can change shale into slate. Slate may be used for chalkboards and floors. Limestone can be changed to marble. Many statues are carved from marble, and some furniture is also made from marble.

Application of reading skills in a science context

Science

UNDERSTANDING

A. Draw a line to connect the name of each type of rock to the word or words it comes from.

1. igneous   a. *sedimentum,* meaning "settling"

2. sedimentary   b. *meta,* meaning "change," and *morph,* meaning "form"

3. metamorphic   c. *ignis,* meaning "fire"

B. Write the name of each rock you read about on page 172 under the correct heading below.

Kinds of Igneous Rocks	Kinds of Sedimentary Rocks	Kinds of Metamorphic Rocks
_____	_____	_____
_____	_____	_____
_____	_____	

C. Beside the name of each kind of rock, list one of its uses.

1. granite _____

2. slate _____

3. marble _____

4. obsidian _____

D. Under each picture, write *igneous, sedimentary,* or *metamorphic* to show which kind of rock would probably be used to make the object.

1. _____   2. _____   3. _____

Application of comprehension skills in a science context

Reading and Writing Wrap-Up

Name _____

THINKING

A. Several students have collected rocks. Each student has written a description of the rock he or she found. Study each description below, and then write the best name for the rock that the student found.

   1. This rock is sandy and rough to the touch. You can almost see little grains of sand in it.

      This rock is likely to be _____.

   2. This rock is shiny and black. You can almost see yourself in it.

      This rock is likely to be _____.

   3. You can see small pieces of shell in this rock.

      This rock is likely to be _____.

   4. This rock looks as if it had been formed in sheets. You can write on it with chalk.

      This rock is likely to be _____.

B. Why might scientists think that an ocean once covered parts of Ohio and Kentucky?

   _____

   _____

   _____

C. Write a word from the box to complete each analogy below.

floors	metamorphic	marble

   1. *Limestone* is to *sedimentary* as *marble* is to _____.

   2. *Granite* is to *buildings* as *slate* is to _____.

   3. *Shale* is to *slate* as *limestone* is to _____.

   Now write an analogy of your own. Use facts from page 172.

   _____ is to _____ as _____ is to _____.

Application of thinking skills in a science context

Name _____

WRITING

Make an outline showing how rocks are formed. Use the facts on page 172. The first part of the outline has been done for you. Do the other parts in the same way. Use complete sentences.

How Rocks Are Formed

I. Igneous Rocks
    A. Igneous rocks are formed from magma.
    B. Granite and obsidian are two kinds of igneous rocks.
        1. Granite is formed from magma that cools slowly.
        2. Obsidian is formed from magma that cools quickly.

II. Sedimentary Rocks

    A. _____

    B. _____
        _____

        1. _____
        _____

        2. _____
        _____

        3. _____
        _____

III. Metamorphic Rocks

    A. _____

    B. _____
        _____

        1. _____
        _____

        2. _____
        _____

Pronunciation Key

/a/ = apple, tap
/ā/ = ate, say
/är/ = car, heart
/ãr/ = hair, care
/b/ = bat, cab
/ch/ = chain, chair
/d/ = door, sad
/e/ = get, egg
/ē/ = even, bee
/f/ = fan, off
/g/ = goat, big
/h/ = her, happy
/hw/ = wheel, why
/i/ = is, fit
/ī/ = ice, tie
/j/ = jump, gentle

/k/ = kick, can
/l/ = laugh, pail
/m/ = mouse, ham
/n/ = nice, ran
/ng/ = ring, song
/o/ = father, hot
/ō/ = old, so
/ȯ/ = ball, dog
/oi/ = boy, oil
/ou/ = house, cow
/p/ = pan, nap
/r/ = ran, race
/s/ = sun, mess
/sh/ = she, rush
/t/ = toy, mat
/Ŧh/ = they, smooth

/th/ = thing, both
/u/ = up, cut
/ü/ = soon, rule
/u̇/ = look, put
/v/ = vine, live
/w/ = wet, away
/y/ = yes, you
/yü/ = use, cute
/yu̇/ = cure, pure
/z/ = zoo, zero
/zh/ = pleasure, beige
/ə/ = a (around)
      e (better)
      i (rabbit)
      o (doctor)
      u (upon)

Hard and Soft C and G

Name

The letters **c** and **g** followed by **e, i,** or **y** usually stand for their soft sounds, as in **cent** and **page.** The letters **c** and **g** followed by any other letters or at the end of words stand for their hard sounds, as in **cat, attic, wagon,** and **bag.**

Read each set of sentences and its list of words. In each blank, write the list word that best completes the sentence.

1. How would you like to hike the mountains of _____California_____
   with a llama as your _____companion_____?

2. Llama trekking is a _____great_____ way to see mountain
   _____country_____ that cannot be reached by car.

3. Instead of _____lugging_____ a heavy pack, you can load your
   goods on a llama.

4. These furry _____creatures_____ can carry sixty to ninety pounds.

lugging
companion
creatures
great
California
country

5. Because they walk at a slow _____pace_____, you will not cover
   great _____distances_____ with a llama.

6. A _____guide_____ who has a good _____knowledge_____
   of forest camping will go with you and seven or eight others in a group.

7. Pine, _____cedar (or lilac)_____, and _____lilac (or cedar)_____ are among
   the sweet-smelling plants and trees that will delight you as you journey.

8. Be _____careful_____ where you walk, though—stepping into a
   patch of poison oak could leave you in an _____uncomfortable_____ state!

lilac
knowledge
cedar
careful
guide
pace
uncomfortable
distances

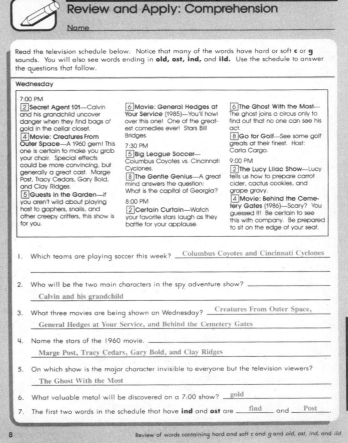

Hard and Soft C and G

Name

Read each sentence and the words beside it. In each blank, write the word that best completes the sentence.

1. There are _____certain_____ dangers to know about while llama trekking.

certain
curtain

2. Rattlesnakes live in mountain _____ranges_____, and
   _____coyotes_____, like other wild animals, may be unfriendly if you frighten them.

rags
ranges
cents
coyotes

3. Don't let these _____creatures_____ worry you too much, though.

creatures
cyclones

4. A llama, when it senses _____danger_____, will give an early
   warning by making a sound like a siren.

danger
digger

5. If you journey near the rocky _____coast_____, you may be able to
   see the _____Pacific_____ Ocean from the path.

circus
coast
Pacific
panic

6. Off in the _____distance_____, in the other direction, you can view the
   _____edge_____ of the desert.

distract
distance
edge
egg

7. All too soon, it will be time to return to the valley, where everyday life and
   _____civilization_____ wait for you.

carnation
civilization

8. When you return home, you may begin making plans for your next
   mountain _____vacation_____.

vacation
vaccination

9. _____Once_____ you've traveled with a llama, you'll want to do it
   _____again_____.

once
orange
again
agent

OLD, OST, IND, and ILD

Name

The letter **o** followed by **ld** or **st** usually stands for the long-**o** sound, as in **cold** and **most.**
The letter **i** followed by **nd** or **ld** usually stands for the long-**i** sound, as in **kind** and **wild.**

Read the list of words below. Then read the sentences that follow. Write the word from the list that best completes each sentence.

winds   bold   postmarked   mild
grinding   goldfinches   childhood   northernmost

1. Our geography book shows new vocabulary words in _____bold_____ print.

2. Long ago, Indians used large flat stones for _____grinding_____ acorns to make bread.

3. A narrow road _____winds_____ its way from the foot of this mountain to a jagged peak two miles above.

4. Winter in the northern part of our state was very _____mild_____ this year.

5. In order to take part in the race, your entry form must be _____postmarked_____ by midnight tomorrow.

6. Going fishing with Aunt Winona is one of my fondest _____childhood_____ memories.

7. The bird watchers spotted five _____goldfinches_____ near a sunflower in the meadow.

8. The Arctic is the _____northernmost_____ point in the world.

Read each clue and the list of words. Write the word from the list that matches the clue.

1. unable to tell one color from another _____colorblind_____

2. not tame _____wild_____

3. fuzzy growth that may appear on old bread _____mold_____

4. cloth used to cover the eyes _____blindfold_____

5. one of two poles on which a crossbar
   is mounted for playing football _____goalpost_____

6. cause a person to remember _____remind_____

7. son or daughter of one's child _____grandchild_____

mold
wild
remind
goalpost
grandchild
blindfold
colorblind

Review and Apply: Comprehension

Name

Read the television schedule below. Notice that many of the words have hard or soft **c** or **g** sounds. You will also see words ending in **old, ost, ind,** and **ild.** Use the schedule to answer the questions that follow.

Wednesday

7:00 PM
2 **Secret Agent 101**—Calvin and his grandchild uncover danger when they find bags of gold in the cellar closet.
4 **Movie: Creatures From Outer Space**—A 1960 gem! This one is certain to make you grab your chair. Special effects could be more convincing, but generally a great cast. Marge Post, Tracy Cedars, Gary Bold, and Clay Ridges.

6 **Movie: General Hedges at Your Service** (1985)—You'll howl over this one! One of the greatest comedies ever! Stars Bill Bridges.

7:30 PM
5 **Big League Soccer**—Columbus Coyotes vs. Cincinnati Cyclones.
8 **The Gentle Genius**—A great mind answers the question: What is the capital of Georgia?

8:00 PM
5 **Guests in the Garden**—If you aren't wild about playing host to gophers, snails, and other creepy critters, this show is for you.
2 **Certain Curtain**—Watch your favorite stars laugh as they battle for your applause.

6 **The Ghost With the Most**—The ghost joins a circus only to find out that no one can see his act.
8 **Go for Golf**—See some golf greats at their finest. Host: Carla Cargo.

9:00 PM
2 **The Lucy Lilac Show**—Lucy tells us how to prepare carrot cider, cactus cookies, and grape gravy.
4 **Movie: Behind the Cemetery Gates** (1986)—Scary! You guessed it! Be certain to see this with company. Be prepared to sit on the edge of your seat.

1. Which teams are playing soccer this week? _____Columbus Coyotes and Cincinnati Cyclones_____

2. Who will be the two main characters in the spy adventure show? _____
   Calvin and his grandchild

3. What three movies are being shown on Wednesday? _____Creatures From Outer Space,
   General Hedges at Your Service, and Behind the Cemetery Gates

4. Name the stars of the 1960 movie. _____
   Marge Post, Tracy Cedars, Gary Bold, and Clay Ridges

5. On which show is the major character invisible to everyone but the television viewers?
   The Ghost With the Most

6. What valuable metal will be discovered on a 7:00 show? _____gold_____

7. The first two words in the schedule that have **ind** and **ost** are _____find_____ and _____Post_____

177

Review and Apply: Composition

Name _____

You have just heard bad news on TV. Due to the carelessness of many humans, several kinds of wild animals in the western part of the country are in danger of becoming extinct. These include the whooping crane (a large bird), caribou (reindeer), wild sheep and goats, and the grizzly bear. Write a letter to a government official explaining your concern about this matter. Use at least twelve of the words below in composing your letter. Notice that each word has a hard or soft **c** or **g** sound or contains **old**, **ost**, **ind**, or **ild**.

remind	almost	certain	creatures	grizzly
convince	panic	danger	trace	caribou
wild	goats	civilization	find	edge
most	country	mind	large	crane
kind	great	old	city	concern

Answers will vary.

_____
_____
_____
_____
_____
_____
_____
_____
_____
_____
_____
_____
_____
_____
_____
_____
_____

Silent Consonants: WR and RH

Name _____

In some words, two consonants together stand for one sound. The letters **wr** and **rh** usually stand for the sound of **r**, as in **write** and **rhyme.**

Read each sentence and the words below the blank. Write the word that best completes the sentence.

1. Dad used the _____rhubarb_____ from his garden to make a wonderful pie.
   (rhino, rhubarb)

2. Our team won first prize in _____wrestling_____ this year.
   (wrecking, wrestling)

3. Divers discovered treasure in the old remains of the _____shipwreck_____
   (shipwreck, songwriter)

4. The _____rhinoceros_____, which is native to Africa and Asia, is a plant-eating
   (rhinoceros, rhythm)
   animal.

5. The plumber used a _____wrench_____ to tighten the water pipes.
   (wren, wrench)

6. Rock and roll music has its roots in another form of music called _____rhythm_____
   and blues.   (rhubarb, rhythm)

7. I hurt my _____wrist_____ while playing football with my brother and sister.
   (wrist, write)

8. A _____wren_____ is a songbird that often builds its nest near a house.
   (wren, wreath)

9. There is no word in the English language that _____rhymes_____ with orange.
   (rhymes, rhythms)

10. The _____rhythmic_____ sound of waves crashing on the shore is my fondest memory
    (rhyming, rhythmic)
    of our summer trip.

11. The hot desert sun left my skin feeling dry and _____wrinkled_____
    (wriggled, wrinkled)

12. A _____rhinestone_____ is a copy of a diamond that is made of glass or paste.
    (rhinoceros, rhinestone)

13. I _____wrung_____ out the wet towel and hung it on the clothesline.
    (wrong, wrung)

Silent Consonants: KN, WH, and SC

Name _____

In some words, two consonants together stand for one sound. The letters **kn** usually stand for the sound of **n**, as in **knot**. The letters **sc** sometimes stand for the sound of **s**, as in **scissors**. The letters **wh** sometimes stand for the sound of **h**, as in **who.**

Complete the unfinished word in each sentence by writing **kn**, **sc**, or **wh**.

1. I bruised my ____kn____eecap when I fell on the ice at the skating rink.

2. Do you know ____wh____ose bicycle is parked in the driveway?

3. The door ____kn____ocker on the large house was made of brass.

4. Vera is helping the stage crew paint ____sc____enery for the school play.

5. The ____sc____ent of blossoms fills the country air each spring.

6. ____Wh____oever called on the telephone hung up before I had a chance to answer it.

7. This ring is too small to fit over my ____kn____uckle.

8. The store owners can offer ____wh____olesale prices to their customers because they buy goods to sell in large numbers.

9. A ____sc____ientist may work outdoors, in an office, or in a laboratory.

10. These ____sc____issors are not sharp enough to cut the thick cardboard.

11. Dan is ____kn____itting a sweater for his mother's birthday.

12. The pancake recipe calls for a half cup of water and a ____wh____ole cup of milk.

13. Jeanette won first prize in the photography contest for her picture of a snowy mountain ____sc____ene.

Silent Consonants: CK and MB

Name _____

In some words, two consonants together stand for one sound. The letters **ck** usually stand for the sound of **k**, as in **duck**. The letters **mb** usually stand for the sound of **m**, as in **lamb.**

Read the list of words below. Then read the sentences that follow. Write the word from the list that best completes each sentence.

| peacock | hammock | cricket | woodchuck |
| padlock | buckles | speckled | crackled |

1. Looking into the sparrow's nest, I saw two tiny _____speckled_____ eggs.

2. I need a key to open the _____padlock_____ on the barn door.

3. A _____woodchuck_____ is sometimes called a groundhog.

4. Star's new coat has gold _____buckles_____ on the sleeves.

5. A _____cricket_____ chirps by rubbing its front wings together.

6. The burning logs popped and _____crackled_____ in the flames of the campfire.

7. When spread, the feathers of a _____peacock_____ look like a brightly colored fan.

8. Gina tied the _____hammock_____ between two tall oak trees.

In each sentence below, circle the two words that have **mb**. Then write the word in which **mb** stands for the sound of **m.**

1. The lost (lamb) was frightened and (trembling) when we found it. _____lamb_____

2. Last (December), two (climbers) reached Mount Runyon's peak. _____climbers_____

3. The huge cedar (limbs) were cut into pieces and used for (lumber). _____limbs_____

4. We (remembered) to spray bug (bomb) to keep insects out of our tent. _____bomb_____

5. A (thimble) is usually worn on any finger except the (thumb). _____thumb_____

6. Two (members) of my family are (plumbers). _____plumbers_____

7. The carpenter (mumbled) when she hit her (thumb) with the hammer. _____thumb_____

8. (Crumble) dry cereal (crumbs) over the casserole before baking it. _____crumbs_____

9. The circus clown carried a (jumbo) size (comb) in his pocket. _____comb_____

Silent Consonants: *GN* and *GH*

Words to use: bought, reign, daughter, resign, freight

In some words, two consonants together stand for one sound. The letters **gn** usually stand for the sound of **n**, as in **sign**. The letters **gh** are usually silent, as in **night**.

Read each clue and the list of words. Find the word in the list that matches the clue. Write the word next to the clue.

1. wear away by chewing _____gnaw_____		slight
2. tallness _____height_____		watertight
3. large snow sled _____sleigh_____		cologne
4. exhale a long, deep breath _____sigh_____		sigh
5. not crooked _____straight_____		gnaw
6. from another country _____foreign_____		sign
7. thick flour mixture used to make bread _____dough_____		foreign
8. try to get votes _____campaign_____		height
9. perfume _____cologne_____		campaign
10. sealed so as not to leak _____watertight_____		straight
11. very small or unimportant _____slight_____		dough
12. write one's name on something _____sign_____		sleigh
13. decorative pattern _____design_____		design

In each sentence below, circle the two words that have **gn** or **gh**. Then write the word in which **gn** stands for the sound of **n** or **gh** is silent.

1. The artist's (signature) was written at the corner of the (design). _____design_____
2. A (foghorn) guided the (freighter) safely to the dock. _____freighter_____
3. Dusty grabbed a (doughnut) and carried it to her (doghouse). _____doughnut_____
4. A (bighorn) sheep had (caught) its foot between two rocks. _____caught_____
5. An SOS (signal) is a (sign) of trouble. _____sign_____
6. My (assignment) is to write a report about (hognose) snakes. _____assignment_____

Review and Apply: Comprehension

Read the groups of words below. Then read the story. In each blank, write the word that best completes the sentence. For paragraphs 1 and 2, choose words from Group A. For paragraphs 3 and 4, choose words from Group B.

Group A				
heights	scenery	sign	known	through
padlock	wrote	who	sight	knew

Group B				
hammock	limbs	flocks	rhinoceros	pecked	night
cricket	thought	crumbs	gnawing	scent	peacocks

1 Last summer Uncle Jake _____wrote_____ and sent a letter inviting us to his farm for an extended weekend. For someone _____who_____ had never _____known_____ any place but the city, it was a great thrill.

2 The _____scenery_____ on the way to Uncle Jake's farm was really breathtaking. I never _____knew_____ mountains could reach such spectacular _____heights_____. Finally a _____sign_____ directed us off the busy highway, and before long the farm came into _____sight_____. Since there was no _____padlock_____ on the fence gate, we drove directly _____through_____ without stopping.

3 How very strange it seemed to me being on a farm! Large _____peacocks_____ with their feathers spread strutted proudly about the yard. Pigs were standing in mud up to their snouts. _____Flocks_____ of geese _____pecked_____ about for _____crumbs_____ of food. A black bull the size of a _____rhinoceros_____ stood _____gnawing_____ peacefully on a fence post. And there under the _____limbs_____ of two maple trees lay my Uncle Jake swinging in a _____hammock_____. I knew from the start what a great weekend it was going to be.

4 That _____night_____ as I lay in bed, I _____thought_____ about everything I wanted to do in the next few days. But the sound of a _____cricket_____ and the _____scent_____ of fresh country air soon soothed me into a deep, deep sleep.

Review and Apply: Composition

You have been asked to give a short speech to a group of parents at your school. It is your job to convince them of the need for some improvements around the school. Use at least twelve of the words below in writing your speech. Notice that each word contains at least one silent consonant.

know	who	thought	write
whole	knock	wrestle	might
sign	scene	limb	chuckle
science	design	rhyme	attack
dumb	rhythm	campaign	high
foreign	plumber	knowledge	taught

Answers will vary.

_____
_____
_____
_____
_____
_____
_____
_____
_____
_____
_____
_____
_____
_____
_____
_____
_____

Vowel Pairs: *AI, AY, EI,* and *EY*

Words to use: braid, clay, neighbor, obey, waist, crayon, reindeer, raise, delay, veil

In some words, two vowels together stand for one vowel sound. The letters **ay** and **ai** usually stand for the long-**a** sound, as in **hay** and **train**. The letters **ei** and **ey** sometimes stand for the long-**a** sound, as in **eight** and **they**.

Read each sentence and notice the word in dark print. Use the sentence to help you figure out the meaning of the word. Check the correct meaning.

1. The woman had been ill so long that she looked thin and **frail.**
   ___ a. happy   ___ b. athletic   ✓ c. weak
2. I think the **beige** jacket looks best with that dark shirt.
   ✓ a. light brown   ___ b. torn   ___ c. tiny
3. The hawk swooped down and, with its sharp claws, snatched its **prey.**
   ___ a. sound made by a large bird   ___ b. wing   ✓ c. animal that is hunted by another animal for food
4. A **veil** of darkness settled over the quiet country village.
   ✓ a. cover   ___ b. wedding gown   ___ c. bright light
5. Gregory carefully **surveyed** the theater crowd, looking for his friend Carlos.
   ___ a. applauded   ✓ b. looked over   ___ c. disliked
6. Because a traffic jam **detained** him, he arrived at the meeting late.
   ___ a. discovered   ✓ b. held back   ___ c. signaled
7. After hurting his foot, the boy had a slow, crooked **gait.**
   ✓ a. way of walking   ___ b. sock   ___ c. opening in a fence
8. When we visit the state fair, I like to spend most of my time on the **midway.**
   ___ a. middle of a sidewalk   ✓ b. rides and amusement area   ___ c. parking lot

179

Vowel Pairs: AI, AY, EI, and EY

Words to use: pain, tray, survey, brain, sleigh, player

Name _____

Read each sentence and the words below each blank. Write the word that best completes the sentence.

1. Many people in large cities live over an hour _____ away _____ from their places of work.
   (await, away)

2. A worker whose job begins at _____ eight _____ o'clock may have to leave home at six o'clock.
   (eight, eighty)

3. Because automobile traffic is so heavy, some people avoid the _____ highway _____
   (halfway, highway)

4. Instead, _____ they _____ may take an underground train, or
   (tray, they)
   _____ subway _____, to work.
   (subway, survey)

5. These high-speed _____ trains _____ stop often and are unlike trains that carry
   (trails, trains)
   _____ freight _____.
   (faint, freight)

6. Some workers who ride the same route every day become _____ acquainted _____ with one another.
   (acquainted, afraid)

7. One subway in Atlanta, Georgia, _____ aids _____ airport passengers who are tired or hurrying to catch planes.
   (aids, aims)

8. Rushing from one end of the huge airport to another can be a _____ strain _____,
   (stain, strain)
   especially for passengers who are carrying much _____ weight _____
   (wail, weight)

9. Because the train has no driver, riders must listen to and _____ obey _____ the train's automated voice.
   (dismay, obey)

10. For example, if you stand too near the _____ doorway _____, the voice politely tells you to move away.
    (delay, doorway)

11. People who are _____ afraid _____ of the trains can still get through the airport.
    (afraid, unpaid)

12. They _____ may _____ ride on moving sidewalks that look like flat escalators.
    (main, may)

13. In this way, passengers can more easily catch their planes without _____ delay _____
    (decay, delay)

Vowel Pairs: EE, EA, and EI

Words to use: knee, sweater, treat, bleed, steady, ceiling, streak, greet, leather, leisure, peace, receipt

Name _____

In some words, two vowels together stand for one vowel sound. The letters **ee** usually stand for the long-e sound, as in **bee**. The letters **ei** sometimes stand for the long-e sound, as in **seize**. The letters **ea** can stand for the long-e sound, as in **bean**, or the short-e sound, as in **bread**.

Read each sentence and the words below each blank. Write the word that best completes the sentence.

1. In order to be _____ healthy _____, you need to _____ eat _____ well every day.
   (heal, healthy)   (eat, speak)

2. By eating foods from each of four groups, your body can _____ receive _____ what it needs for energy, cell growth, and repair.
   (reach, receive)

3. For instance, each day, you _____ need _____ four servings from the milk group.
   (need, repeat)

4. You could have two glasses of milk and two slices of _____ cheese _____
   (cheese, seaweed)

5. For _____ either _____ of these, you could substitute ice _____ cream _____
   (fifteen, either)   (cream, tea)
   or cottage cheese.

6. From the _____ meat _____ group, you need two servings of _____ lean _____
   (mean, meat)   (leaf, lean)
   meat, fish, or poultry.

7. You might decide to have chicken, pork, lamb, or _____ beef _____
   (beef, tea)

8. Also included in the meat group are _____ beans _____, eggs, and nuts.
   (beans, dreams)

9. This is not as odd as it may _____ seem _____
   (seem, seen)

10. They are included because they contain a good portion of _____ protein _____
    (coffee, protein)

11. Instead of meat, you could eat _____ bread _____ with peanut butter
    (bead, bread)
    _____ spread _____ on it.
    (speak, spread)

Vowel Pairs: EE, EA, and EI

Words to use: speech, jealous, leap, deceive, sneeze, health, least, protein, geese, breath, disease, neither

Name _____

Read the list of words below. Then read the sentences that follow. In each blank, write the list word that best completes the sentence.

sweet	need	meals	peach	green
keeps	oatmeal	head	peel	leafy
really	seeds	squeezed	bread	

1. You may hear that "an apple a day _____ keeps _____ the doctor away."

2. This saying is not _____ really _____ true, but it is important to eat fruits and vegetables each day.

3. A fruit is the part of a plant that contains _____ seeds _____, which can be planted.

4. A vegetable is any plant part that can be eaten, such as a carrot, a potato, or a _____ head _____ of lettuce.

5. At breakfast or lunch, you might include fresh-_____ squeezed _____ orange juice and a plump _____ peach _____

6. Perhaps you'd rather _____ peel _____ and eat a banana or have a serving of delicious _____ sweet _____ strawberries.

7. At dinner you may want a _____ green _____, _____ leafy _____ lettuce salad and baked potato.

8. From the grain group of foods, you _____ need _____ four servings such as bread, cereal, rice, or corn.

9. Spaghetti, _____ oatmeal _____, crackers, and wheat _____ bread _____ are good choices.

10. By eating _____ meals _____ that contain food from the four food groups, you can keep your body strong and healthy.

In each sentence below, circle the words that contain a long-e sound.

1. Chung (needs) a (receipt) for this dog collar and (leash).
2. (Three) workers and their (leader) sat down to rest (beneath) a (weeping) willow (tree).
3. (Each) member of our (committee) (agrees) that all club members should (receive) a newsletter.
4. That bus driver (sees) no (need) to (increase) her driving (speed).
5. Scientists found an odd-looking (creature) while diving in (deep seas).

Vowel Pairs: OA, OW, and OE

Words to use: bowl, road, doe, throw, boat, hoe, slow, goat, goes

Name _____

In some words, two vowels together stand for one vowel sound. The letters **oa, ow,** and **oe** often stand for the long-o sound, as in **coat, window,** and **toe.**

Read each sentence and the words below each blank. Complete the sentence by writing the word that makes sense.

1. _____ Potatoes _____ are _____ grown _____ in almost every country around the
   (Potatoes, Tornadoes)   (goals, grown)
   world.

2. Worldwide, _____ growers _____ produce about six billion hundred-pound
   (goats, growers)
   bags of potatoes.

3. Above ground, you might not _____ know _____ a potato plant from any other leafy
   (know, roast)
   green plant.

4. _____ Below _____ the ground is the part of the plant that can be eaten.
   (Below, Blow)

5. This _____ growth _____, which is called a tuber, may weigh a few ounces or several
   (groan, growth)
   pounds.

6. The pink, purple, or white flowers of a potato plant have seedballs that look like small
   green _____ tomatoes _____
   (toast, tomatoes)

7. Farmers use huge machines to plant potatoes in long, _____ narrow _____
   (narrow, shadow)
   _____ rows _____
   (roasts, rows)

8. When the potatoes are ready for harvesting, a machine digs them up and _____ loads _____
   (floats, loads)
   them into trucks.

Vowel Pairs: OA, OW, and OE

Words to use: soap, potatoes, pillow, toast, heroes, know, roast, tomatoes

Name _____

Read each sentence and the words beside it. In each blank, write the word that best completes the sentence.

1. Deer are some of the largest mammals that __roam__ the forests and __meadows__ of North America.	roach roam meadows minnows
2. Deer are the only animals that __grow__ antlers.	glow grow
3. Except for reindeer, a female deer, or __doe__, has no antlers.	doe hoe
4. Depending on its type, a deer's short, smooth __coat__ may be white, reddish-brown, or gray.	coach coat
5. A frightened deer, running up to forty miles an hour, really runs on __tiptoe__	tiptoe tomatoes
6. Its foot is nothing more than two __toes__ protected by a curved hoof.	goes toes
7. Two toes above and behind the hoof never touch the ground but can be seen in tracks left in __snow__	show snow
8. All the contestants are ready for our town's second yearly __soapbox__ derby.	soak soapbox
9. They begin the race near Hanby Park and __coast__ down Snowball Hill.	coast coat
10. As the race cars __approach__ the finish line, a race official waves a checkered flag.	afloat approach
11. Clapping __echoes__ through the crowd as the winner crosses the mark and slides through a __shallow__ puddle.	echoes heroes hollow shallow

Words containing vowel digraphs in context: oa, ow, oe

21

Review and Apply: Comprehension

Name _____

Read the menu below. Many of the words contain the following vowel pairs: **ai, ei, ee, ea, oa, ow, oe.** Use the menu to answer the questions that follow.

The Corner Cafe

Breakfast	Beverages	Main Dishes
Oatmeal $1.00	Tea (hot or cold) . . . . $.75	Veal $7.50
Pancakes $2.00	Coffee . . . . $.50	a lean, tender meat full of
French toast $2.00	Milk . . . . $.95	protein and low in fat
One egg with two	Orange juice . . . . $.80	Maine Lobster Tails $8.75
strips of bacon $1.75	Tomato juice . . . . $.80	three large tails bursting with
Two eggs with two		plump white meat
strips of bacon $2.25	Sandwiches*	Stuffed Pork Chops $6.50
Hash-brown potatoes . . . $1.25	Chicken salad $2.50	overflowing with our famous
	Tuna salad $2.50	cornbread stuffing
Soups	Roast beef $2.75	Roasted Chicken Breast . . . $7.25
Ham and bean $1.50	Ham and cheese $2.75	thick and tender
Vegetable beef $1.50		Shrimp Boat $8.25
Chicken noodle $1.25	*served on raisin, whole-	eight large shrimp served in a
French onion $1.25	grain, or white bread	boat of lettuce
	with lettuce and	
	home-grown tomatoes	

1. Which soups have meat or poultry? __ham and bean, vegetable beef, and chicken noodle__

2. If you order shrimp for dinner, how many will be served? __eight__

3. What hot cereal is on the menu? __oatmeal__

4. Which breakfast food costs $1.25? __hash-brown potatoes__

5. Name three menu items that are made with chicken. __chicken noodle soup, chicken salad sandwich, roasted chicken breast__

6. How are the tomatoes at The Corner Cafe different from those that might be served at another restaurant? __They are home-grown.__

7. What is the least expensive drink on the menu? __coffee__

8. What kinds of bread are served? __raisin, whole-grain, and white__

9. If you were to eat lunch at The Corner Cafe, what foods would you order? __Answers will vary.__

10. Which two menu items contain *both* **oa** and **ea?** __oatmeal and roasted chicken breast__

22

Review of words containing vowel digraphs: ai, ei, ee, ea, oa, ow, oe

---

Review and Apply: Composition

Name _____

Below are nine important steps to follow in planting a vegetable garden. However, these steps are out of order. Write the steps in the correct order. Notice that the steps you write contain words with the following vowel pairs: **ai, ay, ei, ey, ee, ea, oa, ow, oe.** Finally, circle any words you write that have one of these vowel pairs.

Before digging, indicate where each row of seeds will be placed.
Put enough dirt over the seeds so they are covered.
Purchase the seeds you will need at a nursery.
At last, you've reached your goal—eat and enjoy!
Then use a hoe to dig a straight shallow trench in the dirt.
If not, drench it every seven or eight days.
First, determine what item you would prefer to grow. Will it be green beans, sweet peas, beets, or tomatoes?
Lay each seed in a line in the trench.
If the garden receives enough rain, your work is done.

1. First, determine what item you would prefer to (grow.) Will it be (green) (beans,) (sweet) (peas,) (beets,) or (tomatoes?)

2. Purchase the (seeds) you will (need) at a nursery.

3. Before digging, indicate where (each) (row) of (seeds) will be placed.

4. Then use a (hoe) to dig a (straight) (shallow) trench in the dirt.

5. (Lay) (each) (seed) in a line in the trench.

6. Put enough dirt over the (seeds) so (they) are covered.

7. If the garden (receives) enough (rain,) your work is done.

8. If not, drench it every seven or (eight) (days.)

9. At last, you've (reached) your (goal—eat) and enjoy.

_____

_____

Review of words containing vowel digraphs: ai, ay, ei, ey, ee, ea, oa, ow, oe

23

Vowel Pairs: OO, AU, and AW

Words to use: moose, crooked, law, fault, noon, brook, hawk, August, stool, hook, crawl, daughter

Name _____

In some words, two vowels stand for one sound. The letters **oo** can stand for the sound you hear in the middle of **moon** or **book**. The letters **au** and **aw** usually stand for the sound you hear in **auto** and **saw**.

Read the groups of words below. Then read the sentences. In each blank, write the word that best completes the sentence. For sentences 1 through 8, choose words from Group A. For sentences 9 through 13, choose words from Group B.

Group A	because	auditorium	goose	awfully	August
	looked	school	mongoose	foot	zoo	good

Group B	choose	cockatoo	audience	Australia	macaw	squawk

1. Last __August__, Carmen de Molina, the manager of wildlife at the city __zoo__, gave an interesting talk about animals.

2. The meeting was held downtown in the __auditorium__ of my __school__.

3. As Ms. de Molina spoke, we __looked__ at slides of animals from many countries. They included an animal from Africa and southern Asia called a mongoose.

4. __Because__ of its name, I expected it to be a kind of __goose__.

5. But a __mongoose__ looks nothing like a goose at all.

6. Instead, it is a furry mammal, just over a __foot__ long, that looks more like a small beaver.

7. A mongoose can jump upon a rat or snake and kill it __awfully__ fast.

8. In fact, it is so __good__ at hunting and killing its prey the mongoose has been taken to other lands to destroy large numbers of rats.

9. Ms. de Molina showed several slides of a beautiful bird from __Australia__ called a cockatoo.

10. Though not as bright in color, the __cockatoo__ is a member of the parrot family and can be tamed.

11. Some pet-store owners __choose__ not to keep them, though, because they __squawk__ so loudly.

12. A slide of a macaw, a South American bird, really pleased the __audience__.

13. Bright feathers of red, blue, yellow, and green and a long pointed tail make the __macaw__ one of the most beautiful birds in the world.

24

Words containing vowel digraphs in context: oo, au, aw

Vowel Pairs: OO, AU, and AW

Name _____

Words to use: mood, wool, shawl, sauce, scoop, cook, straw, taught, spool, foot, jaw, autumn, gloomy, wood, awkward, pause

Read the groups of words below. Then read the sentences. In each blank, write the word that best completes the sentence. For sentences 1 through 8, choose words from Group A. For sentences 9 through 16, choose words from Group B.

Group A hooked   claws   good   raccoon
taught   paw   looks   swoop

Group B shook   crawled   paused   understood
audience   applause   scooped   food   zoo

1. Ms. de Molina ____taught____ us about birds of prey and then showed a live hawk.

2. Because it had such long, sharp ____claws____, Ms. de Molina did not take the hawk from its cage.

3. Excellent vision allows it to spot a meal from far away and ____swoop____ down upon it with lightning speed.

4. With its strong claws and ____hooked____ beak, the hawk tears its food apart.

5. Next, we saw a young ____raccoon____ that Ms. de Molina had named Bandit.

6. It got its name from the black fur around its eyes that ____looks____ like a mask.

7. Raccoons are ____good____ swimmers and often eat fish they catch in streams.

8. Each ____paw____ has four long toes, and with the front ones, a raccoon handles objects almost as well as if it had human hands.

9. In fact, when Ms. de Molina briefly turned her back, Bandit ____crawled____ across the stage and grabbed the microphone cord.

10. The mike hit the stage with a bang, and Bandit hurried toward the ____audience____.

11. Ms. de Molina ____understood____ that Bandit was only frightened and not really trying to get loose.

12. She quietly followed him up the aisle and ____shook____ a box of seeds and nuts.

13. Bandit remembered that sound from his caretaker at the ____zoo____!

14. He ____paused____, then turned around and followed her back to the stage.

15. Ms. de Molina ____scooped____ out a handful of ____food____ and placed it on the floor of Bandit's cage.

16. Bandit went in; the audience, in amusement and relief, cheered the pair and gave a round of ____applause____.

Words containing vowel digraphs in context: oo, au, aw   25

Vowel Pairs: EW and UI

Name _____

Words to use: stew, crew, fruit, nephew, view, ruin

In some words, two vowels together stand for one vowel sound. The letters **ew** can stand for the sound you hear in **news** or **few**. The letters **ui** can stand for the sound you hear in **suit**.

Read each sentence or the words beside it. Write the word that best completes the sentence.

1. Crops that cannot stand freezing temperatures are well ____suited____ to the warm weather of countries located near the equator. — sewer / suited

2. Bananas, pineapples, and other tropical ____fruits____ are grown in South American countries such as Brazil. — few / fruits

3. Citrus crops such as oranges, lemons, limes, and ____grapefruit____ can be grown farther north. — cruisers / grapefruit

4. Southern California, for example, is cooler than Brazil and sometimes has light frost, but these times are ____few____. — few / flew

5. Florida, also known for its warm weather, is a leading producer of fruit ____juice____. — juice / jewelry

6. Because fruits are so easily ____bruised____, they must be harvested with a great deal of care. — brewed / bruised

7. As a result, most fruit farmers hire fruit-picking ____crews____ to do the work by hand. — chews / crews

8. This is slow and expensive, though, so ____new____ machines have been developed to shake the fruit loose from the trees. — new / nuisance

26   Words containing vowel digraphs in context: ew, ui

Vowel Pairs: EW and UI

Name _____

Words to use: chew, bruise, drew, suitable, jewel, nuisance

Read each sentence and notice the word in dark print. Use the sentence to help you figure out the meaning of the word. Check the correct meaning.

1. The tornado left tree limbs, branches, bricks, and glass **strewn** in its path.
   _✓_ a. scattered   ___ b. growing   ___ c. dead

2. A bed, chest of drawers, bookcase, and night table are included in the bedroom **suit.**
   ___ a. set of clothes   _✓_ b. set of matched furniture   ___ c. closet

3. The **pewter** pitcher made a clanging sound as it crashed to the floor.
   _✓_ a. kind of metal   ___ b. paper   ___ c. liquid

4. After our camping trip, we hung the tent out to dry so that **mildew** would not grow on it.
   _✓_ a. moldlike growth   ___ b. grass   ___ c. dirt

5. Dad will **brew** a fresh pot of coffee when our guests arrive.
   _✓_ a. cook by boiling   ___ b. refrigerate   ___ c. throw away

6. Flies were a **nuisance** at our family picnic.
   ___ a. food   ___ b. butterfly   _✓_ c. something bothersome

7. On week nights, my **curfew** is 8:00, but on Saturdays I don't have to be in until 9:00.
   ___ a. mealtime   ___ b. television program   _✓_ c. time limit for being away from home

8. My pen pal, who lives in Israel, speaks **Hebrew** and English.
   ___ a. softly   _✓_ b. a language   ___ c. coin

9. My father got seasick while he was on a **cruise.**
   ___ a. large tractor   _✓_ b. ocean trip   ___ c. ranch

10. The television reporter showed a **newsreel** about the disaster.
    _✓_ a. short movie that gives news   ___ b. tornado   ___ c. camera

11. Next week, our club will **recruit** helpers to work at the school fair.
    ___ a. fire for doing poor work   ___ b. admire   _✓_ c. try to get people to join

12. The police officer turned on her siren while in **pursuit** of the speeding driver.
    ___ a. automobile   _✓_ b. a chase   ___ c. ticket

13. I **withdrew** fifteen dollars from my savings account to pay for the broken window.
    ___ a. added   _✓_ b. removed   ___ c. helped

14. Since I forgot to **renew** my magazine subscription, I am no longer receiving the magazine.
    ___ a. understand   _✓_ b. make new or good again   ___ c. listen to

Words containing vowel digraphs in context: ew, ui   27

Vowel Pairs: IE

Name _____

Words to use: chief, lie, niece, tried

In some words, two letters together stand for one vowel sound. The letters **ie** can stand for the long-**i** sound, as in **tie**, or the long-**e** sound, as in **shield**.

Read each clue and the list of words. Find the word in the list that matches the clue. Write the word next to the clue.

1. brother's or sister's daughter ____niece____ — die
2. film ____movie____ — believe
3. stop living ____die____ — grief
4. large area of flat land with few trees ____prairie____ — prairie
5. a taking away of pain or discomfort ____relief____ — dried
6. to think that something is true ____believe____ — relief
7. short ____brief____ — niece
8. having no moisture ____dried____ — brief
9. great sorrow ____grief____ — movie
10. cooked in hot oil ____fried____ — fried
11. happy, content ____satisfied____ — untie
12. unfasten by loosening knots ____untie____ — satisfied

In the list above, notice the sound that **ie** stands for in each word. Write the word under the correct heading below.

ie as in **tie**	Order of words may vary.	**ie** as in **shield**	
die		believe	prairie
dried		brief	relief
fried		grief	movie
satisfied		niece	
untie			

28   Words containing vowel digraphs ie in context

182

Vowel Pairs: *IE*

Name _____

Read each set of sentences and its list of words. In each blank, write the list word that best completes the sentence.

1. Marie Curie was a French _____scientist_____ who, in the late 1800's, _____studied_____ radioactivity.

2. During the _____sixties_____, *Lassie* was a well-known television show about a boy and his dog, a _____collie_____

3. The *Mona Lisa*, a painting of a woman with a puzzling smile, is Leonardo da Vinci's most well-known _____masterpiece_____

4. Though most people think of them as vegetables, tomatoes are really large _____berries_____

5. Making colored circles on cloth by tying it in tight bunches before coloring is called _____tie_____ dyeing.

6. A king, queen, and knights are among the _____pieces_____ used to play chess.

Word list: masterpiece, tie, collie, scientist, berries, studied, sixties, pieces

7. Rhubarb, which is often used to make _____pie_____ and other desserts, is sometimes called _____pieplant_____

8. A doctor may be _____qualified_____ to become a surgeon after receiving four to five years of special training.

9. By measuring things such as blood pressure and heart rate, a _____lie_____ detector may help tell whether or not a person is telling the truth.

10. Shetland _____ponies_____, which are only three to four feet tall, were once brought into the United States as children's pets.

11. Because they offer more miles to the gallon than cars that use gasoline, some drivers want cars that use _____diesel_____ fuel.

12. Groups of _____priests_____ began California's raisin business by planting vines around church buildings and harvesting sun-_____dried_____ grapes.

Word list: diesel, lie, pie, dried, priests, ponies, qualified, pieplant

---

Vowel Pairs: *OU*

Name _____

In some words, two vowels together stand for one vowel sound. The letters **ou** can stand for the vowel sounds you hear in **soup, touch, doughnut,** and **should.**

Read the list of words below. Then read the sentences that follow. Write the word from the list that best completes each sentence.

should	various	youth	delicious
coupon	doughnuts	couldn't	tremendous

1. This summer, our neighborhood _____youth_____ group took a trip to Colorado.

2. For three years, we've been raising money by doing _____various_____ jobs.

3. We made a _____tremendous_____ amount of money by having car washes every Saturday.

4. One winter, we sold _____coupon_____ books giving discounts for businesses.

5. One fall, we worked at football games selling whole-wheat _____doughnuts_____

6. The doughnuts tasted great. In fact, they were _____delicious_____

7. We just _____couldn't_____ resist eating most of them ourselves!

8. We _____should_____ have made more money than we did on that project.

Circle the word that best completes each sentence below.

1. Last summer, my (couldn't, **cousin**) and I had a money-raising project of our own to make money for the youth group.
2. We worked on my aunt and uncle's farm picking (**cantaloupes**, couple).
3. Aunt Louise said that for half price, we (**could**, country) buy the cantaloupes we picked.
4. So each day after picking, we carried and sold melons door-to-door, charging (doughnut, **double**) what we had paid.
5. Lugging crates full of ten or twelve cantaloupes is a (trouble, **tough**) job!
6. My (should, **shoulders**) ached, and sometimes I thought my arms would fall off.
7. After only a week, my cousin and I decided we'd had (**enough**, enormous) of that project.
8. So instead, my father taught us to make and can vegetable (soap, **soup**).
9. A (coupon, **couple**) of other youth group members took orders for the soup.
10. Because there were so many of us, we were able to deliver all the soup with no (**trouble**, tough).

Vowel Pairs: *OU*

Name _____

Circle the word that best completes each sentence below.

1. Our youth (ground, **group**) was finally ready for our trip to Colorado by mid-June.
2. We departed from Saint (Loud, **Louis**) Missouri, thrilled and eager to be on our way.
3. We were so (jealous, **joyous**) at having reached our goal, we began singing and clapping.
4. Other travelers on the road must have been (**curious** courageous) about us.
5. Several hours later, we crossed the (Misery, **Missouri**) River, the second largest in the nation.
6. By the end of the day, we had traveled (**through** though) the state of Missouri.
7. We spent the next two days driving through Kansas, which produces more wheat than any other state in the (counting, **country**).
8. We (**would** wound) like to have toured Dodge City, the Cowboy Capital of the world.
9. But since it's in the (soul, **southern**) portion of the state, it was too far off our route.
10. On the morning of our (**fourth** found) day, we crossed the state border and proceeded into Colorado.
11. We headed toward Colorado Springs to see the most (**famous** furious) mountain in the Rockies—Pike's Peak.
12. Approaching from the east, we (cold, **could**) see its snow-capped, 14,000-foot peak.
13. We took a railway car to the top along with other groups of (toughest, **tourists**).
14. My favorite spot near Colorado Springs was Garden of the Gods, an impressive cluster of (enough, **enormous**) sandstone rocks.
15. Several days later in Denver, we took a (tower, **tour**) of the United States mint, a place where American coins are made.
16. The next week, after a day in the city of Boulder, we made (**our** out) way to Rocky Mountain National Park.
17. Trail Ridge Road, the most wonderful highway I've ever seen, allows visitors to enjoy the high (**mountainous** monstrous) country by car.
18. Later, while walking, we saw meadows filled with blooming flowers, (should, **shoulder**)-high banks of snow, and Rocky Mountain wild sheep.
19. (**Through** Thorough) the ages, the mountains have been cut into many different shapes by wind, rain, and glaciers.
20. For me, the breathtaking views of the Rockies were the most (mischievous, **marvelous**) part of the trip.

Review and Apply: Comprehension

Name _____

Read the story below. Many of the words contain the following vowel pairs: **oo, au, aw, ew, ui, ie, ou.** Use the story to answer the questions that follow.

If you've climbed one mountain, you've climbed them all. "Not true," says Reinhold Messner, master mountain climber and the first person to climb the fourteen highest peaks in the world. A mountain climber never tires of achieving that satisfying feeling of touching the skies. It's an interesting test to climb nearly impossible and dangerous cliffs. The enjoyment that comes from being outdoors can't be denied.

Though Messner usually climbs alone, it is good practice for most people to climb in a group. Then if an accident should happen, relief would be close at hand. Since mountain country is pretty rough, it's important to have the right supplies and equipment. Rope, ice hammers and axes, metal spikes, ice screws, and other tools are important to carry. Because the ground may be loose or icy and smooth in spots, shoes with heavy spikes are a necessity as well.

Don't forget to save room for enough food in your pack, too. Dried fruit and a few nuts will give you a tremendous boost. Water, rather than juice, is the best beverage to take. But don't attempt to haul anything too heavy, or you'll soon be exhausted.

Any climber would agree that the sport of mountain climbing is here to stay. And the more enormous the challenge, the more fabulous the thrill.

1. Who is Reinhold Messner? _____a master mountain climber_____

2. A satisfying feeling that mountain climbers never tire of is one of _____touching the skies_____

3. Why are shoes with heavy spikes needed for mountain climbing? _____The ground may be loose or icy and smooth in spots._____

4. What are some good foods to carry while climbing? _____dried fruit and nuts_____

5. Because accidents can happen, what is a good practice for mountain climbers to follow? _____People should climb in a group._____

6. What two items of climbing equipment could you pound into rock or twist into ice? _____metal spikes and ice screws_____

7. What will happen if you carry too many heavy objects while mountain climbing? _____You will soon be exhausted._____

8. Write three words from paragraph 2 in which the same vowel sound is spelled by the letters **ou, oo,** and **ew.** _____group, screws, and tools, loose, or smooth_____

Name _____

Read the unfinished story below. Then look at the list of words beneath it. Notice that each word contains one of the following vowel pairs: **oo, au, aw, ew, ui, ie,** or **ou.** On the lines that follow, write an ending to the story by using at least twelve of the list words.

> When my mother couldn't locate her diamond ring last summer, she really panicked. With our loyal assistance, she turned the whole house inside out. Even the neighbors took up the search. Finally after Mother sat down calmly to retrace her steps, the pieces of the mystery began to fit together. She last remembered taking her ring off when she was outside opening a can of paint. Not wanting it to get damaged, she set her ring on a nearby windowsill.

food	trouble	took	naughty
enormous	jewelry	handkerchief	through
group	afternoon	thieves	young
tried	raccoons	knew	few
pause	lawn	crawl	believe
caught	although	would	newspaper

Answers will vary.

_____
_____
_____
_____
_____
_____
_____
_____
_____
_____
_____
_____
_____

Words to use: ship, thunder, whistle, shrill, shirt, thumb, which, shrubbery, sheep, thanks, why, shriek

Name _____

Two consonants together can stand for one sound. Some consonants that stand for one sound are **sh, th,** and **wh,** as in **shoe, thin,** and **wheel.** At the beginnings of some words, three consonants together stand for special sounds, as in **shrug.**

Read each sentence and the words below the blank. Write the word that best completes the sentence.

1. Fishing crews drag nets across the ocean bottom to catch _____ shrimp _____.
   (shrill, shrimp)

2. James carries a _____ thermos _____ bottle full of hot vegetable soup when he hikes in the snow.   (thermos, thunder)

3. Swimmers should be careful to avoid swimming in waters known to have _____ sharks _____.
   (sharks, shirts)

4. Because _____ whales _____ have lungs, they must swim to the ocean surface in order to breathe.   (whales, while)

5. Plant City was having a sale on _____ shrubs _____, so Tomás bought ten bushes.
   (shrubs, shrugs)

6. Dad won two free _____ theater _____ tickets in our school's marble-guessing contest.
   (theater, thermometer)

7. In the Netherlands, farmers protect their feet from the damp ground by wearing heavy wooden _____ shoes _____.   (shades, shoes)

8. Juanita couldn't find one of the tent stakes, so she _____ whittled _____ one from wood.
   (whittled, whistled)

9. Do not put a wool sweater in a clothes dryer, or it will _____ shrink _____.
   (shriek, shrink)

10. When the body needs water, it sends a signal to the brain, making a person feel _____ thirsty _____.
   (thirty, thirsty)

Words to use: wish, with, ring, polish, moth, lung, brush, hang, cloth, English, month, among

Name _____

Two or three consonants together can stand for one sound. Some consonants that stand for one sound are **sh, th,** and **ng,** as in **wish, with,** and **ring.**

Complete the unfinished word in each sentence by writing **sh, th,** or **ng.**

1. Joggi**ng** on a footpa**th** in Standish Park today, I saw somethi**ng** I'd never seen.

2. In a large open area, a woman was throwi**ng** a curved, flat piece of wood.

3. Each time she flu**ng** it, it would spin forward, rise into the air, and fly in a curved pa**th** back to her.

4. "What is that thi**ng**?" I finally asked, "and why does it keep returni**ng**?"

5. "It's a boomerang," she said. "Each side of the curve is patterned like a wi**ng**."

6. "By throwi**ng** it with just the right motion, a skillful thrower can catch it without movi**ng** from the starti**ng** point."

7. "Would you like to throw it?" the woman asked. "It doesn't require a lot of stren**gth**."

8. I gave it a try, but with a cra**sh**, the boomera**ng** hit a tree and landed under a bu**sh**.

9. "I wi**sh** I weren't so clumsy," I muttered with an embarrassed smile.

10. The woman smiled and said, "Keep trying. Wi**th** a little practice, a good throw is not difficult to accompli**sh**."

Name _____

Read the story below. Many of the words contain the following consonants: **sh, th, shr, ng.** Use the story to answer the questions that follow.

> A shellfish is a water animal that has no backbone but has many legs. One of the most valuable of these animals is shrimp because it is a popular food. Shrimp are found in almost every part of the world in both fresh and salt water. Most shrimp have five pairs of thin front legs and five pairs of back legs. The front legs are used for walking, and the back for swimming. Unlike most animals, if a shrimp damages or loses a leg in a fight with an enemy, it can grow a new one.
> The lobster, another favorite shellfish, has only five pairs of legs. Four of these pairs are thin, but the fifth pair is thick. The thick legs extend in front of the lobster's head and have huge claws on the ends. One of the two claws is heavy and has thick teeth that are used to crush its prey. The other claw has sharp teeth for tearing the food into shreds. Depending on which side has the heavy claw, a lobster is either "right-handed" or "left-handed."

1. Water animals that have many legs but no backbone are called _____ shellfish _____

2. Name two popular kinds of shellfish. _____ shrimp and lobster _____

3. In what kinds of water are shrimp found? _____ fresh and salt water _____

4. What is the difference between the front and back legs of a shrimp? _____ The front legs are used for walking, and the back legs are used for swimming.

5. Tell about two ways in which a lobster's fifth pair of legs is different from the others. The fifth pair is thick and has huge claws on the ends.

6. What does a lobster have on each claw? _____ teeth _____

7. Describe each set of teeth that a lobster has, and tell how each set is used. _____ On one claw, a lobster has thick teeth that are used to crush prey. On the other claw are sharp teeth that are used to tear the food into shreds.

8. Write five words from paragraph 2 that end with these letters: **sh, th, ng.**
   shellfish, fifth, teeth, crush, tearing, Depending

Review and Apply: Composition

Name _____

Look at the photograph below and imagine what it would be like to ride the roller coaster. Then read the list of words that follow. Notice that each word contains **wh, sh, th, shr,** or **ng.** Suppose that a television reporter is interviewing you about your ride. Answer the reporter's questions. Write in complete sentences, and use as many list words as you can.

whirl	shudder	dash	screaming	thump
whoop	shriek	finish	long	whisk
shiny	shrill	path	clang	racing
shook	flash	feeling	thud	winding

1. From the ground, what does the roller coaster look like? _____ Answers will vary. _____
_____

2. As you were sitting in the roller coaster car, how did you feel before the ride began?
_____

3. What sights and sounds did you see or hear during the ride? _____
_____

4. What was the scariest or most thrilling part of the ride? _____
_____

5. How did you feel after the ride was over? _____
_____

6. What could be done to make the ride better? _____
_____

Review of words containing consonant digraphs: sh, th, wh, ng, shr   37

Sounds of *TH*

Name _____

Words to use: think, this, thorn, they, thirsty, these, weather, leather, mother, father, both, path, broth, both, earth, north, south

Two consonants together can stand for one sound. The letters **th** can stand for the sound you hear at the beginning of **think** and **this.**

Circle the word that best completes each sentence below.

1. My (math, (mother) and ((father) feather) have been running ((together) tooth) for (thirsty, (thirteen)) years.
2. They began running as a way to lose weight and improve their ((health) wealth).
3. Mom said that when she and Dad took their first run, they were (bath, (both)) ((breathless) broth) before they had gone around the block.
4. Dad said he didn't (thin, (think)) he had the (south, (strength)) to walk back home.
5. ((Although) Arthur) they were discouraged, they tried not to let their first experience kill their (either, (enthusiasm)).
6. They kept going out, and gradually they increased the (leather, (length)) of their runs.
7. After a few (math, (months)) it was easier to (breath, (breathe)) and they could go (father, (farther)) and farther (wither, (without)) getting tired.
8. (There, (They've)) come a long way in thirteen years.
9. Tomorrow ((they'll) their) run their (teeth, (tenth)) marathon.
10. ((That's) This) a race of over twenty-six miles! Just thinking of it is enough to make me (with, (wither)).
11. I'd ((rather) rhythm) stick with long-distance bicycling.
12. My (bother, (brother)) and I are proud of our parents, ((though) thought), so we'll be (theme, (there)) tomorrow.
13. We want to be with all the (oath, (others)) who'll ((gather) growth) at the finish line to congratulate the runners.

38   Words containing consonant digraph th in context

Consonant Pairs: *CH* and *TCH*

Name _____

Words to use: choose, kitchen, ache, machine, bachelor, scratchy, echo, mustache, teacher, matches, stomach

Two or three consonants together can stand for one sound. The letters **ch** and **tch** usually stand for the sound you hear at the beginning of **chair** and the end of **catch.** The letters **ch** sometimes stand for the sound of **k,** as in **chemist.** The letters **ch** can also stand for the sound of **sh,** as in **chef.**

Read each clue and the list of words. Find the word in the list that matches the clue. Write the word next to the clue.

1. break out of an egg ___hatch___
2. person in a story ___character___
3. small ape known for its intelligence ___chimpanzee___
4. skydiver's equipment ___parachute___
5. a cook ___chef___
6. person who works with machines ___mechanic___
7. winner ___champion___
8. jumping game ___hopscotch___
9. buy ___purchase___
10. light fixture that hangs from a ceiling ___chandelier___
11. group of people who sing together ___chorus___

chimpanzee	
hatch	
parachute	
mechanic	
hopscotch	
champion	
chef	
chorus	
purchase	
chandelier	
character	

In the list above, notice the sound that **ch** or **tch** stands for in each word. Write the word under the correct heading below.

ch and **tch** as in **chair** and **catch**	**ch** as in **chemist**	**ch** as in **chef**
Order of words may vary.		
chimpanzee	character	chandelier
champion	chorus	chef
hatch	mechanic	parachute
hopscotch		
purchase		

Words containing consonant digraphs from definitions: ch, tch. Symbol-sound association of words containing consonant digraphs: ch, tch   39

Consonant Pairs: *PH* and *GH*

Name _____

Words to use: laugh, elephant, enough, telephone, tough, alphabet

Two consonants together can stand for one sound. The letters **gh** and **ph** sometimes stand for the sound of **f,** as in **laugh** and **elephant.**

Read each sentence and notice the word in dark print. Use the sentence to help you figure out the meaning of the word. Check the correct meaning.

1. The feathers of a **pheasant** make a beautiful pattern of bright colors.
   ___ a. fish   _✓_ b. bird   ___ c. automobile
2. Ken filled the pigs' **trough** with corn.
   ___ a. farm   _✓_ b. food tray for livestock   ___ c. dairy cattle
3. The excited child tore the **cellophane** off the new toy before his mother had paid for it.
   _✓_ a. thin plastic wrapping   ___ b. cells   ___ c. aluminum foil
4. My older sister says that this year as a high-school **sophomore** is more enjoyable than last, when she was only in her first year of high school.
   ___ a. principal   _✓_ b. second-year student   ___ c. sixth grader
5. I've been buying my favorite music on tapes because my **phonograph** is broken and cannot be repaired.
   _✓_ a. record player   ___ b. telephone   ___ c. device that takes photographs
6. Mom is unhappy because a **gopher** dug tunnels all through our backyard.
   ___ a. insect that bites   _✓_ b. underground animal   ___ c. freshwater fish
7. From time to time, a snake's skin will **slough** off, and a new skin will take its place.
   _✓_ a. drop; shed   ___ b. jump slowly   ___ c. change colors
8. Before she began painting, the artist penciled her idea on paper as a **rough** sketch.
   ___ a. perfect; ready to be sold   ___ b. colorful   _✓_ c. incomplete; without detail
9. **Dolphins,** which live in salt water, can be trained to jump through hoops and catch balls.
   ___ a. intelligent dogs   _✓_ b. mammals that look like fish   ___ c. seashells
10. I bought a bottle of vitamins at the **pharmacy.**
    ___ a. museum   ___ b. clothing store   _✓_ c. drug store
11. An **oceanographer** may spend much of his or her time working on a ship.
    _✓_ a. person who studies oceans   ___ b. person who studies weather   ___ c. pilot
12. During the first **phase** of life, a baby is helpless and must depend on others to care for it.
    _✓_ a. part   ___ b. wish   ___ c. search

40   Words containing consonant digraphs in context: ph, gh

185

Consonant Pairs: PH and GH

Name _____

Words to use: rough, phonics, laughter, paragraph, cough, nephew

Circle the word that best completes each sentence below.

1. The next time a doctor tells you you're sick, you might try (cough, **laughing**).
2. It may sound strange, but scientists are discovering that (orphan, **laughter**) can help patients feel better.
3. Dr. Frederick Goodwin, a (**physician**, phone), says that jokes give many people a sense of relief and give a feeling of being able to handle frightening situations.
4. Evidence shows that even if you're having a (**rough**, laugh) day, making yourself smile will really help you feel better.
5. Smiling, of course, is a (trophy, **tough**) thing to do when you're feeling sad or angry.
6. But when you laugh, a (**physical**, paragraph) change takes place in your brain.
7. The body makes and uses its own pain relievers, which are called (enough, **endorphins**), and you begin to feel better.

Read the list of words below. Then read the sentences that follow. Write the word that best completes each sentence. You will need to use one word twice.

physically	enough	triumph	laughter
cough	laugh	pharmacy	autobiographical

1. Norman Cousins, who once suffered from a dangerous sickness, says that laughter, in part, helped him in his ____**triumph**____ over disease.
2. Just the touch of his bed sheets was ____**enough**____ to cause him great pain.
3. He had an allergy to the medicine he was getting from the hospital ____**pharmacy**____
4. In an ____**autobiographical**____ account of his sickness, Mr. Cousins tells of checking out of the hospital and into a hotel. With him, he took a film projector and funny movies.
5. "I made the joyous discovery," he writes, "that ten minutes of genuine ____**laughter**____ . . . would give me at least two hours of pain-free sleep."
6. ____**Laughter**____, of course, is not the answer to every sickness.
7. It will not cure a ____**cough**____ or heal a bleeding wound.
8. Good medical care is important when you're not feeling well ____**physically**____
9. But a good rib-tickling can be healthful as well, so go ahead and ____**laugh**____

Review and Apply: Comprehension

Name _____

Read the list of words below. Notice that each word contains **th, ch, tch, ph,** or **gh.** Then read the story that follows. In each blank, write the word that best completes the sentence.

earth	nothing	inch	farthest	parachuting
chase	technique	enthusiasts	trophy	
photographing	catch	tough	school	

Air sports have been popular since the 1700's, when people first began hot-air ballooning. Today the sport includes cross-country races in which the pilot who flies the ____**farthest**____ and fastest wins. In another kind of race, the hare-and-hound, balloon pilots ____**chase**____ after a balloon that has been given a head start. The balloon that comes closest to the "hare," or first balloon, wins a ____**trophy**____.

Another popular air sport is skydiving, or ____**parachuting**____. In some contests, skydivers are judged on their form and ____**technique**____ as they make daring moves while falling through the sky. Once, for example, a team of forty parachutists formed a box shape by holding hands as they fell. Another kind of contest rewards parachutists for landing on or near a six-____**inch**____ circle on the ground. Although it is ____**tough**____ to do, one German who jumps has hit the mark fifty times in a row. Because landing is like jumping from a moving car, it is easy for parachutists to hurt themselves if they land on rough ground. Good safety rules are very important to learn in skydiving ____**school**____.

In hang gliding, fliers hang from a kitelike wing and jump off a cliff or steep bank. They try to ____**catch**____ upward winds that will carry them through the air. One hang glider caught the exciting feel of flying on film by strapping a movie camera to the hang glider and ____**photographing**____ the flight. While some hang gliders try to beat time and distance records, most hang-gliding ____**enthusiasts**____ fly just for the fun of floating high above the ____**earth**____. Says one hang glider who used to drive race cars, "There's ____**nothing**____ like it in the world. The first time I saw it being done, I knew it was the only thing I ever wanted to do."

Review and Apply: Composition

Name _____

Read the paragraphs below. Then read the directions that follow.

> Wild elephants are in danger. In Africa and Asia, the human population has been growing. As a result, more and more people have cleared and settled on land where elephants once lived. The elephants are being crowded into small areas. But because elephants need large areas of land to find enough food to eat, their food supply is shrinking all the time.
>
> In addition, hunters anxious to make money are killing African elephants for their ivory tusks. The tusks, which may sell for over $20,000 a pair, are carved to make beautiful works of art. All the elephants in the northern and southern sections of Africa have been killed already. There are laws that forbid the killing of elephants in special areas where land has been set aside to safeguard them. But because ivory trade can make them wealthy, some hunters shoot elephants anyway.

We must find ways to make enough room for both elephants and humans to live. We must also find ways to keep hunters from killing elephants for profit. On the lines below, tell how we might be able to solve both these problems. You may wish to use some of the words listed below.

tough	population	forbid	limit
laws	protect	sale	wildlife refuge
obey	national parks	hunters	illegal
refuse	control	threaten	ivory trade

Answers will vary.

_____
_____
_____
_____
_____
_____
_____
_____
_____

Vowels With R: AR, ER, IR, OR, and UR

Name _____

Words to use: shark, stern, skirt, fork, curl, artist, anger, thirsty, disturb, starve, nervous, birch, cord, nurse

A vowel that is followed by **r** stands for a special sound that is neither long nor short, as in **jar, fern, bird, horn,** and **burn.**

Complete each unfinished word in each sentence below by writing **ar, er, ir, or,** or **ur.** Choose from the letters shown below the blank.

1. The h__**ar**__monica has been well-known in folk music since its beginning in the (ar, or, ur) early nineteenth cent__**ur**__y. (ar, or, ur)

2. Also called a mouth __**or**__gan, the instrument was made in G__**er**__many in 1821. (ar, ir, or) (ar, er, or)

3. P__**ar**__t of its appeal is its small size; it is easy to put it into a sh__**ir**__t pocket (ar, er, or) (ar, ir, or) or p__**ur**__se. (ar, or, ur)

4. It's not a h__**ar**__d instrument to play; almost any boy or g__**ir**__l can do it. (ar, ir, or) (ar, ir, or)

5. The harmonica is made of a wooden case with ten or more small holes. A brass reed has been ins__**er**__ted in each hole so that it hangs freely. (ar, er, or)

6. By blowing or sucking air through the case, a play__**er**__ can make two tones for each hole. (ar, er, or)

7. Larry Adler, an exp__**er**__t harmonica player of the middle 1900's, became known as a harmonica st__**ar**__. (ar, er, or) (ar, ir, or)

8. He perf__**or**__med in conc__**er**__t halls and even gave one music writer an (ar, or, ur) (ar, er, or) idea for writing a piece that Adler played with the Philadelphia __**Or**__chestra. (Ar, Or, Ur)

Vowels With R: EAR
Words to use: ear, earth, pear, year, bear, clear, learn, near, earn

Name _____

Two vowels followed by the letter **r** stand for a special sound that is neither long nor short. The letters **ear** can stand for the vowel sound you hear in **ear, earth,** or **pear.**

Read each sentence and the words below each blank. In each blank, write the word that best completes the sentence.

1. When ____Earl's____ science teacher told the class to write a ____research____
   (Earl's, Earth's)   (research, search)
   report on animals, Earl had no problem choosing a topic.

2. From the time he was two ____years____ old, Earl had loved ____bears____
   (yearn, years)   (bears, pears)

3. Until he was six, Earl's stuffed brown bear, Teddy, had been his ____dearest____
   companion.   (clearest, dearest)

4. His mother laughs when she recalls how ____near____ Earl always kept his bear.
   (hear, near)

5. "I couldn't ____tear____ the two of you apart," she chuckles as she and Earl
   (smear, tear)
   remember Teddy.

6. "You once forgot to ____wear____ your socks to school, but you never forgot to
   (rear, wear)
   take that bear," she says.

7. "I used to wonder if you'd continue to carry Teddy when you were old enough to grow a
   ____beard____."
   (beard, pearl)

8. When Earl's mother ____heard____ about the science assignment, she knew she
   (heard, rehearse)
   wouldn't be seeing much of her son for a while.

9. Each day after school, Earl brought home another pile of books and ____disappeared____
   into his room.   (disappeared, smeared)

10. He loved ____learning____ about his favorite animals, and in less than a week
    (learning, overhearing)
    the report was written.

11. Earl turned the report in a week ____early____ and ____earned____
    (early, nearly)   (earned, learned)
    an excellent grade for his work.

Words containing *ear* in context   45

Vowels With R: AIR and ARE
Words to use: fair, care, prairie, scare, pair, aware

Name _____

Two vowels followed by the letter **r** stand for a special sound that is neither long nor short. The letters **air** and **are** can stand for the vowel sound you hear in **fair** and **care.**

Read the list of words below. Then read the sentences that follow. In each blank, write the word that best completes the sentence.

air	hare	share	chair	mare
hair	dairy	nightmare	compare	stairs
repair	spare	hardware	millionaire	square

1. Milk, cheese, sour cream, and butter are products made from the milk of
   ____dairy____ cattle.

2. I awoke suddenly last night in the middle of a horrible ____nightmare____.

3. Though its body is bigger, and its ears and legs are longer, a ____hare____ is
   frequently mistaken for a rabbit.

4. Mom was not amused when she had a flat tire and
   discovered that there was no ____air____
   in the ____spare____ tire.

5. Before buying a set of tools, I want to
   ____compare____ prices at three different
   ____hardware____ stores.

6. The ____millionaire____ was generous enough
   to ____share____ her wealth with others.

7. A carpenter will ____repair____ the
   broken banister to make the ____stairs____ safe.

8. The ____mare____ gave birth to a beautiful
   colt with chestnut-colored ____hair____.

9. A shape with four corners and four sides of equal
   length is called a ____square____.

10. Skiers ski down a slope and then ride back to the
    top on a ____chair____ lift.

46   Words containing r-controlled vowels in context: *air, are*

Vowels With R: EAR, AIR, and ARE
Words to use: ear, earth, pear, fair, care, fear, yearn, wear, hair

Name _____

Read each sentence and notice the word in dark print. Use the sentence to help you figure out the meaning of the word. Check the correct meaning.

1. **Spearmint** has long green stems that are topped by white or light purple flowers.
   ____ a. sword-shaped weapon   ____ b. gum   ✓ c. kind of plant

2. Marcia studies at the library every evening in an **earnest** effort to raise her grades.
   ✓ a. serious   ____ b. uninterested   ____ c. illegal

3. I stay out of Dawn's way in the morning because, when she is sleepy, she is a **bear.**
   ____ a. cheerful person   ✓ b. bad-tempered person   ____ c. animal with fur

4. I enjoy reading my sister's funny stories because she has a real **flair** for writing.
   ____ a. flaming light   ✓ b. talent   ____ c. dislike

5. When bicycling, I always carry a **spare** tire in case I have a flat tire.
   ✓ a. extra   ____ b. punctured   ____ c. glass

6. I enjoyed looking through the old family photos that I **unearthed** in Grandma's basement.
   ✓ a. discovered   ____ b. wrote   ____ c. buried

7. Fifth Avenue is one of New York City's busiest **thoroughfares.**
   ____ a. festivals   ✓ b. main roads   ____ c. stores

8. Listening to music that is too loud can **impair** your ability to hear.
   ____ a. make better   ____ b. take away pain   ✓ c. harm

Read each clue and the list of words. Find the word in the list that matches the clue. Write the word next to the clue.

1. very tired ____weary____   rare
2. to practice ____rehearse____   pearl
3. waterproof coat, umbrella, and boots ____rainwear____ weary
4. fix ____repair____   square
5. a precious gem ____pearl____   repair
6. not common ____rare____   rehearse
7. very strong light or reflection ____glare____   glare
8. a shape ____square____   rainwear

Words containing r-controlled vowels in context and from definitions: *ear, air, are*   47

Review and Apply: Comprehension

Name _____

Read the advertisements below. Notice that many of the words contain vowels followed by the letter **r.** Use the advertisements to answer the questions that follow.

FOR SALE	FOR SALE	HELP WANTED	HELP WANTED
Coins. Rare Spanish gold and U.S. silver dollars. Will sell whole collection for $1,000 or make fair trade. Call 555-9668 before 6:00 P.M. **Guitar.** Mason and Cleary six-string electric guitar with orange hard-shell case. One year old, excellent condition. $500. 555-8298. Ask for Chee.	**Bedroom furniture.** Pine three-drawer chest, dresser, nightstand, king-size water-bed frame. $750. Call 555-4777 Saturday only. **Be prepared for winter.** Used snow thrower, 5 horsepower, 24-inch blade. 555-3838. **Pearl necklace** on 15" gold chain. Matching earrings. Worn only once. $25.00. See at 128 W. Witherspoon St.	**Sales Clerk.** Full or part-time position selling women's footwear. Apply in person. The Glass Slipper, 150 E. Kirby St. **Warehouse Worker.** Fast-growing company needs neat, mechanical person to work third shift. Must be at least 18 years old. Apply between 9:00 A.M. and 4:00 P.M., 1543 Corvair Ave.	**Nurse Aide.** Third-shift position open for experienced nurse aide. Top wages and benefits. Call Ms. Martinez at Oak Park Nursing Home, 555-8798. **Hair stylist.** Permanent position. Guaranteed hourly wage, paid vacation, paid holidays, insurance. Applications being taken at Clare's Hair Care, 146 E. Kirby St., 555-3898.

1. What musical instrument is for sale? ____an electric guitar____

2. What four things are being sold in one ad? ____chest, dresser, nightstand, bed frame____

3. What kind of jewelry is for sale? ____a pearl necklace on a gold chain and earrings____

4. Is the jewelry likely to be old or nearly new? ____nearly new____
   How do you know? ____It was worn only once.____

5. How is the nurse aide job like the warehouse worker job? ____Both are third-shift jobs.____

6. What is *The Glass Slipper*? ____a shoe store____

7. Which two businesses are near each other? ____The Glass Slipper and Clare's Hair Care____

8. Why are no telephone numbers given for the sales and warehouse jobs? ____Both places want people to apply in person.____

9. In which street name does **r** follow a vowel twice? ____Corvair Avenue____

48   Review of words containing r-controlled vowels: *ar, er, ir, or, ur, ear, air, are*

Review and Apply: Composition

Name _____

Read the words and look at the picture below. Notice that each word contains a vowel followed by the letter **r**. Think of how you can put together at least ten of the words to make a story about the picture. Then write your story, underlining the listed words.

alarm	shirt	purse	earrings	scare
large	dirty	sure	disappear	careless
discover	store	wear	search	pair
mystery	stormy	tear	pearl	stairs

Answers will vary.

_____
_____
_____
_____
_____
_____
_____
_____
_____
_____
_____
_____
_____
_____
_____
_____
_____

Sounds of S

Name _____

The letter **s** often stands for the sound you hear at the beginning of **sun** or at the end of **nose**. It can also stand for the sound you hear in the middle of **treasure** or at the beginning of **sure**.

Circle the word that best completes each sentence below.

1. Where could you see dinosaur bones, an antique (**sugar**, suggest) bowl, and an old train?
2. If you guessed (**museum**, music), you are right.
3. You could spend many (**leisure**, loose) (**hours**, house) in one and (surgery, **surely**) not see everything.
4. An art museum (pressure, **preserves**) and (delays, **displays**) paintings, carvings, and other art.
5. The largest one in the United States, the Metropolitan Museum of Art, (**includes**, interrupts) over three million works of art in its (**collections**, collisions).
6. Here, you might see (**vases**, veins) from ancient Egypt, clay pots from (**Asia**, Mars), or paintings from present-day Europe.
7. A place such as this (**carries**, cars) a large amount of (issues, **insurance**) to protect against loss or damage.
8. (Becomes, **Because**) the price of insurance and other costs are high, some museums charge for (**admission**, intermission).
9. If you (vision, **visit**) a museum of history, you can see furniture, (tails, **tools**), and other things that show how people lived in the past.
10. Some museums even have old-fashioned villages or (towels, **towns**) from (**various**, vicious) times of history.
11. For example, Greenfield Village in Dearborn, Michigan, has ninety-two (blessings, **buildings**) and landmarks brought in from all (secrets, **sections**) of the United States.
12. Among these shops, homes, (miles, **mills**), and stores are a courthouse where Abraham Lincoln worked as a lawyer and the bicycle shop of the Wright (bothers, **brothers**).
13. Next door, at the Henry Ford Museum, you can see exhibits that show the (permission, **progression**) of transportation, power and machinery, and farming.
14. At a science museum, you can learn about machines such as (summaries, **submarines**) and (division, **television**).
15. Or, if you like, you can study plants, animals, rocks, and (Fridays, **fossils**).

Sounds of S

Name _____

Read each sentence and the words below each blank. In each blank, write the word that best completes the sentence.

1. Some museums have collections that cover only one __**subject**__.
(subject, subtract)

2. The life-size figures of people at a wax museum leave you with the __**impression**__ they are real.
(concussion, impression)

3. The Circus World Museum in Baraboo, Wisconsin, has __**circus**__ wagons, merry-go-rounds, and live circus acts.
(cactus, circus)

4. The Children's Museum in Indianapolis, Indiana, gives __**pleasure**__ to people of all ages.
(pleasure, pleasant)

5. It __**displays**__ over 7,500
(decays, displays)
__**toys**__ and dolls that show how
(toes, toys)
children have played through history.

6. The exhibits show both old and new children's __**treasures**__—from wooden toys of
(tissues, treasures)
the 1700's to today's latest space robots.

7. There are so many kinds of museums to visit, choosing only one could be a hard __**decision**__.
(decision, division)

8. Why not start with a museum __**close**__ by?
(close, clothes)

9. There is __**sure**__ to be one not
(sugar, sure)
far from where you live.

10. If you don't have time to see all the exhibits, you can __**always**__ go back to
(airways, always)
visit again and again.

Sounds of TI and CI

Name _____

The letters **ti** and **ci** can stand for the sound of **sh**, as in **nation** and **special**.

Read each sentence and the words beside it. In each blank, write the word that best completes the sentence.

1. When was the last time you tuned in to watch something on a television __**station**__?
    station / subscription

2. Chances are, while watching a half-hour show, you saw at least ten __**commercials**__.
    commercials / commission

3. Television commercials are the most important way of showing and telling about things for sale among __**national**__ advertisers.
    motion / national

4. One value of television commercials over other kinds of advertising is that people who watch can hear about a product and see it in __**action**__ at the same time.
    action / fractions

5. For example, you may __**appreciate**__ a Treasure Island Park advertisement more on television than on radio or in a newspaper.
    addition / appreciate

6. On television, you could see the park roller coaster in __**motion**__ and hear the riders' screams of delight.
    motion / notion

7. In __**addition**__ to the value of sight and sound, television commercials reach a __**nationwide**__ audience.
    addition / objection / information / nationwide

8. Some commercials are aimed at __**special**__ television audiences such as children, farmers, or sports fans.
    social / special

9. As an example, think about this __**situation**__: If you wanted to sell toys, would you show them on Monday afternoon, Wednesday at midnight, or Saturday morning?
    satisfaction / situation

Sounds of TI and CI

Words to use: artificial, addition, precious, action, social

Name _____

Read each sentence and the words below each blank. In each blank, write the word that best completes the sentence.

1. One way of advertising is to have a well-known or important person give
   __information__ about a product.
   (information, insulation)

2. A well-known rock __musician__ can make young people want to buy a
   certain kind of clothing.
   (magician, musician)

3. The word of a television star who plays the part of a __beautician__ could
   cause people to buy one kind of shampoo.
   (beautician, patient)

4. And who could know more about the best kind of cold medicine than a well-known
   __physician__?
   (physician, position)

5. Even the __initials__ of a favorite football player can rent cars or sell orange
   (infection, initials)
   juice and footballs.

6. In the United States, government __regulation__ states that a well-known
   (regulation, relation)
   person must use the advertised goods at least one time.

7. Becoming known as the __official__ product of some
   (glacier, official)
   __special__ group or happening is another way of getting attention.
   (section, special)

8. People would like to believe that a toothbrush used by astronauts or Olympic athletes
   must offer better __protection__ against tooth decay than all others.
   (detection, protection)

9. One of the best ways to get people to buy a product again and again is to be sure it
   meets the customer's __satisfaction__
   (satisfaction, superstition)

10. By making a high-grade product and building a good __reputation__, a
    (reputation, reservation)
    company can turn its own customers into walking advertisements.

Words containing consonant-vowel combinations in context: ti, ci.   53

Diphthongs: OI, OY, OU, and OW

Words to use: spoil, destroy, trout, tower, poison, voyage, scout, scowl, disappointment, royal, doubt, brownie, choice, annoy, pronounce, powder.

Name _____

The letters **oi** and **oy** stand for the vowel sound in **coin** and **toys.** The letters **ou** and **ow** often stand for the vowel sound in **cloud** and **cow.**

Read the groups of words below. Then read the sentences. In each blank, write the word that best completes the sentence. For sentences 1 through 6, choose words from Group A. For sentences 7 through 12, choose words from Group B.

Group A	wildflowers	point	enjoy	power	crowd	unspoiled	join
Group B	bounce	down	noise	without	avoid	shower	louder	now	wow	pounds

1. Are you looking for fun? Do you __enjoy__ thrill and adventure?

2. Then come and __join__ the wet and wild whitewater __crowd__!

3. The starting __point__ for our journey is along a quiet river bank.

4. Slide the rubber raft into the river and step inside. Don't forget to grab a paddle—this
   raft moves by paddle __power__.

5. At the beginning of our trip, the river is quiet and smooth, so you can enjoy the view of
   the __unspoiled__ wilderness.

6. Along the river banks, you may see beaver, deer, and __wildflowers__.

7. As we float farther down the river, you may hear a rushing, roaring
   __noise__.

8. We are approaching our first set of rapids, and the sound becomes louder and
   __louder__.

9. The rushing water splashes and __pounds__ against the rocks that form
   rapids in the middle of the river.

10. The raft begins to __bounce__ up and __down__ as we rush
    through the foamy water.

11. Don't stop paddling __now__! We've got to keep moving fast to
    __avoid__ flipping the raft.

12. __Wow__! We got through that __without__ dumping over,
    but you look like you took a __shower__!

54   Words containing diphthongs in context: oi, oy, ou, ow

Diphthongs: OI, OY, OU, and OW

Words to use: soil, boy, trousers, eyebrow, voice, oyster, south, towel, point, loyal, shout, allow.

Name _____

Read the list of words below. Then read the sentences that follow. In each blank, write the word that best completes the sentence.

out	bounce	voyage	choice
chow	now	join	point
avoid	around	moist	

1. Now that we're halfway through our whitewater river trip, let's paddle to the shore and
   have some of the __chow__ we brought along.

2. You have your __choice__ of sandwiches—peanut butter and jelly or lunch
   meat and cheese.

3. The person who packed the lunches in these waterproof bags was very careful. The bread
   is not even __moist__.

4. Our river guide says the most exciting part of our __voyage__ is yet to come.

5. A huge rock in the river makes the water turn back upstream and can spin a raft around
   and __around__.

6. In order to __avoid__ that spot, we'll have to shoot through the roughest
   rapid of them all.

7. If you happen to __bounce__ out of the raft, float on your back and
   __point__ your toes downstream.

8. The current is too strong to swim your way __out__ of it, so try to be
   calm and let the river carry you to the shore.

9. We'll paddle to that point and __join__ you there.

10. Are you ready __now__? Check your life jacket and we'll be on our way.

Words containing diphthongs in context: oi, oy, ou, ow   55

Review and Apply: Comprehension

Name _____

Read the groups of words below. Notice that each word contains **s, ti, ci, oi, oy, ou,** or **ow.** Then read the story. In each blank, write the word that best completes the sentence. For paragraphs 1 and 2, choose words from Group A. For paragraph 3, choose words from Group B. For paragraph 4, choose words from Group A again.

Group A	grouchy	station	usually	musicians	choice	annoying
Group B	signals	confuse	explanations	sure	disguise	how	without

1 What happened while you were dreaming last night? Did you find yourself aboard a
mysterious space __station__? Perhaps you were the star singer with a group of
famous rock __musicians__. Whatever you dreamed, it probably seemed very real.

2 Although you may not recall them the next morning, you have several dreams each night.
Each dream is __usually__ connected in some way to a thought or experience you
have had earlier in the day. It may be pleasant, adventuresome, or just plain
__annoying__. Some dreams are so frightening or powerful that they can awaken
you in the middle of the night.

3 No one knows for __sure__ what causes dreams. There are several
different __explanations__. Some doctors think they are a __disguise__
for troublesome thoughts we may be trying to forget. For example, if you are secretly
worried about something, you may dream about taking a test you have forgotten to study
for. Some scientists think electric __signals__ passing through the brain at night
__confuse__ the brain. A dream, they say, is __how__ the brain
tries to make sense of the signals. If you dream of being in a snowstorm __without__
a coat, it may be because the covers have fallen off your bed.

4 No matter why we dream, scientists have discovered that people who are not allowed to
dream during sleep experiments become __grouchy__ and nervous. We haven't
much __choice__ about what our dreams will be, but they do seem to be
important. So when you crawl into bed tonight, your body will be at rest, but your brain will
be at work. Sleep well, and pleasant dreamszzzz
                                        zzz
                                            zzz.

56   Review of words containing s, ti, ci, oi, oy, ou, and ow

189

Review and Apply: Composition

Name

Read the article below. Notice that some of the words contain **s, ti, ci, oi, oy, ou,** and **ow.** Use the paragraphs to answer the questions that follow.

Behind every good motion picture is a good film editor. A movie is not always filmed in the order it is shown in a theater or on television. All the scenes that take place in the same location are shot at the same time. If the beginning and ending of a movie take place in the desert, the scenes are shot one after another. Once the whole movie has been shot, film editors view it and arrange it in the correct order.

Usually, film makers shoot more film than is needed. An uncut movie might last four or five hours. Working in an office or studio, the film editors cut the film down to about two hours. They cut out parts that don't fit in especially well. Sometimes they discover parts that seem to drag. They speed up the action by shortening or cutting slow scenes. Editing a film may take several months. After all the scenes have finally been joined in the correct order, the film is ready for presentation. A film editor who has done his or her job well helps to make sure that the movie will be enjoyed by all who see it.

1. Who is the article about? ___film editors___

2. What do these people do? ___shorten films and put the scenes in order___

3. When do they do this? ___after the film has been shot___

4. Where do they do this? ___in an office or studio___

5. Why do they do this? ___to make the film enjoyable___

6. In one or two sentences, tell what the article is about. Include only the most important points. Use your answers to the questions above to help you. ___After a movie has been shot, film editors view the film. They shorten the film and put the scenes in order so that it will be enjoyed by those who see it. (Wording of answers will vary.)___

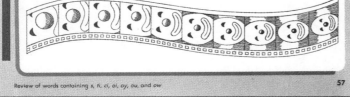

Check-Up Test 1: Phonics

Name

Read the story. Then, using the underlined story words, follow the directions below.

What lives in the ocean and can give you four hugs at once? An octopus, of course. Many people think octopuses are fierce animals, but they're really quite shy. When an enemy is near, an octopus may protect itself in a number of <u>ways</u>. It may hide by changing its color to match its surroundings. It can even turn two colors at once to confuse its enemy. Or it may <u>squeeze</u> its soft body <u>between</u> two rocks so it won't be noticed. If an enemy does spot it, the octopus can swim away by <u>shooting</u> water through a tube on its body. It can also send a liquid that looks like ink <u>through</u> the tube. The liquid makes a black cloud that hides the octopus and confuses the enemy.

Most octopuses are no bigger than an adult's fist. Some are very tiny, <u>measuring</u> only two inches from the tip of one foot to another. The largest ones are about <u>twenty-eight</u> feet long. The bottom of each arm has rows of small round <u>muscles</u> that can grab almost anything. On top of an octopus's <u>head</u> are two large shiny eyes. Good sight helps the octopus spot clams, small crabs, and lobsters. It catches these animals in its arms and may shoot <u>poison</u> into their bodies. The poison paralyzes the shellfish, which then becomes the octopus's <u>meal</u>. Only the blue-ringed octopus has poison strong enough to kill a person. Even though this octopus is tiny and shy, it's best to stay away from an octopus of any <u>kind</u>. So before you step into a bathtub next time, you may want to take a second look . . . just in case.

Follow each of the directions below. Number each underlined word only once.

1. Find three words in which two vowels stand for the long-e sound. Write **1** above each word.

2. Find one word that has the long-i sound. Write **2** above the word.

3. Find two words in which two vowels stand for the short-e sound. Write **3** above each word.

4. Find one word that has the vowel sound you hear in *joy.* Write **4** above the word.

5. Find two words that have the vowel sound you hear in *moon.* Write **5** above each word.

6. Find two words that have the long-**a** sound. Write **6** above each word.

7. Find one word that has one silent consonant in the middle. Write **7** above the word.

Check-Up Test 2: Phonics

Name

Read the story. Then, using the underlined story words, follow the directions below.

Have you ever been so angry that you "saw red"? Perhaps you've had the <u>experience</u> of "feeling blue." These <u>expressions</u> are one way that we link colors with the way we feel. Studies show that color has a <u>powerful</u> effect on our moods. When you see the color red, for example, your breathing, blood <u>pressure</u>, and pulse rate increase. This can make you feel restless or <u>excited</u>. It may contribute to your feeling angry about something that is already bothering you. Red, along with orange and <u>yellow</u>, can make us feel hungry, too. That's why so many fast-food restaurants are decorated in those colors. Wearing a red dress or shirt may also make you feel more <u>energetic</u> or perk you up when you're feeling down.

Blue, green, and violet, on the other hand, can quiet us and make us feel peaceful. They are good colors for a bedroom or any other room where you may want to rest or relax. A person who is tense or nervous may feel better by wearing one of these colors.

Our moods are not the only things that can change depending on the colors in our environment. The quality of our work can be affected, too. Experiments show that we think better and work at a more productive level when we are surrounded by colors we like. The next time you're having trouble <u>concentrating</u> on a task, take a look <u>around</u>. Are you <u>wearing</u> colors that distract you? Is the room painted in dull, drab colors? You may not be able to repaint the room, but perhaps you can wear different <u>clothes</u> or turn so that you <u>face</u> a <u>window</u>. By trying something different, you may find that a <u>change</u> leaves you feeling "tickled pink."

Follow each of the directions below. Number each underlined word only once.

1. Find two words that have a soft-**g** sound, as in *danger.* Write **1** above each word.

2. Find two words in which **s** stands for the sound of **sh**. Write **2** above each word.

3. Find three words that have the long-**o** sound. Write **3** above each word.

4. Find the word that rhymes with *caring.* Write **4** above the word.

5. Find two words that have the vowel sound you hear in *now.* Write **5** above each word.

6. Find four words that have a soft-**c** sound, as in *city.* Write **6** above each word.

Reading and Writing Wrap-Up

Name

READING

A Famous Cherokee

The giant sequoia trees of California are named after a famous Cherokee Indian named Sequoya. He is also well known for something even more important.

Sequoya was born about 1760. He grew up in what is now eastern Tennessee, where his people made their homes. Most of the Cherokee were farmers and hunters, but Sequoya came from a family that was especially interested in Cherokee history and customs. Sequoya dreamed of recording this history so it would not be forgotten. But the Cherokee had no written language. Sequoya decided that he would invent a system of writing for his people. He worked on this task for twelve years, and finally, in 1821, he finished. In Sequoya's alphabet, there were eighty-six signs to represent the sounds of the Cherokee language.

At first the Cherokee refused to accept Sequoya's system of writing. They couldn't believe that their speech could actually be written down and then read by others. But Sequoya proved to them that it was true. A special meeting was held for the chiefs and leaders of the Cherokee. Sequoya had taught his daughter to read and write the alphabet he had created. At the meeting, she wrote down what the chiefs said while Sequoya was in a separate room. Then Sequoya read the chiefs' words back to them. Finally, they were convinced.

Now the Cherokee could learn to write and read in their own language. They could print their own books and newspapers. And they could prepare a written record of their history and customs to share with future generations.

Sequoya was honored by the Cherokee for his work. During the rest of his life, he worked to improve the lives of *all* Indians. A statue of Sequoya stands in the Capitol in Washington, D.C.

Social Studies

UNDERSTANDING

A. Draw a line to connect each phrase on the left with the correct spelling on the right.

1. a giant tree
2. a famous Cherokee

a. Sequoya
b. sequoia
c. Sequoia
d. sequoya

B. Answer the following questions.

1. Where did the Cherokee live? __Tennessee__

2. How did most of the Cherokee make a living in the 1700's?
   Most of the Cherokee made a living by farming and hunting.

3. How many years did Sequoya work on his alphabet? __twelve__

4. Why did Sequoya want to create a system of writing for the Cherokee language?
   He wanted to have a way to record the history and customs of the Cherokee.

5. Why did the Cherokee refuse to accept Sequoya's system of writing at first?
   They couldn't believe that their speech could actually be written down and then
   read by others.

6. How did Sequoya prove to the Cherokee leaders that his writing system really worked?.
   He had his daughter write down what the chiefs said, and then he read it back to
   them.

7. Where do sequoia trees grow? __California__

C. Describe one way in which Sequoya was honored.
   Possible answers: A statue of Sequoya is in the Capitol in Washington, D. C. A tree
   was named after him.

Reading and Writing Wrap-Up

THINKING

A. Write the word from the box that means the same as each word or phrase listed below.

giant	convince	famous	customs	Capitol

1. huge __giant__
2. ways of doing things __customs__
3. building where the government meets __Capitol__
4. well known __famous__
5. persuade __convince__

B. Answer the following questions.

1. About how old was Sequoya when he finished his system of writing? __61__

2. What is the purpose of an alphabet?
   Answers may vary but should be similar to the following: The purpose of an
   alphabet is to represent the sounds of a language in writing.

3. Why might it have been hard for Sequoya's people to accept a written language?
   Answers will vary. Possible answer: Their language may have seemed too
   complicated to put into written form.

C. An alphabet is like a code. Make up your own alphabet, or code, and then write a
   message using it. Exchange messages with your classmates.
   Answers will vary.
   _____
   _____
   _____
   _____

Social Studies

WRITING

Imagine that written language no longer exists. You would not be able to read or write. You
would have to rely on listening and speaking. Write a paragraph telling how this would
change your life. What things could you still do? What things could you not do?

Answers will vary.

_____
_____
_____
_____
_____
_____
_____
_____
_____
_____
_____
_____
_____
_____
_____
_____
_____

Base Words and Endings: -ED and -ING

Words to use: marry, married, marrying; trim, trimmed, trimming; love, loved, loving

A word to which an ending can be added is called a base word. When a word ends with one
vowel followed by a consonant, double the consonant before adding **-ed** or **-ing.** When a
word ends in **e,** drop the **e** before adding **-ed** or **-ing.** When a word ends in a consonant
followed by **y,** change the **y** to **i** before adding **-ed.**

snap snap**ped** snap**ping**   save sav**ed** sav**ing**   hurry hurr**ied** hurry**ing**

Read the words below. Write the base word for each one.

1. clapped __clap__
2. watches __watch__
3. carried __carry__
4. cutting __cut__
5. liked __like__
6. hiding __hide__
7. studied __study__
8. teaching __teach__

Read each sentence below. Complete the sentence by adding **-ed** or **-ing** to the base word
shown below each blank.

1. It was warm this morning, but the temperature has been __dropping__ rapidly
   all afternoon.
   (drop)

2. I __chopped__ carrots and lettuce for the salad while José began
   (chop)
   __preparing__ sauce for the spaghetti.
   (prepare)

3. The dancers were __smiling__ even though they were nervous about giving
   (smile)
   their first performance.

4. __Glancing__ at her watch, Kiku __hurried__ to get to the dentist's
   (Glance)   (hurry)
   office for her appointment.

5. Our history teacher has __planned__ a field trip for our class Friday.
   (plan)

6. Because Ms. Johnston needed a response quickly, I __replied__ to her party
   (reply)
   invitation by telephone.

7. Phyllis __served__ the tennis ball, but it landed beyond the court.
   (serve)

Endings: -S and -ES

Words to use: cough, coughs; dress, dresses; wash, washes; catch, catches; wax, waxes; hurry, hurries

Often, new words can be formed by adding **-s** or **-es** to other words. To change many words, add the ending **-s**. When a word ends in **s, ss, sh, ch, x,** or **z,** add **-es**. When a word ends in a consonant followed by **y,** change the **y** to **i** and add **-es**.

laugh laugh**s**   rush rush**es**   copy cop**ies**

Read each sentence below. Complete the sentence by adding **-s** or **-es** to the base word shown below each blank.

1. My neighbor, Ms. Huntington, _____studies_____ bumblebees as a hobby.
   (study)

2. She _____keeps_____ bees in a glass-walled hive in her backyard.
   (keep)

3. Through the glass panels, Ms. Huntington _____watches_____ the bees as they busily work and communicate with each other.
   (watch)

4. Sometimes Ms. Huntington _____invites_____ me over to observe the bees, and she _____teaches_____ me interesting facts about their unusual habits and lives.
   (invite) (teach)

5. I learned, for example, that when a bumblebee _____hatches_____ from its egg, it _____looks_____ like a teeny white worm.
   (hatch) (look)

6. During this early period of life, the wormlike bee _____relies_____ on other bees to feed it.
   (rely)

7. As the worm eats and grows, it _____pushes_____ through its outer skin and sheds it several different times.
   (push)

8. The bee _____finishes_____ this stage of life by spinning a cocoon.
   (finish)

9. After about two weeks, the bee _____passes_____ into the adult stage of life and _____chews_____ its way out of the cocoon.
   (pass) (chew)

10. Soon the adult bumblebee _____buzzes_____ and _____flies_____ as it begins to produce its delicious honey.
    (buzz) (fly)

Endings: -ER and -EST

Words to use: near, nearer, nearest; young, younger, youngest; tight, tighter, tightest

In many words, the ending **-er** means "more." It is used to compare two things. The ending **-est** means "most." It is used to compare three or more things.

deep   deep**er**   deep**est**

Read the lines from newspaper advertisements below. Add **-er** or **-est** to the base word below each blank to complete the sentence.

1. Our everyday prices are even _____lower_____ than our competitors' sale prices.
   (low)

2. We strive to give you the _____highest_____ quality furniture money can buy.
   (high)

3. At Dealin' Dan's, you'll receive _____greater_____ value for your dollar than at any other car company.
   (great)

4. The Wilson Company offers the _____strongest_____ customer protection plan in the business.
   (strong)

5. Our specialists are trained to use the latest methods and _____newest_____ medical equipment.
   (new)

6. At Accurite, we guarantee our prices to be the _____lowest_____ in town.
   (low)

7. Does our bank pay a _____higher_____ rate on savings than yours? Check our rates.
   (high)

8. We are the city's _____oldest_____ and most experienced carpet cleaning company.
   (old)

9. To find vegetables any _____fresher_____ than Bean's, you'd have to pick your own.
   (fresh)

10. Shopping at Franklin's Food Store may be the _____smartest_____ move you'll ever make.
    (smart)

11. Our automobile gives you more head room, better sound insulation, and a _____smoother_____ ride.
    (smooth)

12. For the _____sharpest_____ photos you've ever seen, let Connelly Camera develop your film today.
    (sharp)

13. At Hagan's Delicious Foods, you'll get the _____fastest_____ service in town.
    (fast)

Endings: -ER and -EST

Words to use: dim, dimmer, dimmest; fine, finer, finest; pretty, prettier, prettiest

When a word ends with one vowel followed by a consonant, double the consonant before adding **-er** or **-est**. When a word ends in **e,** drop the **e** before adding **-er** or **-est**. When a word ends in a consonant followed by **y,** change the **y** to **i** before adding **-er** or **-est**.

wet wet**ter** wet**test**   wise wis**er** wis**est**   cloudy cloud**ier** cloud**iest**

Add **-er** or **-est** to each base word shown below.

1. hot + er = _____hotter_____
2. lovely + est = _____loveliest_____
3. late + est = _____latest_____
4. cranky + er = _____crankier_____
5. sad + er = _____sadder_____
6. brave + er = _____braver_____
7. thirsty + er = _____thirstier_____
8. wide + er = _____wider_____
9. lonely + er = _____lonelier_____
10. big + er = _____bigger_____

Read each sentence below. Complete each one by adding **-er** or **-est** to the base word shown below each blank.

1. A microscope is an instrument that can be used to make objects appear _____bigger_____ than they actually are.
   (big)

2. The Sahara is the _____largest_____ desert in the world and one of the _____hottest_____ places on earth.
   (large) (hot)

3. My sister gets up _____earlier_____ than I because she delivers the morning paper.
   (early)

4. We adopted both puppies from the animal shelter because we couldn't decide which one was _____cuter_____.
   (cute)

5. Marilyn waxed and polished her car until it was the _____shiniest_____ one on the block.
   (shiny)

6. Last night's television special was _____sadder_____ than the one we saw Friday.
   (sad)

7. Which of these two melons do you think is _____riper_____?
   (ripe)

Review and Apply: Comprehension

Read the story below. Complete each unfinished sentence by adding **-s, -es, -ed, -ing, -er,** or **-est** to each word shown in parentheses.

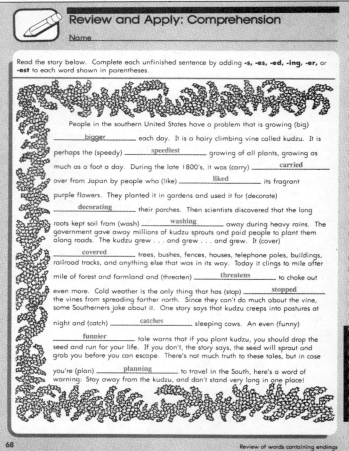

People in the southern United States have a problem that is growing (big) _____bigger_____ each day. It is a hairy climbing vine called kudzu. It is perhaps the (speedy) _____speediest_____ growing of all plants, growing as much as a foot a day. During the late 1800's, it was (carry) _____carried_____ over from Japan by people who (like) _____liked_____ its fragrant purple flowers. They planted it in gardens and used it for (decorate) _____decorating_____ their porches. Then scientists discovered that the long roots kept soil from (wash) _____washing_____ away during heavy rains. The government gave away millions of kudzu sprouts and paid people to plant them along roads. The kudzu grew . . . and grew . . . and grew. It (cover) _____covered_____ trees, bushes, fences, houses, telephone poles, buildings, railroad tracks, and anything else that was in its way. Today it clings to mile after mile of forest and farmland and (threaten) _____threatens_____ to choke out even more. Cold weather is the only thing that has (stop) _____stopped_____ the vines from spreading farther north. Since they can't do much about the vine, some Southerners joke about it. One story says that kudzu creeps into pastures at night and (catch) _____catches_____ sleeping cows. An even (funny) _____funnier_____ tale warns that if you plant kudzu, you should drop the seed and run for your life. If you don't, the story says, the seed will sprout and grab you before you can escape. There's not much truth to these tales, but in case you're (plan) _____planning_____ to travel in the South, here's a word of warning: Stay away from the kudzu, and don't stand very long in one place!

192

Review and Apply: Composition

Name _____

With so much kudzu growing over the southern United States, there must be something useful that could be done with it. One scientist has suggested planting it on tops of buildings. The vines could hang down the sides of the buildings. This would help keep them cool in summer. What are some other ways in which kudzu could be used? Read the words in the boxes below to get some ideas. Add **-s, -es, -ed, -ing, -er,** or **-est** to at least two words from each box, and list your ideas in complete sentences.

fix	catch	fry	pretty	hang	grind	take	squeeze	rip	chop
mix	touch	dry	sticky	yank	thick	save	trade	dip	stop
miss	match	bury	tasty	pick	fasten	poke	shake	dig	scrub
pass	scratch	tiny	healthy	long	gather	rake	stake	tug	snap
crush	pinch	easy	fuzzy	soak	cheap	hire	slice	pop	knot
slash	stretch	carry	hungry	feed	build	bake	scrape	wrap	trap

Answers will vary.

_____

_____

_____

_____

_____

_____

_____

_____

_____

_____

_____

_____

_____

Plurals: -S and -ES

Name _____

Words to use: plant, plants; day, days; monkey, monkeys; dress, dresses; dish, dishes; porch, porches; tax, taxes; penny, pennies

A word that stands for one of something is a singular word. A word that stands for two or more of something is a plural word. Most plurals are formed by adding **-s** to a singular word. When a word ends in **s, ss, sh, ch,** or **x,** add **-es** to form its plural. When a word ends in a consonant followed by **y,** change the **y** to **i** and add **-es.**

Read each sentence below. Complete the sentence by writing the plural form of the word shown below each blank.

1. People have been interested in _____birds_____ almost since the beginning of time.
   (bird)

2. All birds have feathers and wings, though not all birds are _____flyers_____.
   (flyer)

3. _____Ostriches_____, for example, are the fastest birds on land, but they cannot fly.
   (Ostrich)

4. Penguins, which have short, solid _____bodies_____, use their wings like
   (body)
   _____flippers_____
   (flipper)

5. Many birds construct nests on the ground, in tree _____branches_____, or in
   (branch)
   _____bushes_____.
   (bush)

6. Their nests may be made of mud, twigs, leaves, or different kinds of _____grasses_____
   (grass)

7. The nest of the smallest bird in the world, the bee hummingbird, is less than two
   _____inches_____ high.
   (inch)

8. In some species, the _____feathers_____ of the male bird are more brightly colored
   (feather)
   than those of the female.

9. In a few, _____females_____ are brighter; in others, both sexes look alike.
   (female)

10. Many pet birds, such as _____finches_____ and _____canaries_____, are
    (finch)   (canary)
    valued for their beautiful singing voices.

Plurals: Changing F to V

Name _____

Words to use: calf, calves; knife, knives

To form the plural of most words that end in **f** or **fe,** change the **f** or **fe** to **v** and add **-es.**

calf cal**ves**   knife kni**ves**

Read the newspaper headlines below. Using the rule above, complete each headline by writing the plural form of the word shown below the blank.

1. City Cleaning Crews to Pick up _____Leaves_____ Next Week
   (Leaf)

2. Twin Brothers' _____Lives_____ Saved in Daring Rescue
   (Life)

3. Judge Gets Tough on Shoplifters and _____Thieves_____
   (Thief)

4. Children Attend Holiday Party Dressed as _____Elves_____
   (Elf)

5. Workers Demand Insurance for Husbands and _____Wives_____
   (Wife)

6. Farmers Feeding Laboratory-Grown Grain to _____Calves_____
   (Calf)

7. Knights-Chargers Game Scoreless in Both _____Halves_____
   (Half)

8. Audiences Amazed by Daring Performer Who Juggles _____Knives_____
   (Knife)

9. Bakery Donates 1,000 _____Loaves_____ to Food Pantry
   (Loaf)

10. Neighbors Form Lookout Group to Protect Property, _____Selves_____
    (Self)

11. New Library to Include Revolving _____Shelves_____, Computerized Catalogs
    (Shelf)

12. Fairgrounds Pavement Causes Injury to Horses' _____Hooves_____
    (Hoof)

13. Firefighters Collect Used Coats, Boots, _____Scarves_____ for Needy
    (Scarf)

Plurals: Words That End in O

Name _____

Words to use: radio, radios; rodeo, rodeos; photo, photos; piano, pianos; hero, heroes; potato, potatoes

Words that end in a vowel and **o** form their plurals by adding **-s.**
radio**s**   rodeo**s**   kangaroo**s**   igloo**s**   shampoo**s**

Some words that end in a consonant and **o** form their plurals by adding **-s.** Others add **-es.**

photo**s**	soprano**s**	hero**es**
auto**s**	piano**s**	potato**es**
pro**s**	burro**s**	tomato**es**
solo**s**	Eskimo**s**	

Read each clue and the list of words. Find the word in the list whose plural matches the clue. Write the plural form of the word next to the clue.

1. pack animals that look like small donkeys _____burros_____   rodeo
2. jumping animals that carry their young in pouches _____kangaroos_____   igloo
3. musical instruments with black and white keys _____pianos_____   shampoo
4. pictures taken with a camera _____photos_____   kangaroo
5. vegetables from which spaghetti sauce is made _____tomatoes_____   photo
6. people who show great courage or do brave things _____heroes_____   piano
7. vegetables that grow underground _____potatoes_____   burro
8. soaps used to clean hair _____shampoos_____   hero
9. contests in which people ride horses and rope cattle _____rodeos_____   potato
10. dome-shaped houses made of snow blocks _____igloos_____   tomato

Read the list of words below. Then read the sentences that follow. Write the plural form of a word from the list to complete each sentence.
Eskimo   radio   auto   solo   soprano   pro

1. Marta's mother has a job selling televisions, tape players, and _____radios_____.
2. Our school chorus needs two _____sopranos_____ to sing _____solos_____.
3. Sled dogs are often used by _____Eskimos_____ to travel over ice in the far north.
4. I like to watch college football games, but Jan would rather watch the _____pros_____.
5. As a hobby, my brother likes repairing the engines of old _____autos_____.

Irregular Plurals

Words to use: tooth, teeth; child, children; mouse, mice

Name _____

The plurals of some words are formed by changing the spellings of their singular forms.

tooth - teeth	child - children	woman - women	goose - geese
mouse - mice	man - men	foot - feet	ox - oxen

The plural forms of some words can be the same as their singular forms.

deer   sheep   fish   moose

Write the plural form of each word or phrase below.

1. eyetooth   __eyeteeth__
2. cold foot   __cold feet__
3. goldfish   __goldfish (or goldfishes)__

4. grandchild   __grandchildren__
5. reindeer   __reindeer (or reindeers)__
6. ox   __oxen__

In each blank below, write the plural form of the word shown in parentheses. Then use the words you have written to complete the titles of magazine articles that follow.

__sheep__	__teeth__	__mice__
(sheep)	(tooth)	(mouse)
__fish (or fishes)__	__moose__	__feet__
(fish)	(moose)	(foot)
__women__	__geese__	__men__
(woman)	(goose)	(man)
__deer (or deers)__	__children__	
(deer)	(child)	

1. "Do ____Mice____ Really Like Cheese?"
2. "____Fish____ Are Back in Lake Ontario"
3. "Grow Your Own Wooly Sweaters: How to Raise ____Sheep____"
4. "A Birdwatcher's Guide to Wild Ducks and ____Geese____"
5. "Your Body's Chopping, Slicing, Dicing Tools: Your ____Teeth____"
6. "Mammals with Antlers: Elk, ____Deer____, Caribou, and ____Moose____"
7. "Heroes of Science: ____Men____ and ____Women____ Who Changed the World"
8. "Stay on Your Toes by Taking Good Care of Your ____Feet____"
9. "Checkers, Marbles, and Other Favorite ____Children____'s Games"

Review and Apply: Comprehension

Name _____

Read the list of words below. Notice that each word can be made plural by adding -s or -es, by changing letters, or by changing a letter and adding -es. Then read the story that follows. In each blank, write the plural form of the list word that best completes the sentence.

hero	pitch	loss	photo	fly	foot	handkerchief
team	Bobcat	bench	inning	fan	base	story

After eight ____innings____ of play, the two softball ____teams____ were tied. On the scoreboard, each team had a row of zeros. The Tigers were up to bat, but they were feeling gloomy. Earlier, Rita, their best hitter, had hit two grounders and two pop ____flies____. Helene, the pitcher for the ____Bobcats____, had a record of ten wins and only two ____losses____. Rita now faced Helene again, and her confidence was low. Helene's first two ____pitches____ to Rita had been strikes. Helene wound up for the third pitch and hurled the ball toward home plate. Rita eyed the ball carefully and then belted it into a row of wooden ____benches____ three hundred ____feet____ away. The Tiger ____fans____ cheered and waved ____handkerchiefs or handkerchieves____ as Rita circled all three ____bases____. She had regained her playing ability and become one of their ____heroes____. The next day, the newspaper carried several ____stories____ about the game and half a page of color ____photos____.

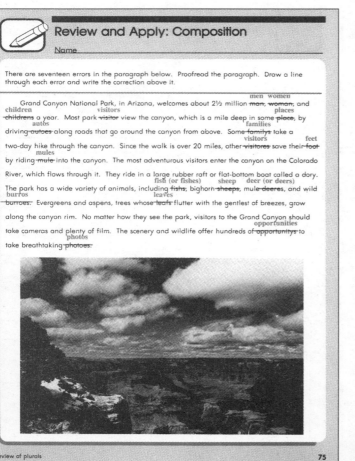

Review and Apply: Composition

Name _____

There are seventeen errors in the paragraph below. Proofread the paragraph. Draw a line through each error and write the correction above it.

Grand Canyon National Park, in Arizona, welcomes about 2½ million ~~man~~, ~~woman~~, and ~~childrens~~ a year. [men, women, children] Most park ~~visitor~~ view the canyon, which is a mile deep in some ~~place~~, by [visitors, places] driving ~~autos~~ along roads that go around the canyon from above. Some ~~familys~~ take a [autos, families] two-day hike through the canyon. Since the walk is over 20 miles, other ~~visitores~~ save their ~~foot~~ [visitors, feet] by riding ~~mule~~ into the canyon. The most adventurous visitors enter the canyon on the Colorado [mules] River, which flows through it. They ride in a large rubber raft or flat-bottom boat called a dory. The park has a wide variety of animals, including ~~fishs~~, bighorn ~~sheeps~~, mule ~~deers~~, and wild [fish (or fishes), sheep, deer (or deers)] ~~burroes~~. Evergreens and aspens, trees whose ~~leafs~~ flutter with the gentlest of breezes, grow [burros, leaves] along the canyon rim. No matter how they see the park, visitors to the Grand Canyon should take cameras and plenty of film. The scenery and wildlife offer hundreds of ~~opportunitys~~ to [opportunities] take breathtaking ~~photoes~~. [photos]

Singular and Plural Possessives

Words to use: teacher, teacher's, teachers, teachers'; student, student's, students, students'; family, family's, families, families'

Name _____

To make most words show ownership, add an apostrophe (') and s. To make a plural word that ends in s show ownership, add just an apostrophe.

Read each sentence below. Complete the sentence by adding ' or 's to the word shown below the blank.

1. The ____morning's____ thunderstorm threatened to close the sidewalk art fair. (morning)
2. The ____storm's____ sudden downpour sent people scurrying for shelter. (storm)
3. A few ____artists'____ exhibits were damaged by high winds and water. (artists)
4. All the ____tents'____ brightly colored covers were soaked and heavy with puddles. (tents)
5. The flowering ____bushes'____ branches were stripped of their petals. (bushes)
6. The ____youngsters'____ face-painting exhibit became a stream of swirling colors as the paint washed over the sidewalk. (youngsters)
7. In less than an ____hour's____ time, the angry storm was over. (hour)
8. The ____sun's____ rays poked through the clouds and seemed to push them away. (sun)
9. The ____churches'____ tall steeples could be seen from far away. (churches)
10. Relief shone on the ____exhibitors'____ faces as they returned to their stands. (exhibitors)

Irregular Plural Possessives

Words to use: child, child's, children, children's; man, man's, men, men's; woman, woman's, women, women's

Name _____

To make a plural word that does not end in **s** show ownership or belonging, add an apostrophe (') and **s**.

Read the lines from bulletin board postings below. Rewrite each group of words, using **'s** to form words that show ownership or belonging.

1. Attention: Basketball Team of Women

   Attention: Women's Basketball Team

2. Breakfast Club of Men to meet Friday

   Men's Breakfast Club to meet Friday

3. Story Hour of the Children cancelled this week

   Children's Story Hour cancelled this week

4. class project of the Freshmen needs volunteers

   Freshmen's class project needs volunteers

5. Remember the birthdays of your grandchildren with this reminder.

   Remember your grandchildren's birthdays with this reminder.

Read the list of words below. Then read the sentences that follow. In each blank, write the **'s** form of the list word that best completes the sentence.

feet   oxen   women   geese   teeth   children   mice

1. Not including their tails, _____mice's_____ bodies are between two and four inches long.

2. It is your _____teeth's_____ hard outer layer of enamel that protects them from decay and from breaking easily.

3. _____Oxen's_____ large, heavy bodies make them able to pull heavy loads.

4. Your _____feet's_____ comfort depends on shoes that fit well.

5. Except for their legs and feet, _____geese's_____ bodies are covered almost entirely with feathers.

6. Many _____children's_____ books have large, colorful pictures and few words.

7. The department store is having a special week-long sale on _____women's_____ dresses.

Review and Apply: Comprehension

Name _____

Read the list of words below. Then read the sentence clues that follow. Fill in the crossword puzzle by adding **'s, s',** or **es'** to the list word that best completes the clue. For two of the list words, you will need to make spelling changes.

wife   piano   canary   child   sheep   box
bus   brush   coach   pilot   fish   ax   watch

ACROSS

2. None of the ____ bands in the jewelry display fit my little sister's wrist.
4. Of the four couples, three of the ____ husbands had grown up in the same community.
7. My ____ name is Sunshine because its feathers are brilliant yellow.
9. The teacher learned all the ____ names in less than a day.
10. Two of the cardboard ____ lids were torn and did not fit tightly.
12. Because the ____ handle was cracked, the painter threw it away.
13. Most of the goldfish looked alike, but one ____ tail was black.

DOWN

1. This ____ keys are made of plastic instead of ivory.
3. The swimming ____ daughter did not make the championship team this year.
5. Twelve of the school ____ tires are being replaced with snow tires.
6. To work for an airlines, a ____ vision must be excellent.
8. That ____ wool will be sheared by the farmer tomorrow.
11. Which ____ blade needs to be sharpened?

Review and Apply: Composition

Name _____

You and Grogan, your space partner, have just returned to your home planet of Urch after visiting the planet Earth. All your Urchin friends have gathered to welcome you and hear about your trip. Grogan has drawn a picture to show the Urchins some of Earth's animal life. Grogan's memory is not very good, though, and there are some mistakes in the drawing. Look at the picture and read the words that follow. Then, using the possessive form of each word, write a paragraph telling Grogan how to correct the picture.

pony   moose   ostrich   foxes   cat   mice
geese   kangaroo   wolves   bushes   pigs   calf

Answers will vary.

_____

_____

_____

_____

Compound Words

Words to use: snowflake, bookcase, somewhere, nobody, anything, waterfall, sunshine, moonbeam, starlight, earthquake, sidewalk, basketball, teammate, seashell

Name _____

A compound word is formed by joining two smaller words together: **rain + bow = rainbow**

Read the groups of words below. Then read the clues that follow. For each clue, join a word from Group A with a word from Group B to form a compound word that matches the clue. Write the word next to the clue. You will use each word in Group A twice.

Group A	bill	book	head	sea	water
Group B	sickness	ache	proof	store	fold
	line	shore	melon	mark	board

1. large bold type printed above a newspaper article _____headline_____
2. place to buy books, magazines, and newspapers _____bookstore_____
3. pain in the head _____headache_____
4. land beside an ocean _____seashore_____
5. paper or thin card used to hold one's place in a book _____bookmark_____
6. water-filled fruit that is green outside and pink inside _____watermelon_____
7. large sign used for advertising _____billboard_____
8. not letting water get through _____waterproof_____
9. wallet for paper money _____billfold_____
10. illness caused by the movement of sailing on an ocean _____seasickness_____

Read the rows of words below. Then read the sentences that follow. Complete each sentence by joining a word from Group A with a word from Group B to form a compound word. Use each word only once.

Group A	flash	pass	straw	eye	suit
Group B	sight	light	port	case	berries

1. I took so many clothes on our trip, I had to sit on my _____suitcase_____ to shut it.
2. The miner's _____flashlight_____ shone dimly because it needed new batteries.
3. In the summer, many people eat _____strawberries_____ they have grown in their gardens.
4. Before taking a trip to a foreign country, you must have a _____passport_____.
5. My brother's new glasses have improved his _____eyesight_____ greatly.

Compound Words

Words to use: snowstorm, suitcase, anywhere, somebody, sunlight, teamwork, seashore, birthday, popcorn, houseboat, lifeguard, housework, chairperson

Read the list of compound words below. Then read the incomplete book titles and descriptions that follow. In each description, circle two compound words. Then write the best compound word from the list to complete the book title.

Wildlife	Handbook	Baseball	Upside	
	Houseplants	Cookbook	Shortcuts	

1. **Favorite Brand Name Recipe** ___Cookbook___ An illustrated collection of popular recipes that have appeared on food packages for ages. (Everything) from a simple family snack to an elegant meal. 416 pages, (hardcover) book. $15.95.

2. **The New 35MM Photographer's** ___Handbook___ 400 photos in color and black and white. This guide is easy to read and gives all the tips you need for successful picture taking, (indoors) or out. 1987 (copyright) 240 pages. $14.95.

3. **The New Complete Book of Collectible** ___Baseball___ **Cards** Fascinating, fun, and (overflowing) with facts about this great sport. Find out why these cards are such a hot item, why they bring high prices, what makes a card rare, and more. Price guide plus information on buying, selling, and trading. Book (Warehouse) special price $14.98.

4. **How a Fly Walks** ___Upside___ **Down and Other Curious Facts** Why is the sky blue? What are freckles? Is (quicksand) really dangerous? These and dozens of other questions are answered in this interesting and entertaining book. 256 (softbound) pages. $6.95.

5. **The Encyclopedia of North American** ___Wildlife___ A treasure for (anyone) interested in animal life. Alphabetically arranged listings cover hundreds of animals, answering questions about habits, breeding, size, diet, and history. Originally sold for $35.00, now selling for (closeout) price of $14.98.

6. **Quilting** ___Shortcuts___ Now you can make your own beautiful quilts and (bedspreads) in less time than you ever dreamed possible! A wealth of ideas that save time for the beginning or advanced quilter. Includes photos, drawings, patterns, and (patchwork) designs. 8½ x 11 inches, $9.95.

7. **Illustrated Guide to Popular** ___Houseplants___ Provides all the details you need to know for growing plants at home or in your (greenhouse) Covers many kinds of cacti, plus other flowering and non-flowering plants. Full of pictures, this guide includes color photos and (artwork) $9.98.

Contractions

Words to use: you + are = you're, should + not = shouldn't, must + not = mustn't

A contraction is a short way to write two words. It is written by putting two words together and leaving out a letter or letters. An apostrophe (') takes the place of the letters that are left out. **Won't** is a special contraction made from the words **will** and **not**.

was + not = wasn't   I + have = I've   will + not = won't

Below are some people's comments about movies they have seen. Read each comment and the pair of words shown below each blank. Complete the comment by writing the contraction that stands for each word pair.

1. "If you ___don't___ love *Animal Sense*, you ___haven't___ got any."
   (do not)   (have not)

2. "For all those adults who think ___they've___ outgrown fairy tales, *Puppy*
   (they have)
   Longstocking will be a real pleasure."

3. "*Space Train* is out of this world. ___You've___ got to see it."
   (You have)

4. "*A Chorus Lion* is the funniest movie ___we've___ seen in a long time.
   (we have)
   ___You'll___ roar with laughter."
   (You will)

5. "*The Umpire Strikes Out* may be the best comedy ___we'll___ see all year.
   (we will)
   The script-writers ___must've___ been batty."
   (must have)

6. "I ___didn't___ expect to be so enthusiastic about a race-car movie. But *The*
   (did not)
   Brake Fast Club will be a winner, ___I'm___ sure."
   (I am)

7. "You ___shouldn't___ miss *Smokey and the Band*. You ___won't___
   (should not)   (will not)
   see a better musical this year."

8. "See *Toastbusters*. ___It's___ far from crummy."
   (It is)

9. " ___I've___ seen lots of boxing films, and ___I'll___ tell you
   (I have)   (I will)
   Eddie and the Bruisers is bound to be a hit."

Contractions

Words to use: was + not = wasn't, I + have = I've, will + not = won't

Read the word pairs below. Then read the sentences that follow. Complete each sentence by forming a contraction from one of the word pairs. For sentences 1 through 8, choose word pairs from Group A. For sentences 9 through 15, choose words from Group B.

Group A	would not	she is	could not	what is	can not
	did not	I am	there is	she will	have not	must have
Group B	could not		I am		she had	let us
	it is		that is	I have	I will	who is

1. Last week, when I ___couldn't___ find Rascal, I was really worried.

2. She is usually well-behaved, and ___there's___ no dog more loyal.

3. It ___must've___ been while Mom was taking out the trash that she left the door open and Rascal slipped out.

4. We ___didn't___ discover until two hours later that she had disappeared. I was especially anxious because Rascal was due to have puppies any day.

5. "___What's___ the matter?" Sam Fenton asked as I ran up the street desperately calling Rascal's name.

6. "Rascal has escaped and I ___can't___ find her," I explained.

7. "___I'm___ sorry, but I ___haven't___ seen her," Sam replied.

8. "I ___wouldn't___ worry," he went on. "___She'll___ reappear like magic when ___she's___ hungry."

9. Then Mrs. Lynch, ___who's___ Sam's neighbor, came out and suggested that we drive around town to look for Rascal.

10. "___Let's___ take the pick-up truck," she said. "___It's___ parked in the garage. You get in it, and ___I'll___ get the keys."

11. I hurried into the Lynch's garage, and ___that's___ when I knew my worries were over.

12. Somehow, Rascal had managed to get into the back of the truck. ___She'd___ snuggled down into a pile of old rags and blankets.

13. Nestled beside her were three newborn pups—the most adorable ones ___I've___ ever seen.

14. Rascal looked up at me as if to say, "___I'm___ glad to be found."

15. I, of course, ___couldn't___ have been happier.

Review and Apply: Comprehension

Read the article below. Complete each unfinished sentence by writing the contraction that stands for the two words shown below each blank. Then reread the article and circle all the compound words. There are thirteen compound words.

___Who's___ the wealthiest person in the world, and ___what's___
(Who is)   (what is)
his or her (income?) ___Where's___ the tallest (flagpole) or the oldest (lighthouse?)
              (Where is)
___You'll___ find the answers to these and other interesting questions in the
(You will)
Guinness Book of World Records. While glancing through this (paperback)
___you're___ sure to find some odd achievements. For example, Jay Gwaltney's
(you are)
record for eating trees ___hasn't___ been broken since he set it in Chicago in 1980.
                         (has not)
Deciding he must be the $10,000 (prizewinner) in a contest, he ate an 11-foot birch tree.
Gwaltney finished the meal in 89 hours and commented that its taste ___wasn't___
                                                                      (was not)
bad.

If ___you're___ thinking Gwaltney is (somewhat) crazy, ___you'll___
   (you are)   (you will)
really be astonished by Michel Lotito of France. Lotito, also known as "Mr. Eat (Anything,)
___doesn't___ eat things as tasty or tender as trees. Since 1966, ___he's___
(does not)   (he has)
eaten 10 bicycles, a (supermarket) cart, 7 television sets, 6 chandeliers, and a small passenger
(airplane.) As if that ___weren't___ enough, he has also eaten a coffin! As one
                        (were not)
(newspaper) writer points out, ___let's___ hope (nobody) was (inside) at the time.
                                (let us)
The Guinness book doesn't say why Lotito does such strange things.

If ___you'd___ like to earn a place in the Guinness book by beating Lotito's
   (you would)
record, don't try it. Its editors write that ___they've___ published this unusual stunt
                                              (they have)
only since ___it's___ unlikely to be challenged. They ___won't___
            (it is)   (will not)
list records for eating (anything) else that could be dangerous.

Review and Apply: Composition

Name _____

The paragraph below could appear in the *Guinness Book of World Records*. Read it and notice that it contains three compound words that have been underlined. Then read the list of words that follows. Notice that each word can be joined with at least one other list word to form a compound word. Choose words from the list to form at least ten compound words. Use the ten compound words in two short paragraphs of your own that could appear in the *Guinness Book of World Records*. Underline the compound words you write.

> In 1980, Jerry Mercer and Arden Chapman stood at opposite ends of the <u>Northeast</u> Louisiana University <u>football</u> field. Twenty times, Mercer threw a grape at Chapman. On the twentieth throw, Chapman caught the grape <u>inside</u> his mouth. It was a distance of 319 feet, 8 inches.

breath	back	paint	apple	down	tub
earth	cat	ship	pop	fish	corn
jelly	gold	skate	board	fall	worm
basket	tooth	snow	quake	ball	cycle
bare	grand	touch	fall	foot	wreck
bath	motor	water	taking	sauce	brush

Answers will vary.

_____

_____

_____

_____

_____

_____

_____

_____

_____

_____

_____

_____

_____

_____

Review of compound words and contractions   85

Prefixes, Suffixes, and Roots

Name _____

Words to use: unhappy, rewrap, midyear; hopeless, player, treatment; conductor, inaudible

Many words can be divided into small parts that have meaning. Understanding the meaning of word parts can help you understand the meaning of whole words.

A prefix is a letter or group of letters that can be added to the beginning of a word. Write the prefix of each word below.

1. unfair	un-	5. dislike	dis-
2. rebuild	re-	6. imperfect	im-
3. prepay	pre-	7. nonliving	non-
4. mistreat	mis-	8. incomplete	in-

A suffix is a letter or group of letters that can be added to the end of a word. Write the suffix of each word below.

1. useless	-less	5. restful	-ful
2. loudly	-ly	6. childish	-ish
3. rusty	-y	7. illness	-ness
4. breakable	-able	8. enjoyment	-ment

A root is a word part to which a prefix, suffix, or another root can be added. The root of *transportation* is **port.** Complete each sentence below by writing the root of the given word.

1. The root of *reporter* is _____ port _____
(re-, port, -er)

2. The root of *prediction* is _____ dict _____
(pre-, dict, -ion)

3. The root of *geography* is _____ graph _____
(geo-, graph, -y)

4. The root of *introduction* is _____ duct _____
(intro-, duct, -ion)

5. The root of *projector* is _____ ject _____
(pro-, ject, -or)

86   Identifying prefixes, suffixes, and roots

Prefixes: *UN-*, *MIS-*, and *PRE-*

Name _____

Words to use: unfriendly, unable, untie, unwrap; misbehave, misspell; prefix, prewar

A prefix is a letter or group of letters that can be added to the beginning of a word.

Prefix	Meaning	Example
un-	not, opposite of	**un**tied (not tied)
mis-	badly, wrongly	**mis**treat (to treat badly)
pre-	before	**pre**pay (to pay before)

Read the clues below. Add **un-**, **mis-**, or **pre-** to each underlined word to form a word that matches the clue. Write the new word in the blank.

1. not <u>expected</u> _____ unexpected
2. <u>understand</u> wrongly _____ misunderstand
3. <u>arrange</u> before _____ prearrange
4. <u>pronounce</u> wrongly _____ mispronounce
5. not <u>aware</u> _____ unaware
6. bad <u>behavior</u> _____ misbehavior
7. <u>test</u> before _____ pretest
8. bad <u>fortune</u> _____ misfortune
9. not <u>common</u> _____ uncommon
10. <u>view</u> before _____ preview

Read the sentences below. Complete each unfinished word by writing **un-**, **mis-**, or **pre-** in the blank.

1. It is not easy to buy food or pay bills if you are _____ un employed.
2. Finding a word in a dictionary is a good way to avoid _____ mis spelling it.
3. While boating, it is a good idea to take the _____ pre caution of wearing a life jacket.
4. Many toddlers attend _____ pre school before going to kindergarten.
5. Fortunately, the driver of the automobile was _____ un hurt in the accident.
6. Because I do not speak French, I'm afraid I may have _____ mis pronounced the girl's name.
7. Maria was late for school because she _____ mis placed her umbrella and was looking for it.

Forming words with prefixes in isolation and in context: un-, mis-, pre-   87

Prefixes: *NON-*, *RE-*, and *FORE-*

Name _____

Words to use: nonbreakable, nonstop, nonwashable, nonprofit; reappear, rearrange, return, repay; forecast, forehead, foresee

A prefix is a letter or group of letters that can be added to the beginning of a word.

Prefix	Meaning	Example
non-	not, opposite of	**non**living (not living)
re-	back, again	**re**write (to write again)
fore-	in front, before	**fore**warn (to warn before)

Read the groups of words below. Then read the sentences that follow. Write the word that best completes each sentence. For sentences 1 through 5, choose words from Group A. For sentences 6 through 10, choose words from Group B.

Group A	foretold	nonsense	forecasts	foretells	respin
Group B	readjust	nonscientific	foretell	rebuilding	reconsider

1. Long ago, people did not have the aid of up-to-date weather _____ forecasts _____ on radio or television.

2. By watching nature's patterns, though, people were able to predict the weather. These patterns were often described in poems that _____ foretold _____ the weather.

3. One poem, for example, _____ foretells _____ the coming of good weather after bad: "When spiders weave their webs by noon, fine weather is coming soon."

4. It may sound like _____ nonsense _____, but there is some truth to this old saying.

5. Because damp air absorbed by spider webs makes their silk threads shorten and snap, spiders must _____ respin _____ their damaged webs during a damp day.

6. As drier air comes near, the webs break less, are easier to spin, and do not need repeated _____ rebuilding _____

7. Swallows adjust their flying height depending on the air pressure. When changing weather causes air-pressure changes, swallows _____ readjust _____ their flying height.

8. So, this poem to _____ foretell _____ weather came into being: "Swallows fly high; clear blue sky. Swallows fly low; rain we shall know."

9. Of course, predicting weather by _____ nonscientific _____ ways is not always reliable. But then, scientific methods aren't always failproof, either.

10. So the next time you see a beautiful morning sky as you head out the door with no umbrella, think about this: "Red sky at night; sailors' delight. Red sky at morning; sailors take warning." You may want to _____ reconsider _____ taking the umbrella.

88   Using words with prefixes in context: non-, re-, fore-

Prefixes: IR-, INTER-, and SEMI-

Name _____

A prefix is a letter or group of letters that can be added to the beginning of a word.

Prefix	Meaning	Example
ir-	not, opposite of	**ir**responsible (not responsible)
inter-	between, among	**inter**national (between nations)
semi-	half, partly	**semi**circle (half circle)

Read the list of words below. Then read the sentences that follow. Add **ir-**, **inter-**, or **semi-** to a list word to form a word that best completes each sentence.

gloss	mission	resistible	circle	national
view	responsible	regular	annually	conscious

1. A person who cannot be depended on or be trusted with important matters is an _____irresponsible_____ person.

2. A paper that is cut in the shape of half a circle is a _____semicircle_____

3. Something that is not average or not as it should be is _____irregular_____

4. News that tells about happenings that have taken place between or among countries is _____international_____ news.

5. A hospital patient who is only partly alert, awake, and aware of what is happening is _____semiconscious_____

6. Paint that is only half as shiny as paint with a full gloss, or shine, is _____semigloss_____ paint.

7. If you make trips to your dentist's office every six months, you visit him or her _____semiannually_____

8. If you have an overwhelming desire to eat lemons every night at midnight, you have an _____irresistible_____ urge to eat sour foods.

9. A break between two parts of a concert, play, or other performance is an _____intermission_____

10. A meeting between people in which one person asks for information from the other is an _____interview_____

Prefixes: DIS-, EN-, and POST-

Name _____

A prefix is a letter or group of letters that can be added to the beginning of a word.

Prefix	Meaning	Example
dis-	not, opposite of	**dis**like (not like)
en-	in, into	**en**trust (trust in)
post-	after, later, behind	**post**war (after war)

Read each clue and the list of words. Write the word from the list that matches the clue.

1. the opposite of "put something together" ____disassemble____   postwar
2. to place in an unsafe situation ____endanger____   enclose
3. a note added to the end of a friendly letter ____postscript____   discontented
4. to close in, surround ____enclose____   disassemble
5. not happy ____discontented____   postscript
6. involve ____entangle____   disappear
7. after a war ____postwar____   entangle
8. become invisible or unable to be seen ____disappear____   endanger

Read the base words below and notice that **dis-** or **en-** can be added to each one. Then read the paragraphs that follow. Complete the sentences in each paragraph by writing the same base word in both blanks and correctly adding **dis-** or **en-** to each word.

able	closed	courage

1. After a witness ____disclosed____ information about the crime, police went to the scene. An officer dusted for fingerprints and ____enclosed____ the evidence in a large bag.

2. Although Dad tried to ____discourage____ me from playing football, he let me decide about joining the team. He still fears I may be hurt, but he does ____encourage____ me to play my best.

3. Polio can ____disable____ a person by destroying nerves and causing muscles to become paralyzed. Fortunately, a vaccine will ____enable____ a person to develop antibodies that fight against and prevent polio.

Prefixes: IN-, SUB-, and BI-

Name _____

A prefix is a letter or group of letters that can be added to the beginning of a word.

Prefix	Meaning	Example
in-	not, opposite of	**in**complete (not complete)
sub-	under, below	**sub**marine (under water)
bi-	two	**bi**cycle (two wheels)

Read the list of words below. Then read the lines from advertisements that follow. Add **in-**, **sub-**, or **bi-** to a list word to form a word that completes each sentence. The new word should have the same meaning as the words shown below the blank.

standard	freezing	digestion	expensive
focal	cycle	visible	weekly

1. Dr. Ken C. Better will fit you with contacts, a pair of reading glasses, or _____bifocal_____ glasses quick as a wink!
   (for seeing both near and far)

2. Just two teaspoons of Yummy Tummy will cure your _____indigestion_____ faster than you can say "oink."
   (stomachache)

3. Buy Armor Auto Shine today. It's like putting an _____invisible_____ screen of protection on your car.
   (unable to be seen)

4. Best of all, a telephone from Wright Connections is so _____inexpensive_____ you'll want to buy two of them!
   (not costly)

5. When you buy windows from The Glass House, you get the best! If you buy windows anywhere else, you may be accepting a _____substandard_____ product.
   (below average)

6. Believe it or not, this _____bicycle_____ from Wheely Small, Inc. folds to a small carrying size in less than twenty seconds.
   (two-wheeled vehicle)

7. *Hollywood Happenings* will arrive in your mailbox _____biweekly_____. You'll have time to read each copy from cover to cover before a new one arrives.
   (every fourteen days)

8. A wool-lined coat from Cloaks for Waggers will keep your fuzzy friend warm even in _____subfreezing_____ temperatures.
   (below 32° F.)

Prefixes: IM-, OVER-, and TRI-

Name _____

A prefix is a letter or group of letters that can be added to the beginning of a word.

Prefix	Meaning	Example
im-	not, opposite of	**im**perfect (not perfect)
over-	too much	**over**eat (eat too much)
tri-	three	**tri**angle (three angles)

Read the sentences below. Complete each unfinished word by writing **im-**, **over-**, or **tri-** in the blank.

1. I entered Jansen's Department Store and headed through the narrow, ____over____crowded aisles toward the toy department.

2. "I bought this ____tri____cycle here yesterday," I said to the department manager. "However, there are some things wrong with it."

3. "When I put the parts together," I went on, "the ____tri____angular seat did not fit."

4. "Besides that, the box shows ____tri____color streamers hanging from the ends of the handlebars. But there weren't any in the box."

5. "Anything else?" the manager snapped rather ____im____patiently.

6. "Yes," I continued, feeling slightly annoyed. "I believe I was also ____over____charged."

7. For a moment, the manager looked as though she might leap over the counter at me. Then she took a deep breath and said, "I'm sorry, ma'am. I didn't mean to be ____im____polite.

8. "It's been an ____im____possible day," she quickly explained. "First I ____over____slept and was late for work."

9. "At lunchtime my car ____over____heated, and I had to walk two miles to a service station."

10. "When I finally got back to work, my head sales clerk went home ill. Now the other clerk is saying that she's ____over____worked."

11. "I guess an ____im____perfect tricycle doesn't make your day any better," I said.

12. "No, but it's ____im____proper to take my troubles out on you," she said with an apologizing smile. "Wait here, and I'll get another tricycle from the back room."

13. When she returned with a fully assembled tricycle, my face brightened. "I don't look forward to customer complaints," she said. "But the ____over____joyed look on your face has changed my day from bad to better."

198

Prefixes: IN-, CO-, and MID-

Name _____

Words to use: inbound, inbred, inborn; coauthors, coeducational; midsummer, midpoint

A prefix is a letter or group of letters that can be added to the beginning of a word.

Prefix	Meaning	Example
in-	in, into	intake (take in)
co-	with, together	copilot (pilot together)
mid-	middle	midnight (middle of night)

Read the list of words below. Then read the sentences that follow. In each blank, write the word from the list that best completes the sentence. You should use one word twice.

coauthors	in	June	Wednesday
July	into	with	middle
incoming	live	noon	look

1. If you live at the midpoint of a city block, you live at or near the ___middle___ of the block.

2. When you pick up the receiver of a ringing telephone, you are answering an ___incoming___ phone call.

3. If you have a midyear birthday, your birthday is in ___June___ or ___July___.

4. To cooperate with someone means to work or get along ___with___ him or her.

5. If you have arranged to see a doctor at midday, you should be at the doctor's office by ___noon___.

6. To exist means to "live," so the word coexist means to "___live___ ___with___."

7. To indent the first line of a paragraph means to set it ___in___ from the left side.

8. Two people who write a book together are ___coauthors___.

9. If you belong to a club that meets midweek, the club meetings are held on ___Wednesday___.

10. Spect is a word part that means "look," so the word inspect means to "___look___ ___into___."

Using words with prefixes in context: in-, co-, mid-

93

Review and Apply: Comprehension

Name _____

The newspaper headlines below have words with prefixes. Read the headlines. Then answer the questions that follow.

Subfreezing Temperatures Endanger Bicyclists; Midwinter Race Postponed
Two Coworkers Discover Impurities in Milk; 3,000 Gallons Recalled
Nonprofit Cancer-Research Organization Holds Semiannual Fund-Raising Carnival
Misprinted Forecast Calls for 10 Feet of Snow in Miami
Association of International Scientists Hopes to Uncover Mystery of Bermuda Triangle
Illinois Workers' Income Up This Year; Unemployment Down
Overweight Postoperative Patients Develop Irregular Heartbeats
Homeowners Take Precautions Against Invisible Radon Gas

1. Did heart trouble appear in certain people before or after surgery? ___after___
   What might such people do to avoid the trouble? ___lose weight___

2. What Florida city had an odd weather prediction? ___Miami___ Why was it odd? ___It called for snow in a place where it never snows.___

3. To what group might an African chemist, a European geologist, and an Asian biologist all belong? ___Association of International Scientists___
   What area of the world will this group be studying? ___the Bermuda Triangle___

4. The weather caused what sporting event to be moved to a later date? ___a bicycle race___ Why? ___It was too cold for bicyclists to ride.___

5. Were most people in Chicago richer or poorer this year than last? ___richer___

6. What group is holding a twice-yearly event? ___a cancer-research organization___
   What is the purpose of the event? ___to raise money___

7. What is radon? ___an invisible gas___ Is it dangerous to people? ___yes___ Where might radon be found? ___in people's homes___

8. What problem occurred at a dairy? ___Impurities were discovered in milk.___
   Who found the problem? ___two coworkers___ What did the dairy do about the problem? ___They recalled 3,000 gallons of milk.___

9. Which prefix has two different meanings and appears twice in the headlines? ___in-___

Review of words with prefixes

94

Review and Apply: Composition

Name _____

Members of the school board in your town are thinking of making school days shorter by making the school year longer. Instead of going to school from 9:00 A.M. to 3:30 P.M., September through mid-June, you would go from 8:30 A.M. to 12:00 noon, all year round. The school board has agreed to listen to students' opinions on the matter. Your class is against the idea. They have elected you to be their spokesperson. Write a paragraph or more telling the school board why the school year should not be changed. Use at least eight of the words below or eight words of your own that have prefixes.

nonsense	reconsider	ineffective	substandard	unfair
misjudge	foresee	disagree	encourage	impossible
overworked	irresponsible	cooperate	indoors	midyear	predict

Answers will vary.

_____
_____
_____
_____
_____
_____
_____
_____
_____
_____
_____
_____
_____
_____
_____
_____

Review of words with prefixes

95

Suffixes: -ENCE, -IVE, and -FUL

Name _____

Words to use: preference, existence; active, possessive; careful, wasteful, harmful

A suffix is a letter or group of letters that can be added to the end of a word.

Suffix	Meaning	Example
-ence	state or condition of being	silence (state or condition of being silent)
-ive	having, tending to	expensive (having expense)
-ful	full of	restful (full of rest)

Read each clue and the list of words. Write the word from the list that matches the clue.

1. state of being unlike others ___difference___   frightful
2. full of hurt and aching ___painful___   attractive
3. tending to cost a great deal ___expensive___   interference
4. having the power to draw attention ___attractive___   difference
5. full of terror ___frightful___   painful
6. the condition of getting in the way of something ___interference___   adhesive
7. state of waiting calmly ___patience___   forgetful
8. having the ability to adhere or be sticky ___adhesive___   expensive
9. act of carrying out someone's orders ___obedience___   patience
10. full of not remembering ___forgetful___   obedience

Read the list of words below. Then read the sentences that follow. Write the word from the list that best completes each sentence.

intelligence	reflective	careful	absence	powerful

1. Although I still suffered from a cold, I returned to school after an ___absence___ of three days.

2. Coyotes, wolves, and foxes have ___powerful___ jaws that can close on their prey like a steel trap.

3. Eva wrapped her bicycle with ___reflective___ tape so it would be easy to see when she carried newspapers after dark.

4. Chimpanzees, known for their ___intelligence___, are able to learn a few words and signs that allow them to "talk" with people.

5. Dad warned the movers to be ___careful___ when they packed the antique china.

Using words with suffixes in definitions and in context: -ence, -ive, -ful

96

199

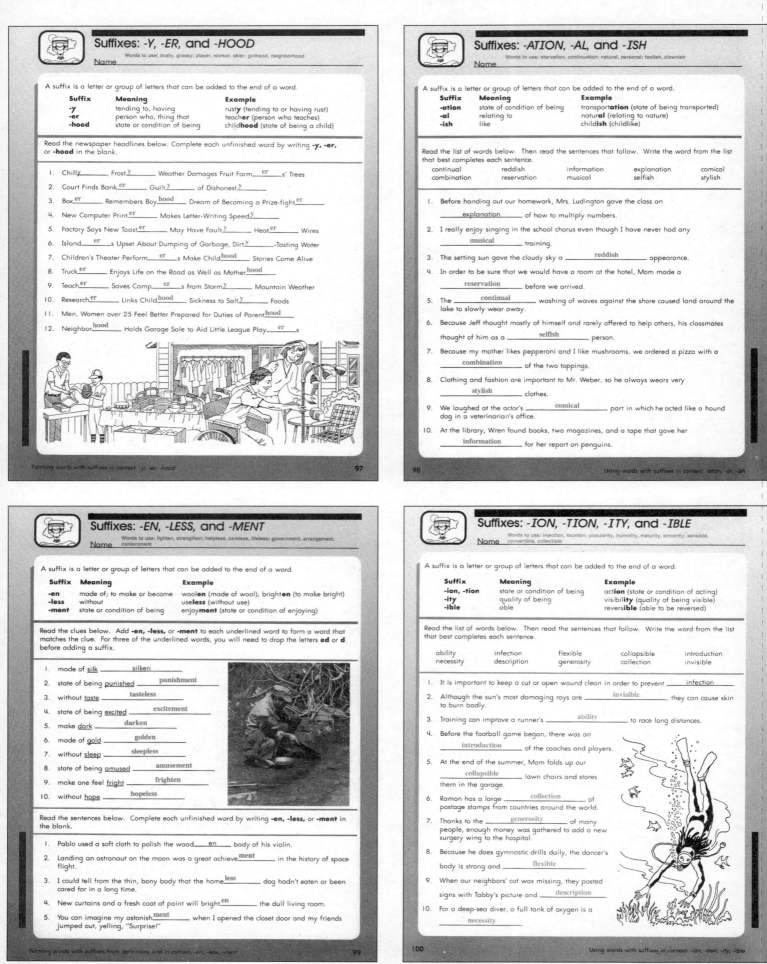

Suffixes: -Y, -ER, and -HOOD

Name _____

Words to use: dusty, grassy; player, worker, skier; girlhood, neighborhood

A suffix is a letter or group of letters that can be added to the end of a word.

Suffix	Meaning	Example
-y	tending to, having	rust**y** (tending to or having rust)
-er	person who, thing that	teach**er** (person who teaches)
-hood	state or condition of being	child**hood** (state of being a child)

Read the newspaper headlines below. Complete each unfinished word by writing **-y, -er,** or **-hood** in the blank.

1. Chilly____, Frost_y____ Weather Damages Fruit Farm___er__s' Trees
2. Court Finds Bank__er__ Guilt_y__ of Dishonest_y__
3. Box__er__ Remembers Boy_hood__ Dream of Becoming a Prize-fight__er_
4. New Computer Print__er_ Makes Letter-Writing Speed_y___
5. Factory Says New Toast_er__ May Have Fault_y__ Heat__er__ Wires
6. Island____er_s Upset About Dumping of Garbage, Dirt_y____-Tasting Water
7. Children's Theater Perform____er_s Make Child_hood__ Stories Come Alive
8. Truck__er___ Enjoys Life on the Road as Well as Mother_hood__
9. Teach__er___ Saves Camp____er_s from Storm_y___ Mountain Weather
10. Research__er____ Links Child_hood_ Sickness to Salt_y____ Foods
11. Men, Women over 25 Feel Better Prepared for Duties of Parent_hood__
12. Neighbor_hood__ Holds Garage Sale to Aid Little League Play____er_s

97

Forming words with suffixes in context: -y, -er, -hood

98

Suffixes: -ATION, -AL, and -ISH

Name _____

Words to use: starvation, continuation; natural, personal; foolish, clownish

A suffix is a letter or group of letters that can be added to the end of a word.

Suffix	Meaning	Example
-ation	state or condition of being	transport**ation** (state of being transported)
-al	relating to	natur**al** (relating to nature)
-ish	like	child**ish** (childlike)

Read the list of words below. Then read the sentences that follow. Write the word from the list that best completes each sentence.

| continual | reddish | information | explanation | comical |
| combination | reservation | musical | selfish | stylish |

1. Before handing out our homework, Mrs. Ludington gave the class an __explanation__ of how to multiply numbers.
2. I really enjoy singing in the school chorus even though I have never had any __musical__ training.
3. The setting sun gave the cloudy sky a __reddish__ appearance.
4. In order to be sure that we would have a room at the hotel, Mom made a __reservation__ before we arrived.
5. The __continual__ washing of waves against the shore caused land around the lake to slowly wear away.
6. Because Jeff thought mostly of himself and rarely offered to help others, his classmates thought of him as a __selfish__ person.
7. Because my mother likes pepperoni and I like mushrooms, we ordered a pizza with a __combination__ of the two toppings.
8. Clothing and fashion are important to Mr. Weber, so he always wears very __stylish__ clothes.
9. We laughed at the actor's __comical__ part in which he acted like a hound dog in a veterinarian's office.
10. At the library, Wren found books, two magazines, and a tape that gave her __information__ for her report on penguins.

Using words with suffixes in context: -ation, -al, -ish

Suffixes: -EN, -LESS, and -MENT

Name _____

Words to use: lighten, strengthen; helpless, careless, lifeless; government, arrangement, contentment

A suffix is a letter or group of letters that can be added to the end of a word.

Suffix	Meaning	Example
-en	made of; to make or become	wool**en** (made of wool); bright**en** (to make bright)
-less	without	use**less** (without use)
-ment	state or condition of being	enjoy**ment** (state or condition of enjoying)

Read the clues below. Add **-en, -less,** or **-ment** to each underlined word to form a word that matches the clue. For three of the underlined words, you will need to drop the letters **ed** or **d** before adding a suffix.

1. made of silk __silken__
2. state of being punished __punishment__
3. without taste __tasteless__
4. state of being excited __excitement__
5. make dark __darken__
6. made of gold __golden__
7. without sleep __sleepless__
8. state of being amused __amusement__
9. make one feel fright __frighten__
10. without hope __hopeless__

Read the sentences below. Complete each unfinished word by writing **-en, -less,** or **-ment** in the blank.

1. Pablo used a soft cloth to polish the wood__en__ body of his violin.
2. Landing an astronaut on the moon was a great achieve__ment__ in the history of space flight.
3. I could tell from the thin, bony body that the home__less__ dog hadn't eaten or been cared for in a long time.
4. New curtains and a fresh coat of paint will bright__en__ the dull living room.
5. You can imagine my astonish__ment__ when I opened the closet door and my friends jumped out, yelling, "Surprise!"

99

Forming words with suffixes from definitions and in context: -en, -less, -ment

---

100

Suffixes: -ION, -TION, -ITY, and -IBLE

Name _____

Words to use: injection, location; popularity, humidity, maturity, sincerity; sensible, convertible, collectible

A suffix is a letter or group of letters that can be added to the end of a word.

Suffix	Meaning	Example
-ion, -tion	state or condition of being	act**ion** (state or condition of acting)
-ity	quality of being	visibil**ity** (quality of being visible)
-ible	able	revers**ible** (able to be reversed)

Read the list of words below. Then read the sentences that follow. Write the word from the list that best completes each sentence.

| ability | infection | flexible | collapsible | introduction |
| necessity | description | generosity | collection | invisible |

1. It is important to keep a cut or open wound clean in order to prevent __infection__.
2. Although the sun's most damaging rays are __invisible__, they can cause skin to burn badly.
3. Training can improve a runner's __ability__ to race long distances.
4. Before the football game began, there was an __introduction__ of the coaches and players.
5. At the end of the summer, Mom folds up our __collapsible__ lawn chairs and stores them in the garage.
6. Ramon has a large __collection__ of postage stamps from countries around the world.
7. Thanks to the __generosity__ of many people, enough money was gathered to add a new surgery wing to the hospital.
8. Because he does gymnastic drills daily, the dancer's body is strong and __flexible__.
9. When our neighbors' cat was missing, they posted signs with Tabby's picture and __description__.
10. For a deep-sea diver, a full tank of oxygen is a __necessity__.

Using words with suffixes in context: -ion, -tion, -ity, -ible

Suffixes: -SION, -NESS, and -ABLE

Name

A suffix is a letter or group of letters that can be added to the end of a word.

Suffix	Meaning	Example
-sion	state or condition of being	divi**sion** (state of being divided)
-ness	state or condition of being	ill**ness** (state or condition of being ill)
-able	able to be, can be	break**able** (can be broken)

Read the list of words below. Then read the sentences that follow. Write the word from the list that best completes each sentence.

extension	sadness	comfortable	collision
weakness	unbelievable	valuable	rudeness
decision	forgetfulness	enjoyable	nervousness

1. When you make up your mind about something, you are making a _____decision_____.

2. If your ankles are not strong enough to hold you up while ice skating, you have a _____weakness_____ in your ankles.

3. When one automobile hits another, a _____collision_____ has taken place.

4. If you are often not able to remember things, you have a habit of _____forgetfulness_____.

5. If you take pleasure in taking pictures with a camera, photography is a hobby that is _____enjoyable_____ for you.

6. An electric cord that makes another electric cord longer by plugging into it is an _____extension_____ cord.

7. A person who is not polite to others may be disliked for his or her _____rudeness_____.

8. The things that you own and are of great worth to you are your _____valuable_____ possessions.

9. A sofa with soft cushions on which you are able to take it easy and fall asleep is a _____comfortable_____ sofa.

10. A person who feels ill or nervous about going on stage before a large group is suffering from a kind of _____nervousness_____ called stage fright.

11. A story that you find hard to accept as true is an _____unbelievable_____ story.

12. A person who cries in sorrow is feeling _____sadness_____.

Suffixes: -ANCE, -IST, and -OUS

Name

A suffix is a letter or group of letters that can be added to the end of a word.

Suffix	Meaning	Example
-ance	state or condition of being	appear**ance** (state of appearing)
-ist	person or thing that makes or does	art**ist** (person that makes art)
-ous	full of, having	joy**ous** (full of joy)

Below are people's notes about a jazz concert. Read each sentence and the word shown below the blank. Complete the word by adding **-ance, -ist,** or **-ous**. If a word has a line through the last letter, drop the letter before adding the suffix.

1. "I enjoyed last night's _____performance_____ by Razzmatazz Jazz more than any other music show I've ever attended."
   (perform)

2. "They may not be world-_____famous_____, but they certainly put on a first-class, entertaining show."
   (famé)

3. "For such a well-known artist, I thought Robin Earl seemed more than a little bit _____nervous_____ in front of her fans."
   (nervé)

4. "I really liked the way the _____guitarist_____ played the strings and came up with a ringing sound."
   (guitar)

5. "Razzmatazz Jazz is the finest team of jazz _____artist_____s this city has hosted in five years."
   (art)

6. "I saw Razzmatazz Jazz in their first live _____appearance_____ five years ago. They were good then, but they're really great now!"
   (appear)

7. "I wish the _____pianist_____ could have played another piece or two."
   (pianó)

8. "They're as much fun to watch as they are to listen to. Their jokes and silly dances are quite _____humorous_____."
   (humor)

9. "Gary Lotilla's skill with the strings and bow makes me wish I'd stuck with music lessons and become a _____violinist_____."
   (violin)

Suffixes: -LY, -OR, and -SHIP

Name

A suffix is a letter or group of letters that can be added to the end of a word.

Suffix	Meaning	Example
-ly	in a way that is like; every	loud**ly** (in a loud way); year**ly** (every year)
-or	person who, thing that	sail**or** (person who sails)
-ship	state or condition of being	friend**ship** (state of being a friend)

Read the sentences below. Complete each one by adding **-ly, -or,** or **-ship** to each word shown in parentheses.

1. An (act) _____actor_____ from the college theater spoke to us about ways to raise the (member) _____membership_____ of our drama club.

2. A favorite character in *The Wizard of Oz* is the (coward) _____cowardly_____ lion who, at the end of a frightening journey, discovers he really does have courage after all.

3. The band (conduct) _____conductor_____ raised her baton (slow) _____slowly_____, and the band began playing (soft) _____softly_____.

4. Lee Ying, a well-known (sculpt) _____sculptor_____, will be an (exhibit) _____exhibitor_____ at the stone-carvers' fair.

5. One of the rights and duties of (citizen) _____citizenship_____ is to be a responsible (elect) _____elector_____ at voting time.

6. The swim team has been in training four times (week) _____weekly_____ in hope of winning the city (champion) _____championship_____.

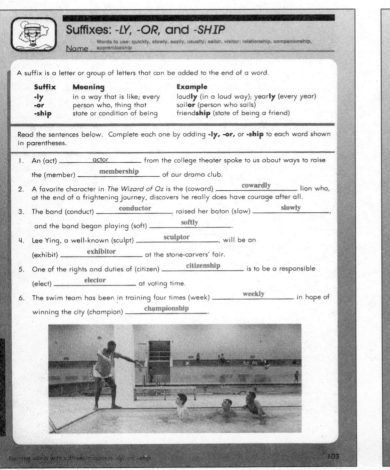

Words With More Than One Suffix

Name

A suffix is a letter or group of letters that can be added to the end of a word. Some words have more than one suffix.

hope + ful + ness = hope**fulness**   act + ive + ly = act**ively**

Read the suffixes below. Then read the items that follow. Follow the item directions, using the suffixes to form new words.

-al   -less   -ness   -ive   -ful   -ly   -ish   -ous

1. Form a new word by adding two suffixes to the word *music*. _____musically_____

2. Form two new words by adding two suffixes each to the word *fool*.
   _____foolishly_____   _____foolishness_____

3. Form two new words by adding two suffixes each to the word *attract*.
   _____attractively_____   _____attractiveness_____

4. Form two new words by adding two suffixes each to the word *nerve*. Before adding the suffixes, drop the final **e** from nerve. _____nervously_____   _____nervousness_____

5. Form four new words by adding two suffixes each to the word *care*. _____carelessness_____
   _____carelessly_____   _____carefulness_____   _____carefully_____

Use the words you wrote above to complete the sentences below.

1. Some _____musically_____ talented youngsters have begun learning to play the piano as young as two years of age.

2. The _____attractiveness_____ of the store's window case caused people walking by to stop and look at the goods.

3. Shaking hands and a cracking voice were signs of my _____nervousness_____ while giving a report to the class.

4. The police officer taught the children to look _____carefully_____ in all directions before crossing the street.

5. Before the invention of the airplane, most people thought the idea of a flying machine was pure _____foolishness_____.

6. Clothes, papers, and books were _____carelessly_____ scattered across the teenager's bedroom.

Words With More Than One Suffix

Name _____

Words to use: naturally, nervousness, usefulness, thoughtlessly

Read the suffixes below. Then read the sentences that follow. Complete each sentence by adding two suffixes to the word shown below the blank.

| -al | -ly | -ous | -ful | -ish | -less | -ness |

1. I knew how to answer the questions on the math test, but my __carelessness__ caused me to score lower than I should have. (care)

2. The circus acrobat swung from a trapeze, dropped to a trampoline below, and __gracefully__ landed on his toes. (grace)

3. I have no lunch money today because I __foolishly__ spent my last dollar yesterday. (fool)

4. The firefighter was honored for her __courageousness__ in the daring rescue. (courage)

5. The puppy's wide eyes, floppy ears, and friendly __playfulness__ made me want to take it home. (play)

6. The weather this spring has been __exceptionally__ warm and dry. (exception)

7. Thinking mostly of yourself and caring very little about other people is known as __selfishness__. (self)

8. A great flash of lightning came __dangerously__ close to hitting the hundred-year-old oak tree. (danger)

9. I felt a sense of wonder and reward as I __breathlessly__ dashed toward the finish line of the ten-mile footrace. (breath)

Solve the word puzzles below by writing a word or suffix in each blank to form new words.

1. fear + ful + ly = __fearfully__ – ful + less = __fearlessly__
2. childishness – __ness__ = childish + ly = __childishly__
3. joy + ous + ly = __joyously__ – ous + ful = __joyfully__
4. hopelessness – __less__ + ful = hopefulness – ness + ly = __hopefully__
5. help + __ful__ + __ly__ = helpfully – ful + less – ly + ness = __helplessness__

Forming words with more than one suffix in context and in isolation

105

Review and Apply: Comprehension

Name _____

Read the words and suffixes below. Then read the story. In each blank, write the word or suffix that makes sense. For paragraph 1, choose words and suffixes from Group A. For paragraph 2, choose from Group B. For paragraph 3, choose from Group C.

Group A	companions	possibility	aviation	-er	-al	-ly	-ful	-ment	-hood
Group B	happiness	scientists	creative	immeasurable	-y	-en	-or	-ish	-ous
Group C	influence	visible	-ance	-ship	-less	-ment			

1 You've likely heard of the Wright brothers and their contribution to __aviation__. But did you know there was a Wright sister? Katherine Wright was one of Wilbur and Orville's most faith__ful__ believers. The three had become close __companions__ after their mother died during Katherine's late child__hood__. Later, Katherine's brothers, who had always been interested in mechanic__al__ things, became serious__ly__ interested in the __possibility__ of flying. Katherine, eager to lend encourage__ment__ and be a help__er__, stitched cloth covers for the wings of gliders.

2 Though many folks laughed at the Wright brothers' fool__ish__ ideas, Katherine was proud of their courage__ous__ efforts and __creative__ ideas. She talked her invent__or__ brothers into attending a meeting where they could share ideas with other __scientists__. Later, as flight experiments failed, one after another, it was Katherine's cheer__y__ spirit that helped bright__en__ Wilbur and Orville's days. Finally, in 1903, when the brothers sent home a wire from Kitty Hawk, saying, "Success/ four flights/ engine power alone," Katherine's __happiness__ was __immeasurable__.

3 As the brothers carried on their work, Katherine kept up her involve__ment__. She became Orville's nurse after he crashed in a test flight, and journeyed with both brothers through Europe. Though her place in history has not been as __visible__ as her brothers', history might have been different had it not been for Katherine Wright's __influence__. Without her friend__ship__ and assist__ance__, her brothers might have become hope__less__ during their early days of failure. It seems that Katherine was indeed the "Wright" sister for Wilbur and Orville—in more ways than one!

106

Review of words with suffixes

Review and Apply: Composition

Name _____

You've just returned from a trip to Jupiter. You unexpectedly landed in the middle of a neighborhood of creatures called Jupes. Now that you've returned to Earth, a reporter is interviewing you about the trip. Answer the reporter's questions, using at least one word that has a suffix for each answer. You may want to use some of the words listed below.

achievement	weightless	famous	scientist	ability	protection
incredible	exploration	television	darkness	portable	friendship
neighborhood	fearful	ticklish	frighten	active	natural
talker	survivor	carefully	furry	difference	assistance

Answers will vary.

1. After landing, what was the first thing you saw from your spaceship? _____

2. What did the Jupes look like? _____

3. What did you think when you saw the Jupes coming toward your ship? _____

4. What did the Jupes do when you got out of your spaceship? _____

5. How did the Jupes seem to feel about your landing in the middle of their neighborhood? _____

6. How did you communicate with the Jupes? _____

7. What do Jupes do all day? _____

8. What is the most amazing thing about Jupes? _____

9. What unusual habit or custom did you observe among the Jupes? _____

10. In what way are Jupes like human beings? _____

Review of words with suffixes

107

Roots

Name _____

Words to use: transport, inspect, conduct, propel, transcribe, compose, transmit, inject, precede

A root is a word part to which a prefix, suffix, or other root can be added to form a new word.

Root	**Meaning**	**Example**
port	carry	transport
spect	look, watch, see	inspect
duct	take, lead	conduct

Read the roots and their meanings below. Then read the sentences that follow. Complete the unfinished word in each sentence by writing the correct word.

scribe - write	**mit** - send	**cede** - go
pel - drive, push	**spect** - see, look, watch	**duct** - lead, take
pos - put, place	**ject** - throw, force	**port** - carry

1. Pro- means "forward," so to push forward is to pro__pel__. To throw forward is to pro__ject__. To look forward is to pro__spect__.

2. Trans- means "across," so to send across is to trans__mit__. To carry across is to trans__port__.

3. De- means "away from," so to take away from is to de__duct__. De- can also mean down, so to write down is to de__scribe__.

4. In- means "into," so to look into is to in__spect__. To write into is to in__scribe__. To force into is to in__ject__.

5. Re- means "back," so to throw back is to re__ject__. To push back is to re__pel__. To go back is to re__cede__.

6. Com- means "together," so to put together is to com__pos__e.

7. Pre- means "before," so to go before is to pre__cede__. To write before is to pre__scribe__.

In each sentence below, circle the word that correctly completes the sentence.

1. This coupon allows a customer to (describe (deduct)) 25¢ from the cost of a bar of soap.
2. Friday is the day that ((precedes) prescribes) Saturday.
3. A bug bomb is used to ((repel) report) flies, bees, and other insects.
4. A songwriter's job is to (reject (compose)) music.
5. To write your name on the inside cover of a book is to ((inscribe) inject) the book.

108

Forming words with roots in isolation; Using words with roots in context

---

202

A root is a word part to which a prefix, suffix, or other root can be added to form a new word.

Read the roots and their meanings below. Then read the sentences that follow. Using the underlined word as a clue, complete the unfinished word in each sentence by writing the correct root. In one sentence, the root will form a word by itself.

aud - hear, listen   **dict** - say, declare   **puls** - drive, push
miss - send   **spec** - see, look, watch   **script** - write

1. To _say_ words aloud so that another person may write them down is to _____ **dict** ate.
2. A powerful ruler who _declares_ laws and gives orders is a _____ **dict** ator.
3. _Diction_ is the way in which a person uses words, so a book that tells how words can be used is a _____ **dict** ionary.
4. If something is loud enough to be _heard_, it is _____ **aud** ible.
5. A group of people who gather to _hear_ something, such as a speech, is an _____ **aud** ience.
6. A room in which a crowd gathers to _hear_ something is an _____ **aud** itorium.
7. _Handwriting_, or a kind of print that looks like handwriting, is called _____ **script**
8. An object that is _sent_ through the air with force is a _____ **miss** ile.
9. A duty or task that a person is _sent_ elsewhere to attend to is a _____ **miss** ion.
10. The beating of blood vessels as blood _pushes_ through them is a _____ **puls** e.
11. Glass or plastic lenses that help a person _see_ better are _____ **spec** tacles.
12. Something that is wonderful to _look_ at is _____ **spec** tacular.
13. People who _watch_ something, such as a sports game, are _____ **spec** tators.

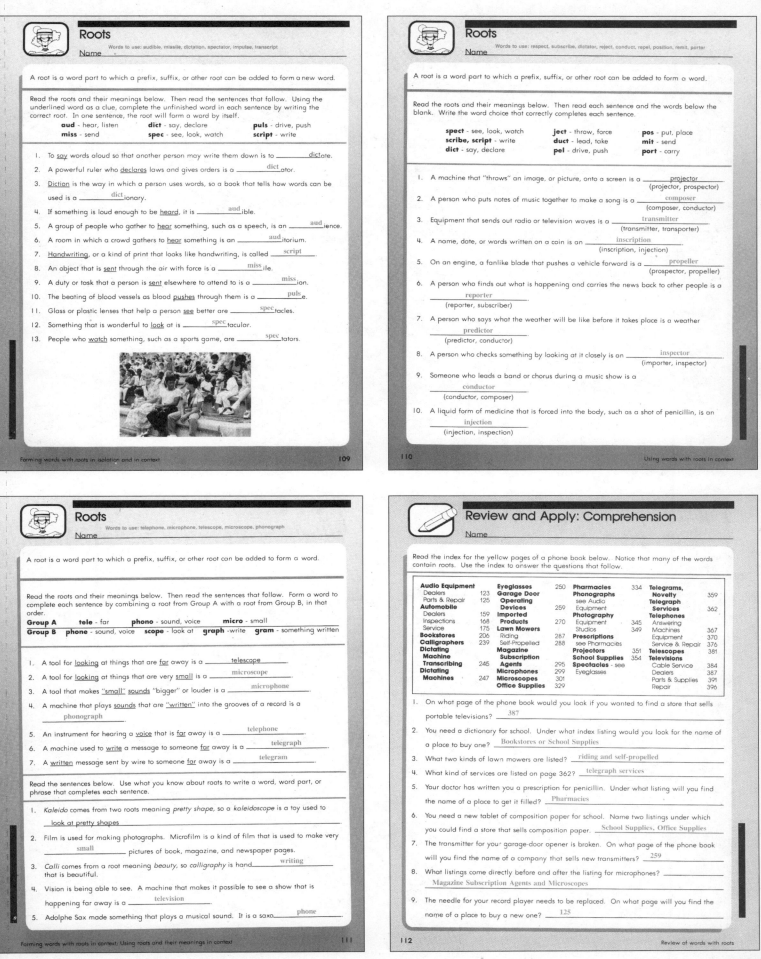

A root is a word part to which a prefix, suffix, or other root can be added to form a word.

Read the roots and their meanings below. Then read each sentence and the words below the blank. Write the word choice that correctly completes each sentence.

spect - see, look, watch   **ject** - throw, force   **pos** - put, place
scribe, script - write   **duct** - lead, take   **mit** - send
dict - say, declare   **pel** - drive, push   **port** - carry

1. A machine that "throws" an image, or picture, onto a screen is a _____ projector
(projector, prospector)
2. A person who puts notes of music together to make a song is a _____ composer
(composer, conductor)
3. Equipment that sends out radio or television waves is a _____ transmitter
(transmitter, transporter)
4. A name, date, or words written on a coin is an _____ inscription
(inscription, injection)
5. On an engine, a fanlike blade that pushes a vehicle forward is a _____ propeller
(prospector, propeller)
6. A person who finds out what is happening and carries the news back to other people is a _____ reporter
(reporter, subscriber)
7. A person who says what the weather will be like before it takes place is a weather _____ predictor
(predictor, conductor)
8. A person who checks something by looking at it closely is an _____ inspector
(importer, inspector)
9. Someone who leads a band or chorus during a music show is a _____ conductor
(conductor, composer)
10. A liquid form of medicine that is forced into the body, such as a shot of penicillin, is an _____ injection
(injection, inspection)

A root is a word part to which a prefix, suffix, or other root can be added to form a word.

Read the roots and their meanings below. Then read the sentences that follow. Form a word to complete each sentence by combining a root from Group A with a root from Group B, in that order.

Group A **tele** - far   **phono** - sound, voice   **micro** - small
Group B **phone** - sound, voice **scope** - look at **graph** - write **gram** - something written

1. A tool for _looking_ at things that are _far_ away is a _____ telescope
2. A tool for _looking_ at things that are very _small_ is a _____ microscope
3. A tool that makes _"small"_ sounds "bigger" or louder is a _____ microphone
4. A machine that plays _sounds_ that are _"written"_ into the grooves of a record is a _____ phonograph
5. An instrument for hearing a _voice_ that is _far_ away is a _____ telephone
6. A machine used to _write_ a message to someone _far_ away is a _____ telegraph
7. A _written_ message sent by wire to someone _far_ away is a _____ telegram

Read the sentences below. Use what you know about roots to write a word, word part, or phrase that completes each sentence.

1. _Kaleido_ comes from two roots meaning _pretty shape_, so a _kaleidoscope_ is a toy used to _____ look at pretty shapes
2. Film is used for making photographs. Microfilm is a kind of film that is used to make very _____ small _____ pictures of book, magazine, and newspaper pages.
3. _Calli_ comes from a root meaning _beauty_, so _calligraphy_ is hand _____ writing that is beautiful.
4. Vision is being able to see. A machine that makes it possible to see a show that is happening far away is a _____ television
5. Adolphe Sax made something that plays a musical sound. It is a saxo _____ phone

---

Read the index for the yellow pages of a phone book below. Notice that many of the words contain roots. Use the index to answer the questions that follow.

Audio Equipment		**Eyeglasses**	250	**Pharmacies**	334	**Telegrams,**
Dealers	123	**Garage Door**		**Phonographs**		**Novelty** 359
Parts & Repair	125	Operating		see Audio		**Telegraph**
Automobile		Devices	259	Equipment		**Services** 362
Dealers	159	**Imported**		**Photography**		**Telephones**
Inspections	168	**Products**	270	Equipment	345	Machines 367
Service	175	**Lawn Mowers**		Studios	349	Equipment 370
Bookstores	206	Riding	287	**Prescriptions**		Service & Repair 376
Calligraphers	239	Self-Propelled	288	see Pharmacies		**Telescopes** 381
Dictating		**Magazine**		**Projectors**	351	**Televisions**
Machine		**Subscription**		**School Supplies**	354	Cable Service 384
Transcribing	245	**Agents**	295	**Spectacles -** see		Dealers 387
Dictating		**Microphones**	299	Eyeglasses		Parts & Supplies 391
Machines	247	**Microscopes**	301			Repair 396
		Office Supplies	329			

1. On what page of the phone book would you look if you wanted to find a store that sells portable televisions? _____ 387
2. You need a dictionary for school. Under what index listing would you look for the name of a place to buy one? _____ Bookstores or School Supplies
3. What two kinds of lawn mowers are listed? _____ riding and self-propelled
4. What kind of services are listed on page 362? _____ telegraph services
5. Your doctor has written you a prescription for penicillin. Under what listing will you find the name of a place to get it filled? _____ Pharmacies
6. You need a new tablet of composition paper for school. Name two listings under which you could find a store that sells composition paper. _____ School Supplies, Office Supplies
7. The transmitter for your garage-door opener is broken. On what page of the phone book will you find the name of a company that sells new transmitters? _____ 259
8. What listings come directly before and after the listing for microphones? _____ Magazine Subscription Agents and Microscopes
9. The needle for your record player needs to be replaced. On what page will you find the name of a place to buy a new one? _____ 125

Review and Apply: Composition

Ward Root, an inventor, invented each of the things pictured below. However, Ward did not name any of his inventions, and now he has forgotten what they do. Your job is to figure out what each thing does and to give it a name that uses at least two word roots. You may add letters such as **a, i, o, er,** or **or.** After you decide on a name for each invention, write it beside the picture. Then tell what the invention does.

port - carry	**micro** - small	**aud** - hear, listen	**script** - write	**tele** - far
dict - say	**spect** - see	**phone** - voice, sound	**scope** - look at	**graph** -write
mit - send	**ject** - throw	**duct** - take	**pos** - put	**pel** - drive, push

1. _microjector_ - This is a machine that picks up small pieces of trash and throws
   them away.

   Answers will vary.

2. _____

3. _____

4. _____

5. _____

Syllables

Words are made of small parts called syllables. Each syllable has one vowel sound, so a word has as many syllables as it has vowel sounds.

stone - 1 syllable   raincoat - 2 syllables   butterfly - 3 syllables

Name the pictures. Write the number of syllables you hear in each picture name.

jellyfish   3   moose   1   alligator   4

pigeon   2   woodpecker   3   caterpillar   4

A compound word should be divided into syllables between the words that make it compound.

Read the list of words below. Divide each word into syllables by drawing a line between the syllables. Then read the sentences and write the list word that best completes each one.

star/fish   catfish   bluebird
sheepdog   greyhound   stinkbug

1. Many animals, such as the ____starfish____, which has five arms, take their names from the shapes of their bodies.

2. Others, such as the ____bluebird____ and ____greyhound____, have been named because of their body color.

3. Some animals, such as the ____catfish____, with its whiskerlike feelers, have a name that is a combination of two animal names.

4. The ____sheepdog____ also has a combination of two animal names, but the reason is different. This animal is known for guarding and herding flocks of sheep.

5. A few animals are named for their more unpleasant qualities. The ____stinkbug____, as you can guess, is one of these.

Syllables

A word that has a prefix or suffix can be divided into syllables between the prefix or suffix and the base word.

re/pay   un/tie   cheer/ful   dark/ness

Read the words below. Then write each word and draw a line between its syllables.

1. nonsense ____non/sense____
2. sleepy ____sleep / y____
3. disease ____dis / ease____
4. wooden ____wood / en____
5. impure ____im / pure____

6. forecast ____fore / cast____
7. artist ____art / ist____
8. lovely ____love / ly____
9. homeless ____home / less____
10. poorly ____poor / ly____

Read the sentences below. Choose the best word from those you wrote above to complete each sentence.

1. Because stream water may be ____impure____, people who camp and must use it for drinking should boil it thoroughly.

2. Grandma Moses was a well-known ____artist____ who did not begin painting until she was seventy-six years old.

3. We took Wags to the veterinarian because she was eating ____poorly____ and was always ____sleepy____.

4. Eating foods low in fats and watching how much you weigh are two ways to lower your chances of developing heart ____disease____.

5. Mrs. Richards grows roses in her yard. She gave our family a ____lovely____ bunch of flowers last week.

6. Today's weather ____forecast____ calls for several inches of snow.

7. *Huckleberry Finn* is a book about a ____homeless____ boy and an escaped slave who float down the Mississippi River on a ____wooden____ raft.

8. Children learn to talk by repeating the sounds they hear, even though their talk may sound like nothing more than ____nonsense____ to us.

Syllables

Some words have two consonants between two vowels. These words can usually be divided between the two consonants.

but/ter   mon/key   cir/cus
vc/cv   vc/cv   vc/cv

Read the sentences and the words shown below each blank. In each blank, write the word that has the VC/CV pattern.

1. If you ever think some of your parents' rules are silly, you may feel ____better____ (thankful, better) after reading some very old city laws that ____concern____ (concern, relate to) children.

2. Although they may have been reasonable when they were ____written____ (written, created), today they make no sense at all.

3. For example, in Janesville, Wisconsin, it is illegal for a child to pull a ____dentist's____ (baby, dentist's) tooth. Parents who ____permit____ (approve of, permit) such behavior can be sent to jail.

4. If you hate to take baths, move to Pickens, Oklahoma. It's against the law to take a bath in that town during the ____winter____ (autumn, winter) months.

5. A law in Columbia, Pennsylvania, ____forbids____ (keeps, forbids) an adult from tickling a child ____under____ (under, beside) the chin with a feather in ____order____ (order, trying) to get the child's attention.

6. If you visit Wakefield, Rhode Island, do not ____enter____ (enter, exit) a movie theater sooner than four hours after eating ____garlic____ (onions, garlic), or you'll be breaking the law.

7. By all means, watch your eating habits while in Halstead, ____Kansas____ (Kansas, Texas). It is a violation for a child to eat ice cream with a fork in a ____public____ (public, quiet) place. ____Perhaps____ (Perhaps, Surely) it would be more sensible to use a knife!

Syllables

Name _____

Words that have one consonant between two vowels can be divided into syllables in two ways. When you see such a word, say it. If the first vowel sound is long, divide the word after the first vowel. If the first vowel sound is short, divide the word after the consonant that follows the vowel.

1. ē/ven	pā/per	2. vĭs/ĭt	mĕt/al
v/cv	v/cv	vc/v	vc/v

Listed below are some things that Tracy and Robert need to buy at the grocery store. One word in each item contains the V/CV or VC/V pattern. Divide the shopping list into two parts by writing the items with a V/CV-pattern word under Tracy's name. Write the items with a VC/V-pattern word under Robert's name.

Grandma's Gravy Mix
Wagon Wheel Dog Food
Chef's Salad Dressing
Redman Radish Dip
Sur-Cheap Tuna

Good Flavor Orange Juice
Ame's Silver Polish
Never-Fail Pie Crusts
Chelsea Paper Plates
World-Famous Pea Soup

Magic Dusting Spray
Farm Time Bacon
Petal-Soft Tissues
Citril Lemon Juice
Fiber-Rich Bread

Tracy (V/CV)	**Robert** (VC/V)
Grandma's Gravy Mix	Wagon Wheel Dog Food
Sur-Cheap Tuna	Chef's Salad Dressing
Good Flavor Orange Juice	Redman Radish Dip
Chelsea Paper Plates	Ame's Silver Polish
World Famous Pea Soup	Never-Fail Pie Crusts
Farm Time Bacon	Magic Dusting Spray
Fiber-Rich Bread	Petal-Soft Tissues
	Citril Lemon Juice

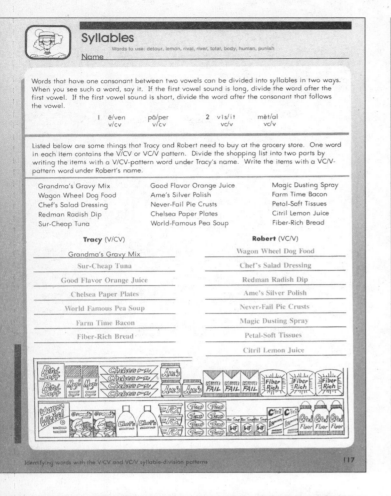

Review and Apply: Comprehension

Name _____

Below is a key that shows five patterns for dividing words into syllables. Study the key and read the story that follows. In each blank, write the word whose syllable pattern matches the pattern shown by the key number. Then draw a line to divide the word into syllables.

1 = prefix or suffix   2 = compound word   3 = VC/CV   4 = V/CV   5 = VC/V

A few years ago, Richard Dean lost his job. To make ends meet, he made and sold

___bas/kets___ One day he met a ___farm / er___ who had planted
3 - (jewelry, baskets)   1 - (lady, farmer)

willow trees just a foot apart. Because the ___sap / lings___ grew straight, Richard
                                           3 - (saplings, branches)

could make fine baskets from them. The farmer gave Richard some plans for making a chair

from the willow saplings. Learning by trial and error, Richard ___fin / ished___ his
                                                                5 - (finished, painted)

chair and took it to the ___Bench / works___ Gallery, a small shop in Columbus, Ohio.
                          2 - (Benchworks, Nature)

When the chair sold almost immediately, Mr. Dean decided to go ___in / to___ the
                                                                2 - (study, into)

business of furniture making. Working in a barn near Johnstown, Ohio, Richard makes

beautiful furniture from bent ___wil / lows___ and twigs. Richard spends about five
                              3 - (branches, willows)

hours making a simple piece of furniture such as a chair or ___night / stand___. He
                                                             2 - (nightstand, table)

makes chairs, ___head / boards___, and swings in different sizes—all from willow
              2 - (headboards, sofas)

saplings. Using ___on / ly___ green wood, he gently bends saplings to form the
                3 - (only, mostly)

___grace / ful___ curving arcs and spokes that give the pieces their special look. From
1 - (special, graceful)

Alaska to the ___South / east___, Richard's ___i / tems___ of furniture
              2 - (desert, Southeast)   4 - (items, anthems)

add interest to kitchens, patios, and courtyards throughout the country.

Review and Apply: Composition

Name _____

Each word puzzle below stands for a familiar phrase. For example, puzzle 1 stands for the words *monkey around*. Look at each puzzle. Then read the words that follow. Notice that the words have different syllable patterns. Using the syllable patterns as clues, figure out the meaning of each puzzle and write the missing word in the correct blank.

1	2	3	4	5	6
m y o n k	hold second	flightflign tflightfli ghtflightff lightfligh tflightflig	he art	HchAanNgeD	↓↓↓ counter

checkout   nonstop   monkey   second   handful   broken

1. ___monkey___ around   4. ___broken___ heart
       (VC/CV)   (V/CV)

2. Hold on a ___second___   5. ___handful___ of change
            (VC/V)   (suffix)

3. ___nonstop___ flight   6. ___checkout___ counter
      (prefix)   (compound word)

Now try making some puzzles yourself. The phrases are given below the boxes. Fill in each box to match its phrase by arranging the words in a special way.

1.	2.	3.	4.
league	head heels	noon good	lovelovelovelovelo
little league	head over heels	good afternoon	endless love

Answers will vary. Given answers are suggestions only.

5.	6.	7.	8.
busines	everything pizza	life other planets	2 cycle cycle
unfinished business	pizza with everything on it	life on other planets	bicycle built for two

---

Check-Up Test 3: Structural Analysis

Name _____

There are seventeen errors in the story below. Proofread the story. Draw a line through each error and write the correction above it. Then follow the directions below the story.

1 Have you ever wondered how actors and actress make movies without getting hurt in the dangerous scenes? Well, the truth is, they don't act in those scenes themselves. Men and women called stunt people play those parts instead. Stunt people fall from windows, roofs, and bridges. They drive autos that end up in crashes. They play the parts of thiefs, fighters, or other people who may get hurt while filming.

2 Being a stunt person isn't an easy way to make a living. These people spend hours practicing their tricks. They must be able to roll, fall, jump, and land without hurting their bodies. Each trick must be carefully planned and done in the safest way possible. At the same time, the trick must be convincing enough for an audience to believe.

3 No matter how well a stunt has been planned, there's always a chance that something can go wrong. Just one incorrect move or one misjudged distance can cause an accident. An air bag that a stunt person is to fall on may break. A car seat that is supposed to collapse during a crash may get stuck. An unexpected breeze may throw a falling actor off course. Even though other jobs are safer and easier, most stunt people love what they do. The danger is just part of the job. Besides, a difficult stunt pays off in two ways. The harder the stunt, the more the person gets paid. It also pays off by giving the person something to be proud of.

1. Circle the three words in paragraph 1 that have a suffix. Write **1** above each word.
2. Circle the word in paragraph 2 that has two suffixes. Write **2** above the word.
3. Divide the compound word in paragraph 2 into syllables. Write **3** above the word.
4. Circle the word in paragraph 2 that has a root meaning "hear." Write **4** above the word.
5. Circle the three words in paragraph 3 that have a prefix. Write **5** above each word.

Read and follow each set of directions below.

1. Write the base word of each of these words.   advising ___advise___
   marries ___marry___   confided ___confide___

2. Add **-ed** to these words.   wrap ___wrapped___   ignore ___ignored___

3. Add **-ing** to these words.   soothe ___soothing___   obey ___obeying___

4. Add **-er** to these words.   clear ___clearer___   dizzy ___dizzier___

5. Add **-est** to these words.   dreary ___dreariest___   cute ___cutest___

6. Write the plural forms of these words.   potato ___potatoes___
   life ___lives___   goose ___geese___   nursery ___nurseries___

7. Rewrite each group of words below to show ownership.
   the dishes of the restaurant ___the restaurant's dishes___
   the customers of the merchants ___the merchants' customers___
   books of children ___children's books___

8. Circle the words that are compound words: combine (strawberry) prevent (throughout)

9. Write the contractions for these words.   they are ___they're___
   there is ___there's___   will not ___won't___

10. Add one of these prefixes or suffixes to each underlined word to form a word that matches each clue.   **im-   over-   pre-   -ish   -ist   -less**
    one who makes art ___artist___   not proper ___improper___
    without worth ___worthless___   sleep too much ___oversleep___
    pay before ___prepay___   like a fool ___foolish___

11. Write one of these words to match each clue.   **repel   spectators   report   audience**
    people who listen ___audience___   to push back ___repel___
    to carry back ___report___   people who watch ___spectators___

12. Draw a line to divide each of these words into syllables.
    wid/ow   tex/tile   wood/en   ri/fle   re/build   snow/storm

---

READING

Friendship

Adapted from *The Wind in the Willows* by Kenneth Grahame

This story tells about four friends who live in the country. Here, two of the friends talk over a problem.

The Mole had long wanted to make friends with the Badger. He seemed, by all accounts, to be an important person, though rarely visible. Still, his unseen nearness was felt by everybody about the place. But whenever the Mole mentioned his wish to the Water Rat, he always found himself put off. "It's all right," the Rat would say. "Badger will turn up some day or other—he's always turning up—and then I'll introduce you. The best of fellows! But you must not only take him as you find him, but *when* you find him."

"Couldn't you ask him here—dinner or something?" said the Mole.

"He wouldn't come," replied the Rat simply. "Badger hates company, and invitations, and dinner, and all that sort of thing."

"Well, then, supposing we go and call on *him?*" suggested the Mole.

"Oh, I'm sure he wouldn't like that at *all*," said the Rat, quite alarmed. "He's so very shy, he'd be sure to have his feelings hurt. I've never even dared to call on him at his home myself, though I know him so well. Besides, we can't. It's quite out of the question, because he lives in the very middle of the Wild Wood."

"Well, supposing he does," said the Mole. "You told me the Wild Wood was all right, you know."

"Oh, I know, I know, so it is," replied the Rat, avoiding the Mole's concern. "But I think we won't go there just now. Not *just* yet. It's a long way, and he wouldn't be at home at this time of year anyhow, and he'll be coming along some day, if you'll wait quietly."

The Mole had to be content with this. But the Badger never came along, and it was not till summer was long over, and cold and frost and muddy roads kept them much indoors, and the swollen river raced past their windows with a speed that mocked at boating of any sort or kind, that he found his thoughts dwelling again on the lone gray Badger, who lived his own life by himself, in his hole in the middle of the Wild Wood.

UNDERSTANDING

A. Under each word, write the name of the story animal that it best describes.
   friendly   cautious   shy
   ___the Mole___   ___the Rat___   ___the Badger___

B. In each group, check the sentence or sentences that are true.
   1. ___✓___ The Mole wants to meet the Badger.
      _____ The Badger wants to meet the Rat.
      _____ The Rat wants to meet the Mole.
   2. ___✓___ The Badger lives in the Wild Wood.
      ___✓___ The Badger lives in a hole.
      _____ The Mole and the Rat live in the city.

C. What reasons does the Rat give for not inviting the Badger to dinner?
   The Rat says that the Badger hates company, and invitations, and dinner, and all
   that sort of thing.

D. Draw a line to connect each word on the left with its meaning on the right.
   1. introduce   a. hardly ever
   2. mentioned   b. swelled up
   3. replied   c. interest
   4. visible   d. put off
   5. concern   e. spoke of
   6. rarely   f. able to be seen
   7. avoiding   g. answered
   8. swollen   h. meet
   9. delay   i. keeping away from

THINKING

A. Check each reason that might explain why the Rat puts off introducing the Mole to the Badger.
   1. _____ The Rat does not like to eat dinner with his friends.
   2. ___✓___ The Rat wants to keep the Mole as a friend for himself alone.
   3. ___✓___ The Rat wants to keep the Badger as a friend for himself alone.
   4. ___✓___ The Rat does not know the Badger as well as he says he does.
   5. ___✓___ The Rat does not want the Mole and the Badger to become friends.
   6. _____ The Rat is afraid of going into the Wild Wood to find the Badger.
   7. _____ The Rat does not know where the Badger lives.
   8. ___✓___ The Rat is afraid the Mole and the Badger will become friends and he will be left out.

B. Check the answer that tells how much time passes during the story. Then write the words from the story that prove your answer is true.
   _____ a few days   ___✓___ many months   _____ several years
   "... and it was not till summer was long over, and cold and frost and muddy
   roads kept them much indoors, ..."

C. A summary is a brief statement that gives the main points of a story. It tells only the important parts of the story. In your own words, write a summary of the story on page 122.
   The Mole wants to meet the Badger, but the Rat keeps putting him off. The
   Mole suggests inviting the Badger to dinner, but the Rat explains why this
   wouldn't work. Then the Mole suggests visiting the Badger, and again the Rat
   objects. The Rat says they must just wait for the Badger to come along, but
   many months pass and the Mole has still not met the Badger.
   Answers may vary but should be similar to the summary given above.

Page 125

Name _____

WRITING

Choose one of the following writing suggestions.

What Is a Friend?

Describe your best friend by telling what it is about this person that you especially like. You might write an advertisement praising your friend. Or you might retell a particular incident that shows why this person is a good friend to you. Or you might write a poem describing the qualities you like in your friend.

Mole Meets Badger

Write a conclusion for the story on page 122. You might begin with the following sentence if you need help getting started.

One cold winter afternoon while the Rat was dozing in his armchair before the fire, the Mole decided to go out by himself and explore the Wild Wood in the hope of at last meeting the Badger.

Answers will vary.

_____

_____

_____

Application of writing skills in a literature context   125

Page 126

Antonyms

Words to use: backward–forward, always–never, young–old, late–early, open–closed, first–last, clean–dirty, easy–hard, hot–cold, wrong–right

Name

An antonym is a word that has the opposite meaning of another word.   wet - dry

Read each row of words below. In the first blank beside the row, write the word that is shown in dark print. In the second blank, write the antonym of the word in dark print.

1.	**create:**	make, destroy, creature	create	destroy
2.	**flood:**	drought, rain, desert	flood	drought
3.	**clumsy:**	awkward, fool, graceful	clumsy	graceful
4.	**alert:**	awake, delighted, drowsy	alert	drowsy
5.	**poverty:**	dollar, wealth, poor	poverty	wealth
6.	**severe:**	bad, mild, miserable	severe	mild
7.	**thaw:**	freeze, snow, ice	thaw	freeze
8.	**victory:**	win, game, defeat	victory	defeat
9.	**purchase:**	buy, sell, merchandise	purchase	sell
10.	**imaginary:**	make-believe, dream, real	imaginary	real

Read the list of words below. Then read the sentences that follow. Write the word from the list that is an antonym for the underlined word in each sentence.

gradually   precious   obedient   nervous   swelling   dreadfully

1. We had to postpone our Saturday picnic plans because the weather was <u>delightfully</u> cold and rainy.   dreadfully

2. Although Carmen said she was <u>calm</u> about her piano performance, she played remarkably well.   nervous

3. As rain continued to fall, the river <u>immediately</u> rose until it overflowed its banks.   gradually

4. It took several months of patience and training to teach Muttsy to be <u>naughty</u>.   obedient

5. Melinda found a shiny glasslike stone that turned out to be a <u>worthless</u> gem.   precious

6. Pain, redness, and <u>shrinkage</u> are indications that a wound has become infected.   swelling

126   Identifying antonyms in isolation and in context

Page 127

Synonyms

Words to use: large, big, huge, enormous, gigantic; pretty, lovely, attractive, beautiful; strange, unusual, peculiar, odd, curious; happy, glad, joyous, cheerful, merry

Name

A synonym is a word that has the same or nearly the same meaning as another word.

big - large   bright - shiny   small - little

Read the list of words below. Then read the sentences that follow. Write the word from the list that is a synonym for the underlined word in each sentence.

journeys   trade   simple   enjoy   major   performers
demands   marry   hard   twirl   remain

1. Circus <u>actors</u> and stagehands lead lives very different from most of us.   performers

2. A circus group <u>travels</u> from town to town for ten months of every year.   journeys

3. While traveling across the country, the circus stops in almost every <u>important</u> city.   major

4. The journey is <u>difficult</u>, but the circus people get used to it.   hard

5. Many of them would not like to <u>stay</u> in one town for long.   remain

6. They <u>like</u> seeing different parts of the country.   enjoy

7. Most circus members grow up in the circus and <u>wed</u> other circus people.   marry

8. Many circus tricks look <u>easy</u>, but the performers are highly skilled athletes.   simple

9. Trapeze artists, for example, must be exact in every move as they hang, swing, flip, and <u>spin</u>.   twirl

10. The <u>duties</u> of circus life leave the members little time for outside friends or entertainment.   demands

11. The circus is a way of life for these people, though, and most of them wouldn't <u>exchange</u> it for any other.   trade

Identifying synonyms in context   127

Page 128

Synonyms

Words to use: clothes, clothing, dress, costume, garments; little, small, tiny; way, custom, habit, manner, method, fashion, practice; certain, sure, convinced, clear

Name

Read the groups of words below. Then read the story that follows. For each underlined word, choose a list word that is a synonym. For paragraph 1, choose words from Group A. For paragraph 2, choose from Group B. For paragraph 3, choose from Group C. Write the synonym in the blank whose number matches the number of the underlined word.

Group A						
caverns	stream	winds	pools	point	experience	trip

Group B						
clinging	pitched	fall	enjoyed	chilly	swiftly	struggled

Group C						
immediately	survived	crew	realizes	crouched	attempted	ledge

1   In June, 1985, Roman Lazowski and Michael Hall planned a (1) <u>journey</u> through the (2) <u>caves</u> of Spring Mill State Park. Both men had made the trip before, and Michael had a good deal of (3) <u>practice</u> exploring caves. The underground tunnel closely follows a narrow, deep (4) <u>brook</u>. At one (5) <u>spot</u>, the cave ceiling drops to four feet. After a distance, the passageway (6) <u>turns</u> through chest-deep (7) <u>puddles</u> of water.

2   At first, the two cavers (8) <u>liked</u> wading through the (9) <u>cool</u> water, but then rain began to (10) <u>descend</u> outside. Soon the water in the cave stream was running deep and (11) <u>fast</u>. The strong current (12) <u>tossed</u> the two men from wall to wall as they desperately (13) <u>fought</u> to get through the cave. Somehow they managed to pull themselves from the water. (14) <u>Grabbing</u> onto the tunnel wall, they thought the water would soon go down.

3   Unfortunately, Roman fell backward into the rushing water. After hitting a wall of rock, he blindly felt around and found a three-foot-long (15) <u>shelf</u>. (16) <u>Stooped</u> on the ledge, Roman watched the stream steadily rise. Michael bravely (17) <u>tried</u> to reach Roman, but the current quickly carried him a hundred yards downstream to daylight. Michael was rushed to a hospital (18) <u>instantly</u>. Two days later, a (19) <u>team</u> of rescuers reached Roman and pulled him to safety. Roman (20) <u>understands</u> he is fortunate to have (21) <u>lived</u>. Now every day seems especially meaningful to him.

1.	trip
2.	caverns
3.	experience
4.	stream
5.	point
6.	winds
7.	pools
8.	enjoyed
9.	chilly
10.	fall
11.	swiftly
12.	pitched
13.	struggled
14.	clinging
15.	ledge
16.	crouched
17.	attempted
18.	immediately
19.	crew
20.	realizes
21.	survived

128   Identifying synonyms in context

Synonyms

Name _____

Words to use: speak, say, talk, converse, communicate; almost, nearly, approximately; street, road, avenue, way, boulevard, highway; quiet, calm, patient, unexcited

Read the list of words below. Then read the sentences that follow. In each blank, write the list word that is a synonym of the word shown below the blank.

recordings	survive	ocean	headed	coast	creature
commotion	encourage	beat	dangerous	spectators	attempted
environment	toward	course	strayed	professors	promptly

1. In October, 1985, a whale stirred up quite a ____commotion____ near the
   (disturbance)
   ____coast____ of California.
   (shore)

2. The whale, a ____creature____ so large that its home is the Pacific Ocean, swam
   (animal)
   under the Golden Gate Bridge and ____headed____ up the Sacramento River.
   (went)

3. Humphrey, as ____spectators____ named the whale, was in a ____dangerous____
   (watchers)   (unsafe)
   situation.

4. A shallow river is too small for a forty-ton whale. Besides that, whales, like other
   ____ocean____ animals, need salt water.
   (sea)

5. In an ____environment____ of fresh water, a whale cannot ____survive____
   (surrounding)   (live)
   more than a few weeks.

6. Scientists, ____professors____, and fishing guides ____attempted____ to get
   (teachers)   (tried)
   Humphrey to turn around.

7. They ____beat____ on pipes, played sound ____recordings____ of other
   (banged)   (tapes)
   whales, and used tugboats to ____encourage____ him to swim back to the Pacific.
   (urge)

8. After more than three weeks, Humphrey finally reversed his ____course____ and
   (direction)
   swam back ____toward____ the ocean.
   (to)

9. A few days later, another whale ____strayed____ into the same area.
   (wandered)

10. This one ____promptly____ headed out, though. Perhaps Humphrey had given it a
    (quickly)
    warning!

Using synonyms in context   129

Review and Apply: Comprehension

Name _____

Read the groups of words below. Then read the story that follows. In each blank, write the list word that is either a synonym (S) or antonym (A) of the word shown below the blank. For synonyms, choose words from Group 1. For antonyms, choose from Group 2.

Group 1: Synonyms	kinds	road	helpful	perhaps	folks	student	prize
	ideas	device	because		pedestrian	created	lid

Group 2: Antonyms	straight	won	enjoy	dark	rainy
	problem		bottom	young	could

Young ____folks____ ____enjoy____ entering contests of all
(people-S)   (dislike-A)

____kinds____. In a contest held for ____young____ inventors, about
(types-S)   (elderly-A)

80,000 ideas were mailed in. A five-year-old ____student____ ____won____
                                          (pupil-S)   (lost-A)

a $250 ____prize____ for making an umbrella with a flashlight attached to it.
        (award-S)

Using the umbrella, a ____pedestrian____ ____could____ easily see and be
                      (walker-S)   (couldn't-A)

seen on ____dark____, ____rainy____ days. A second-grade child
        (bright-A)   (sunny-A)

thought of a ____device____ to help keep a class of children in a
             (thing-S)

____straight____ line while walking along a ____road____. One
(crooked-A)   (street-S)

eighth-grade pupil ____created____ a peanut butter jar that has a
                   (made-S)

____lid____ on both ends. That way, there's no ____problem____
(cover-S)   (solution-A)

reaching the peanut butter at the ____bottom____ of the jar, ____because____
                                  (top-A)   (since-S)

the jar has no bottom. Young people have a lot of good ____ideas____ for
                                                       (thoughts-S)

____helpful____ inventions. ____Perhaps____ you have an idea or two of
(useful-S)   (Maybe-S)

your own!

130   Review of antonyms and synonyms

Review and Apply: Composition

Name _____

Read the words below. Then read the paragraph that follows. The underlined words in it are vague or overused. They could be replaced with synonyms that are more descriptive. Using the word list and any words of your own, rewrite the paragraph, replacing the underlined words with synonyms.

continued	major	illness	officials	prevented	challenge
crippling	task	illnesses	vaccinate	efforts	poverty-stricken
youngsters	plenty	disease	nations	diseases	accomplishing
funding	deadly	achieved	scarred	action	realize

Workers at the World Health Organization (WHO) have a hard problem. They know that far too many of the world's children die from sicknesses that could be stopped. For example, there has been a lot of polio vaccine in the United States for over thirty years. But many children in poor countries have not been protected from this bad, killing sickness. One of WHO's jobs is to protect all the world's children against preventable sicknesses. One of the big problems in doing this job is money. Much has been done since WHO began stepping up its work in 1974. Smallpox, for example, a sickness that marked, blinded, or often killed its victims, was completely wiped out in the late 1970's, thanks to the work of WHO. With lasting work, WHO workers hope that all preventable sicknesses may one day be sicknesses of the past.

Answers will vary. The given paragraph is a suggestion only.

Workers at the World Health Organization (WHO) have a challenge. They realize that far too many of the world's children die from sicknesses that could be prevented. For example, there has been plenty of polio vaccine in the United States for over thirty years. But many youngsters in poverty-stricken nations have not been protected from this crippling, deadly disease. One of WHO's jobs is to vaccinate all the world's children against preventable illnesses. One of the major problems in accomplishing this task is funding. Much has been achieved since WHO began stepping up its efforts in 1974. Smallpox, for example, a disease that scarred, blinded, or often killed its victims, was completely wiped out in the late 1970's, thanks to the action of WHO. With continued work, WHO officials hope that all preventable diseases may one day be sicknesses of the past.

Review of antonyms and synonyms   131

Homophones

Name _____

Words to use: died–dyed, great–grate, break–brake, rap–wrap, plane–plain, waist–waste, pain–pane

Homophones are words that sound the same but have different spellings and different meanings.

would - wood   right - write   flour - flower

Read the sentences below. In the blanks, write the pair of homophones from each sentence.

1. Talking aloud in the library is not allowed because it disturbs others.
   ____aloud____ ____allowed____

2. If you bury these seeds, in two months a berry bush will sprout.
   ____bury____ ____berry____

3. There is a ten percent discount on these boots if you buy them by the end of the week.
   ____buy____ ____by____

4. Please hang these clothes in the bedroom closet and then close the door.
   ____clothes____ ____close____

5. Three crews of sailors went with us on our tropical ocean cruise.
   ____crews____ ____cruise____

6. Do you remember what day these library books are due?
   ____Do____ ____due____

7. If the police find your car illegally parked, you will be given a ticket and fined.
   ____find____ ____fined____

8. Next year, the company will hire new workers at salary levels higher than this year's.
   ____hire____ ____higher____

9. Because heavy fog and mist slowed the airport traffic, we missed our flight to Boston.
   ____mist____ ____missed____

10. Mom planted two rows of tulips in the garden near a pink rose.
    ____rows____ ____rose____

11. I felt tired, weak, and feverish because I had the flu last week.
    ____weak____ ____week____

132   Identifying homophones in context

Homophones

Name _____

Words to use: I–eye, or–oar–ore, pall–pale, threw–through, to–too–two, principal–principle

Read the list of homophones and their meanings below. Then read the sentences that follow. In each blank, write the homophone that correctly completes the sentence.

aisle - pathway   **isle** - island
coarse - rough   **course** - class
find - locate   **fined** - charged money as punishment
passed - went by   **past** - history
presence - nearness, being there   **presents** - gifts
principal - head of a school   **principle** - rule or truth
their - belonging to them   **there** - in that place   **they're** - they are
threw - tossed   **through** - between
to - toward   **too** - also   **two** - a number
wood - what trees are made of   **would** - past tense form of *will*

1. Mrs. Lin walked down the supermarket ___aisle___
(aisle, isle)

2. She ___passed___ the grapefruit display because she couldn't decide between
(past, passed)
pink grapefruit and the regular kind.

3. ___There___ were ___two___ kinds of cherries.
(There, Their, They're)   (two, to, too)

4. Next she wondered where she might
___find___ the salad dressings.
(find, fined)

5. Noticing the ___presence___ of a stock clerk,
(presence, presents)
Mrs. Lin asked her in what ___aisle___ she
(aisle, isle)
should look.

6. After finding the dressings, she ___threw___
(through, threw)
a coin in the air to determine her choice of French
dressing.

7. She wondered if one of the schools in town offered a
___course___ on the ___principles___
(course, coarse)   (principals, principles)
of grocery shopping.

Homographs

Name _____

Words to use: story, second, date, bark, down

Homographs are words that have the same spelling but different meanings. Sometimes they are pronounced differently.

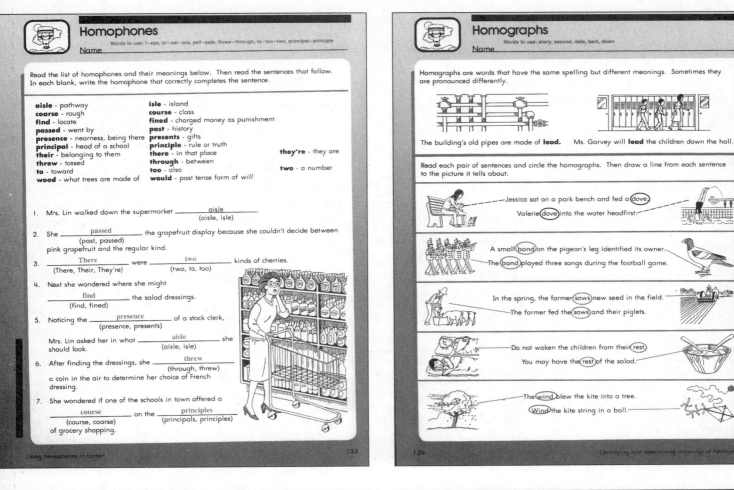

The building's old pipes are made of **lead**.   Ms. Garvey will **lead** the children down the hall.

Read each pair of sentences and circle the homographs. Then draw a line from each sentence to the picture it tells about.

- Jessica sat on a park bench and fed a (dove).
- Valerie (dove) into the water headfirst.

- A small (band) on the pigeon's leg identified its owner.
- The (band) played three songs during the football game.

- In the spring, the farmer (sows) new seed in the field.
- The farmer fed the (sows) and their piglets.

- Do not waken the children from their (rest).
- You may have the (rest) of the salad.

- The (wind) blew the kite into a tree.
- (Wind) the kite string in a ball.

Homographs

Name _____

Words to use: mine, nap, rose, pitch, can, mold

Read the list of homographs below. Then read each pair of meanings that follow. Write the homograph from the list that matches both meanings.

bill   tire   bow   wind   bank
close   ring   yard   tear   row

1. a. place to save money   b. land beside a river   ___bank___
2. a. jewelry for a finger   b. bell-like sound   ___ring___
3. a. strong breeze   b. to twist   ___wind___
4. a. knotted ribbon on a gift   b. to bend in greeting   ___bow___
5. a. near   b. to shut   ___close___
6. a. rubber around a wheel   b. become weary   ___tire___
7. a. move a boat with oars   b. straight line   ___row___
8. a. paper telling how much to pay   b. bird's beak   ___bill___
9. a. drop of water from the eye   b. to rip   ___tear___
10. a. grassy area around a house   b. thirty-six inches   ___yard___

Read the homographs and their meanings below. Then read the sentences that follow. In each sentence, decide the meaning of the underlined homograph. Write the letter of the correct meaning in the blank.

coast - a. seashore   b. to ride or slide without power
light - a. not heavy   b. not dark
palm - a. tree that grows in warm climates   b. flat side of a hand
present - a. opposite of absent   b. to give something to another person
pupil - a. a student   b. part of the eye
spoke - a. wire that supports a bicycle wheel   b. did speak

1. Hundreds of people take winter vacations on the Atlantic <u>coast</u>. ___a___
2. Last year, I was a <u>pupil</u> in Mrs. Yee's class. ___a___
3. The <u>palm</u> offered the sunbathers very little shade. ___a___
4. We plan to <u>present</u> our teacher with a surprise for her birthday. ___b___
5. The author <u>spoke</u> to the audience about her trip to South America. ___b___
6. It was not yet <u>light</u> when I got out of bed yesterday morning. ___b___

Review and Apply: Comprehension

Name _____

Read the list of homophones and their meanings below. Then read the story that follows. In each blank, write the homophone that correctly completes the sentence.

feat - daring act   **feet** - part of the body for walking
hall - long, narrow room   **haul** - carry
heard - listened   **herd** - group of animals
hole - opening   **whole** - entire
night - opposite of day   **knight** - king or queen's servant
our - belonging to us   **hour** - sixty minutes
peak - top of a mountain   **peek** - look
stairs - steps   **stares** - fixed looks

We were relaxing in the living room while watching a television mystery (last)
___night___. Suddenly Nikki sprang to her ___feet___ and
(night, knight)   (feat, feet)
whispered, "What's that noise?" Mom grabbed a (bat) from the corner of the room and crept
down the ___hall___ toward the kitchen. By this time, my sister had scurried up
(hall, haul)
the ___stairs___ to (hide) in her bedroom closet. Meanwhile, I stayed in the
(stairs, stares)
living room and hid my face in my (arms). Every once in a while, I looked up briefly to take a
___peek___ at anything that might be happening. Soon I ___heard___
(peek, peak)   (heard, herd)
laughter coming from the kitchen. Coming into the living room, Mom explained, "Lucky
jumped to the window ledge and climbed through a ___hole___ in the screen!"
(hole, whole)
After showing ___our___ neighbors' cat to the front door, Mom and I sat back
(hour, our)
down to watch the news. Nikki, in the meantime, fell asleep on her closet floor.

Read the homographs and their meanings below. Then find each of the listed homographs in the story above and circle them. Decide the meaning of each homograph as it is used in the story. Write the letter of the correct meaning in the blank beside the homograph below.

1. last ___a___   a. the one just past   b. go on and on; continue; endure
2. bat ___b___   a. a flying mammal   b. piece of baseball equipment
3. hide ___a___   a. stay out of sight   b. animal skin
4. arms ___a___   a. part of the body   b. weapons

Read the list of homophones and their meanings below. Then read the story that follows. In some sentences, the wrong homophone has been used. Circle those homophones. Write the correct homophones above them. You should find twelve errors.

aisles - pathways	**isles** - islands
be - exist	**bee** - buzzing insect
by - near, beside	**bye** - good-bye
for - in order to do something	**four** - number after three
hall - long, narrow room	**haul** - carry
in - within	**inn** - hotel
new - not old	**knew** - did know
not - meaning *no*	**knot** - tangled string
oar - long paddle used to row a boat	**or** - word that gives a choice
one - single	**won** - did win
their - belonging to them	**there** - in that place
to - toward	**too** - also
way - direction	**weigh** - find the heaviness of something

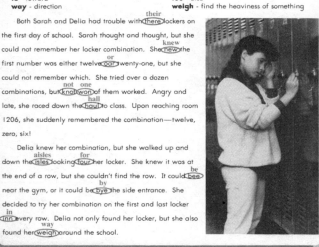

Both Sarah and Delia had trouble with ~~There~~ *their* lockers on the first day of school. Sarah thought and thought, but she could not remember her locker combination. She ~~new~~ *knew* the first number was either twelve ~~oar~~ *or* twenty-one, but she could not remember which. She tried over a dozen combinations, but ~~knot~~ *not* ~~won~~ *one* of them worked. Angry and late, she raced down the ~~haul~~ *hall* to class. Upon reaching room 1206, she suddenly remembered the combination—twelve, zero, six!

Delia knew her combination, but she walked up and down the ~~isles~~ *aisles* looking ~~four~~ *for* her locker. She knew it was at the end of a row, but she couldn't find the row. It could ~~bee~~ *be* near the gym, or it could ~~bye~~ *by* the side entrance. She decided to try her combination on the first and last locker ~~inn~~ *in* every row. Delia not only found her locker, but she also found her ~~weigh~~ *way* around the school.

Many words have more than one meaning. Most dictionaries show the different meanings of a word by placing a number before each meaning.

Read the dictionary entries below. Then read the sentences. Use the entries to decide the meaning of each underlined word. In the blank, write the number of the correct meaning.

camp er /kam'pər/ *n* **1** a person who lives outdoors in a tent or other temporary shelter **2** a vehicle designed for camping that is either self-propelled or pulled by an automobile

cast /kast/ *n* **1** the act of throwing or tossing: *The sea workers made a cast of the fishing net.* **2** a mold into which a hot liquid substance, such as wax, can be poured so that when it hardens, the substance takes the shape of the mold **3** a group of actors in a play **4** a hard bandage made of plaster of paris put on a part of the body to keep it still while healing

faint /fānt/ *adj* **1** weak, dizzy feeling of the body: *The crowded room was so hot, I felt faint.* **2** not strong or distinct; pale: *The handwriting in the old book was very faint.*

tis sue /tish'/ *n* **1** the substance that forms the parts of animals and plants **2** a paper handkerchief

vol ume /vol' yəm/ *n* **1** one of a series of books forming a collection **2** amount of sound: *Please turn down the volume on your radio.* **3** the amount of space taken up by something: *This trunk has a volume of three cubic feet.*

1. Use this <u>tissue</u> to wipe the glue off your hands.   **2**
2. Our family rented a <u>camper</u> for our trip to the Smoky Mountains.   **2**
3. Because I had a fever, I felt <u>faint</u> and unsteady on my feet.   **1**
4. Our class is collecting orange juice cans to use as <u>casts</u> for candle making.   **2**
5. The third <u>volume</u> of the library's encyclopedia set is missing.   **1**
6. Although Mom is a <u>camper</u>, Dad would rather stay in a hotel while on a trip.   **1**
7. After the show, the members of the <u>cast</u> gave their acting teacher a dozen roses.   **3**
8. If you stay in the sun too long without being protected, the <u>tissue</u> that forms the surface of the skin will burn.   **1**
9. Our new refrigerator has greater <u>volume</u> than our old one, so it holds more food.   **3**
10. The voice on the other end of the telephone was so <u>faint</u> I could hardly hear it.   **2**
11. Dee wasn't able to go swimming last summer because her arm was in a <u>cast</u>.   **4**
12. The band's <u>volume</u> increased as it neared the end of the song.   **2**
13. That artist is known for the <u>faint</u> pink and purple skies in her paintings.   **2**
14. The worm flew off my fishing line when I made a quick <u>cast</u>.   **1**
15. The homesick <u>camper</u> felt better after she received a letter from her parents.   **1**

Read the dictionary entries below. Then read the sentences. Complete each sentence by writing the correct entry word. You will use some words more than once. In the blank that follows the sentence, write the number of the word's correct meaning.

land /land/ *n* **1** soil; earth: *Mrs. Smith grows wheat on her land.* **2** a country: *He comes from a land far away.*

odd /od/ *adj* **1** unusual; STRANGE: *Aunt Gert told us an odd story about Mars.* **2** only one from a pair or set: *There is an odd glove in the closet.* **3** not even; having one left over when divided by two

or ange /or inj, är' inj/ *n* **1** a round, sweet, juicy fruit: *I will eat an orange for lunch.* **2** the color made by mixing red and yellow: *That shade of orange is really bright.*

pitch er /pich' ər/ *n* **1** a jug or container used to hold and pour liquids: *The pitcher of milk fell to the floor.* **2** a baseball player who throws the ball to the batter: *Li is our team's pitcher.*

quar ter /kwôr' ər/ *n* **1** an American or Canadian coin worth twenty-five cents **2** one of four equal parts: *One quarter of eight is two.*

show er /shour, shou' ər/ *n* **1** a brief rainfall **2** a party given by friends who bring gifts for a particular occasion **3** a bath in which water pours down on a person from an overhead nozzle

1. Pedro will like this jogging suit because his favorite color is ___orange___ . **2**
2. A ___quarter___ of the students in our class are absent with the flu. **2**
3. An anteater is an ___odd___-looking creature that catches ants with its long, sticky tongue. **1**
4. The waiter filled our glasses with water from a metal ___pitcher___ **1**
5. Our neighbor took a ___shower___ at our house because his hot water heater had broken. **3**
6. We dug up a small area of ___land___ in the backyard to be used as a vegetable garden. **1**
7. Because there was an ___odd___ number of players, one team had seven members, and the other had eight. **3**
8. We had a ___shower___ for Mr. and Mrs. Wilson before their baby arrived. **2**
9. I prefer to cut rather than peel an ___orange___ because I don't like getting the sticky juice on my hands. **1**
10. The neighborhood children held a carnival and charged a ___quarter___ for admission. **1**

Read the dictionary entries below. Notice that each word has more than one meaning. Then read the story. Complete each unfinished sentence by writing the correct entry word in the blank. In the parentheses at the end of the blank, write the number of the word's meaning.

ap pear /ə pir'/ *v* **1** to come into sight: *The stars appear at night.* **2** seem: *You appear to be ill.* **3** to come out in print; be published: *The book will appear in bookstores next month.*

ar ti cle /ärt' i kəl/ *n* **1** a nonfiction piece of writing in a magazine or newspaper **2** a thing: *A scarf is an article of clothing.* **3** a word such as *a, an,* or *the* used before a noun to limit its meaning

cer tain /surt' ən/ *adj* **1** sure: *Are you certain you locked the door?* **2** specific but not named: *Carlita can repair the engine after she buys a certain part.*

char ac ter /kar' ik tər/ *n* **1** the qualities that make up a person: *Jeremy has a gentle character.* **2** a strange or odd person: *Gus was quite a character.* **3** a person in a story: *An outlaw is the main character in the movie.*

film /film/ *n* **1** a roll or strip of plastic material used in a camera for taking photographs **2** a motion picture; movie

scout /skout/ *n* **1** one sent ahead to get information **2** one sent to search for talent: *He is a basketball scout.* **3** boy scout **4** girl scout

ti tle /tīt' əl/ *n* **1** a legal right to something, such as property: *Who has title to that land?* **2** a paper showing ownership: *Juan keeps the title to his car in the glove box.* **3** the name of a book or film **4** a name that shows a person's condition, rank, or occupation, such as *Ms., Doctor,* or *Uncle*

Gone With the Wind, the most widely read novel in history, is a love-and-war story set in the South during the Civil War. The author, Margaret Mitchell, had never written a novel before writing *Gone With the Wind.* She had become a skilled writer some years earlier as a writer of ___article___s (**1**) for the *Atlanta Journal.* After writing the book, Mitchell was not ___certain___ (**1**) of her writing talent. She called the book "lousy" and did not try to sell it. However, a talent ___scout___ (**2**) from the Macmillan Company talked Mitchell into sending him her unfinished book and offered to buy the publishing rights. The book had to go through some changes before it could ___appear___ (**3**) in stores. For example, the original ___title___ (**3**) had been *Tomorrow Is Another Day.* A main ___character___ (**3**), Scarlett O'Hara, was named Pansy until just a few weeks before the book was published in 1936. In 1939, the story was made into a ___film___ (**2**) that is still popular today.

Review and Apply: Composition

Name _____

Read the list of words and their meanings below. For each word, write one sentence that uses both meanings of the word.

patient	a. person under medical care	b. willing to wait	
pitcher	a. container for pouring liquid	b. baseball player	
bowl	a. play a game with pins and a ball	b. rounded dish	
husky	a. sled dog	b. big and strong	
loaf	a. to be lazy	b. shaped mass of bread	
palm	a. inside of the hand	b. kind of tree	
racket	a. something used to hit a tennis ball	b. loud noise	

1. A doctor's patient must sometimes be patient while waiting to be seen.

Answers will vary.

Idioms

Name _____

An idiom is a phrase or expression that cannot be understood by the meaning of its separate words. For example, **run into** is an idiom. To run into a friend has nothing to do with running into or with hitting a person. It means "to meet."

Read the words and phrases below. Then read the sentences that follow. Complete each sentence by writing a word or phrase that has the same meaning as the idiom shown below the blank.

fly	reject	found	visit
not laugh	became angry	rest	went to bed
stop	waited near		

1. After the football game, the news people _____ waited near _____ the locker room to talk to the players. (hung around)

2. Mrs. Bilington _____ became angry _____ when, by accident, I slammed a baseball through her front picture window. (blew a fuse)

3. The lifeguard blew her whistle at the two girls and told them to _____ stop _____ the splashing. (cut out)

4. Luis was awake past midnight last night, so he _____ went to bed _____ early tonight. (hit the sack)

5. A comedian who can _____ not laugh _____ while telling a joke usually gets laughs by surprising an audience. (keep a straight face)

6. I _____ found _____ this old photograph while cleaning out my bedroom closet. (ran across)

7. While on vacation, Dina plans to swim, read books, and _____ rest _____. (take it easy)

8. Our neighbors are moving out of town, but they've invited us to _____ visit _____ whenever we're near their new home. (drop in)

9. I had to _____ reject _____ Sue Lee's party invitation because I'd already made plans to attend a concert. (turn down)

10. The quickest way to get from Indianapolis to St. Louis is to _____ fly _____. (catch a plane)

Figures of Speech

Name _____

A figure of speech is a phrase that compares two things that are not really alike but are similar in at least one way. A figure of speech may use the words *like* or *as* to tell how one thing is like another. For example, a person's hair may be described as *black as night* or *like silk*. A figure of speech may compare two things by saying that one thing *is* another. For example, in describing what your hair looks like when you get out of bed, you might say *My hair is a mop*.

Read the figures of speech below. Then read the sentences that follow. Complete each sentence by writing the figure of speech that has the same meaning as the words shown below the blank.

is a clown	like two cents	is a snail
hard as a rock	is a walking encyclopedia	as smooth as glass
like a bull in a china shop	is a chicken	am a real bear

1. My little brother _____ is a chicken _____ when it comes to going to sleep in a darkened room all by himself. (is afraid)

2. Because the cornbread had not been tightly sealed in its wrapper, after a week it was _____ hard as a rock _____. (stale)

3. There was not even a breeze, and the lake water was _____ as smooth as glass _____. (calm)

4. If I don't get enough sleep at night, I _____ am a real bear _____ when I have to get up the next morning. (am grumpy)

5. Uncle Fred causes lots of accidents because he's _____ like a bull in a china shop _____. (clumsy)

6. I was so embarrassed at forgetting my neighbor's name, I felt _____ like two cents _____. (almost worthless)

7. Whenever her bedroom needs cleaning, Marlena _____ is a snail _____ about getting it done. (is slow)

8. Because my friend Harold _____ is a clown _____, the teacher sometimes has to speak sternly to him. (is silly)

9. My mother always knows the answers to quiz game questions because she _____ is a walking encyclopedia _____. (is smart)

Review and Apply: Comprehension

Name _____

Read the words and phrases below. Then read the story and notice the idiom or figure of speech below each blank. In each blank, write the word or phrase that has the same meaning as the words below the blank. You will use one word twice.

waiting	first thing	get angry	saw	calm
hurry	finally	quickly	reach	stuck

Today has really been horrible. _____ First thing _____ this morning, I broke my (Right off the bat)

mother's expensive necklace, and she gave me a scolding. Then I moved _____ quickly _____ to get downstairs for breakfast and tore the hem of my pants. After (like mad)

putting on another pair, I _____ saw _____ myself in a mirror and noticed they had (caught sight of)

shrunk from many washings. By this time, I knew I'd have to _____ hurry _____, or I'd (step on it)

be late for school. I dashed up the street toward the bus stop, but looking ahead, I saw the bus

had left me behind. I was ready to _____ get angry _____, but instead I sat down on the (throw a fit)

curb to _____ calm _____ myself. Before long, Mom drove by on her way to work. (get a hold of)

"Maybe the bus is hung up in traffic," I said. "Let's follow its usual route and see if we can

_____ reach _____ it." Sure enough, we found the bus a mile away, (catch up with)

_____ stuck _____. Mom dropped me off at the intersection, and I ran down the (caught like a bug in a web)

sidewalk _____ quickly _____ and motioned to the bus driver. _____ Finally _____ (like greased lightning)   (At last)

seated on the bus, I began to feel sick as I rode to school. I realized I had forgotten my math

homework. "What a great way to start a Monday," I thought, quietly laughing at myself. "I

can't imagine what else today has _____ waiting _____ for me!" (in store)

Review and Apply: Composition

Name _____

Imagine that you're spending the week at summer camp. Using at least six of the idioms and figures of speech below, write a letter to a friend. Tell about your adventures. You may also use your own idioms and figures of speech.

drives me buggy	as hungry as a bear	hang in there
like cats and dogs	take care	is a blast
is a doll	is a ball of energy	like a refrigerator
got carried away	as cold as ice	broke out
as hard as a rock	got the hang of	hit it off
is a riot	drop a line	as dry as a bone
let off steam	looks like a tornado struck	threw a party
worked like a horse	like a bottomless pit	is a sport

_____

_____

_____

Dear _____

Answers will vary.

_____

_____

_____

_____

_____

_____

_____

_____

_____

_____

Review of idioms and figures of speech   145

Analogies

Name _____

Words to use: *Toe is to foot as finger is to hand. Boot is to winter as sandal is to summer. Bat is to baseball as racket is to tennis.*

An analogy is a way to compare two things. It shows their relationship. The relationship between the first pair of words is the same as the relationship between the second pair of words. Analogies can be stated in two ways.

Finger is to *hand* as *toe* is to *foot*.   *Big* is to *little* as *cold* is to *hot*.
finger : hand : : toe : foot   big : little : : cold : hot

Read the list of words below. Then read the sentences that follow. Complete each sentence by writing the list word that completes the analogy.

sour   cow   calendar   gas   night   car

1. *Sun* is to *day* as *moon* is to _____ night _____
2. *Sugar* is to *sweet* as *lemon* is to _____ sour _____
3. *Lamp* is to *electricity* as *car* is to _____ gas _____
4. *Ride* is to *bike* as *drive* is to _____ car _____
5. *Time* is to *clock* as *date* is to _____ calendar _____
6. *Egg* is to *hen* as *milk* is to _____ cow _____

Read each analogy below. Figure out the relationship between the first pair of words. Then complete the second pair by writing the word from parentheses that has the same relationship.

1. cold : cool : : hot : _____ warm _____ (weather, snow, warm, oven)
2. painter : picture : : author : _____ book _____ (book, pencil, paint, read)
3. chair : sit : : bed : _____ sleep _____ (table, television, stand, sleep)
4. mother : daughter : : father : _____ son _____ (sister, son, family, man)
5. fish : swim : : rabbit : _____ hop _____ (bunny, hop, ears, water)
6. stop : go : : in : _____ out _____ (out, over, above, around)
7. basketball : court : : baseball : _____ diamond _____ (bat, diamond, play, football)
8. mud : dirty : : soap : _____ clean _____ (clean, wash, bathtub, dishes)
9. spider : web : : bird : _____ tree _____ (tree, fly, branches, nest)
10. horse : colt : : cow : _____ calf _____ (barn, calf, farm, pony)

146   Completing analogies

Analogies

Name _____

Words to use: *Yellow is to bananas as green is to peas. Oak is to tree as tulip is to flower. Ring is to finger as bracelet is to wrist.*

Read the sentences below. Complete each one by writing the word from parentheses that completes the analogy.

1. *Butterfly* is to *fly* as *fish* is to _____ swim _____ (cocoon, swim, moth, water)
2. *Smile* is to *frown* as *happy* is to _____ sad _____ (sad, mouth, glad, face)
3. *Leaf* is to *tree* as *bloom* is to _____ flower _____ (garden, branch, soil, flower)
4. *Dime* is to *ten* as *nickel* is to _____ five _____ (money, fifteen, one, five)
5. *Lend* is to *borrow* as *beautiful* is to _____ ugly _____ (steal, ugly, pretty, give)
6. *Carrot* is to *bean* as *apple* is to _____ orange _____ (food, fruit, orange, peel)
7. *Crayon* is to *color* as *violin* is to _____ music _____ (guitar, music, paint, drum)
8. *Orchard* is to *trees* as *garden* is to _____ flowers _____ (flowers, dig, grass, pick)
9. *Bill* is to *William* as *Bob* is to _____ Robert _____ (Robert, boy, Smith, John)
10. *Oar* is to *row* as *scissors* is to _____ cut _____ (paper, sharp, boat, cut)

Read the list of words below. Then read the analogies that follow. Complete each one by writing the correct list word.

| neck | arm | fire | wheel | win |
| girl | see | nation | whale | string |

1. shirt : button : : shoe : _____ string _____
2. door : knob : : car : _____ wheel _____
3. desert : camel : : ocean : _____ whale _____
4. glacier : ice : : sun : _____ fire _____
5. lungs : breathe : : eyes : _____ see _____
6. collar : neck : : sleeve : _____ arm _____
7. gift : present : : country : _____ nation _____
8. ring : necklace : : finger : _____ neck _____
9. brother : boy : : sister : _____ girl _____
10. defeat : loss : : victory : _____ win _____

Completing analogies   147

Review and Apply: Comprehension

Name _____

Look at each pair of pictures below. Think about the ways in which the picture parts are alike. Then write an analogy to show the comparison. If you wish, you may use some of the following words in your analogies.

canvas	curtains	antler	rain	bird	feather	cloud
wing	pour	vase	pond	tusk	picture	glass
window	trunk	cage	milk	bloom	leaf	elephant
pitcher	flower	fall	nose	bowl	frame	deer

1. **Answers will vary. Given answers are suggestions only.**

Tusk is to elephant as antler is to deer

2. Milk is to pitcher as rain is to cloud

3. Window is to curtains as picture is to frame

4. Cage is to bird as vase is to flower

148   Review of analogies

212

Review and Apply: Composition

Name _____

Questions, questions, questions! Your four-year-old cousin, for whom you are babysitting, is always asking questions. Below are some of your cousin's questions. Answer each one and then write an analogy that illustrates your answer.

1. How is a toothbrush like a broom? __Both a toothbrush and a broom__ __are used for cleaning.__

   __Toothbrush__ is to __teeth__ as __broom__ is to __floor__ .
   Answers will vary. Given answers are suggestions only.

2. How is a house like a fish bowl? __Both a house and a fish bowl are places for living.__

   __Person__ is to __house__ as __fish__ is to __fish bowl__ .

3. How is a violin like a drum? __Both are musical instruments that are played__ __with separate pieces.__

   __Drumstick__ is to __drum__ as __bow__ is to __violin__ .

4. How is a door like a zipper? __Both can be opened and closed.__

   __Zipper__ is to __jacket__ as __door__ is to __house__ .

5. How is baseball like hockey? __Both are sports in which an object is hit.__

   __Ball__ is to __bat__ as __puck__ is to __stick__ .

6. How is a button like a shoestring? __Both are used to fasten articles of clothing.__

   __Button__ is to __shirt__ as __shoestring__ is to __shoe__ .

7. How is a refrigerator like a silo? __Both are used to store food.__

   __Milk__ is to __refrigerator__ as __corn__ is to __silo__ .

Check-Up Test 5: Vocabulary

Name _____

Read the story. Then, using the underlined story words, follow the directions below.

When a baby kangaroo is born, it is as big as your thumb. The baby, which is called a joey, cannot see, hear, walk, or jump. It crawls into a pouch on its mother's stomach and remains there about eight months. During that time, its body grows and develops more fully.

A full-grown kangaroo is 6 to 7 feet tall and weighs 100 to 150 pounds. Its hind legs are much larger than the front ones because they are used for jumping. A long, muscular tail helps the kangaroo keep its balance when it stands, walks, and jumps. The kangaroo has a small head, similar to a deer's, with a pointed nose. Its large ears stand upright on top of its head. They can turn from front to back, allowing the kangaroo to pick up sounds like radar.

The kangaroo is the pogo stick of the animal world. It can cover short distances at speeds up to 40 miles an hour and leap over trees and bushes that are 6 feet tall. About this animal that begins life the size of a thumb but later jumps higher than even the finest basketball player, one thing is certain: The kangaroo is surely an animal that grows by leaps and bounds!

Follow each of the directions below. Use the underlined words from the story above.

1. Write the words that are synonyms for these words.   stays __remains__
   jump __leap__   sack __pouch__

2. Write the words that are antonyms for these words.   worst __finest__
   ends __begins__   uncertain __certain__

3. Write the words that are homophones for these words.   ways __weighs__
   tale __tail__   our __hour__

4. Write the phrases that have these meanings.   small __as big as your thumb__
   jumps well __is the pogo stick of the animal world__
   hear well __pick up sounds like radar__

5. Write the words that can have either of these two meanings.
   (a) parts of the body used for walking   (b) units of 12 inches __feet__
   (a) go over; travel   (b) blanket __cover__

6. Complete the sentence by writing the same word in both blanks.
   The worker __pounds__ the heavy metal stakes into the ground with a sledge hammer that weighs five __pounds__

Check-Up Test 6: Vocabulary

Name _____

Read the words below. Use them to answer the questions that follow.

content	time	orange	solution	seller	guard	find
finger	week	seal	humorous	weave	backward	fair
left	decide	loaf	leave	unhappy	towed	

1. Write the antonyms of these words.   forward __backward__
   problem __solution__   arrive __leave__

2. Write the synonyms of these words.   protect __guard__
   funny __humorous__   miserable __unhappy__

3. Write the homophones of these words.   we've __weave__
   toad __towed__   cellar __seller__

4. Complete each sentence below by writing the same homograph in both blanks.
   After three weeks of work, Jim was __content__ with the __content__ of his history report.
   Peter __left__ the room, walked down the hall, and turned __left__ .
   To keep the contest __fair__ , there were five judges at our county-__fair__ tractor pull.

5. Write the words that can have either of these two meanings.
   (a) to be lazy   (b) a large shape of baked bread __loaf__
   (a) sea mammal   (b) to close or fasten tightly __seal__
   (a) reddish-yellow color   (b) a citrus fruit __orange__

6. Write the word that has the same meaning as each underlined phrase below.
   If you run across my old photograph album, please let me know. __find__
   I can't make up my mind about what color to paint the room. __decide__

7. Complete each analogy below.
   Date is to calendar as __time__ is to watch.
   December is to year as Saturday is to __week__ .
   Belt is to waist as ring is to __finger__ .

Reading and Writing Wrap-Up

Name _____

READING

Exercise and Health

Exercise comes from a Latin word that means "to keep busy." Keeping busy is a way of keeping healthy. You need exercise for your mind, your body, and your personality.

Exercising Your Mind
Exercise helps improve your mind. It keeps your mind working well. Everyone should do some mental exercises every day. These kinds of exercises help you think clearly. They help you solve problems quickly and easily. They help you understand your feelings better. They help you study and learn new things to make life more interesting.

You can do mental exercises by yourself or with other people. Reading and thinking are two kinds of exercises for your mind that you can do by yourself. You can write a poem or do arithmetic. You can put together a puzzle with a friend or play a thinking game with your family.

Exercising Your Body
Exercise helps keep your body healthy. You must use your muscles to keep your body in good shape. When you exercise your body, your muscles become strong. A healthy body helps you sleep well and work well. Physical exercise helps control your weight, improves your blood flow, and makes you look and feel fit and healthy.

Some kinds of physical exercise are good for your whole body. These include walking, running, jumping rope, and swimming. You can also work on different parts of your body. You can stretch and bend and lift weights. Playing sports is still another way to keep your body in good shape. It exercises your mind, too.

Exercising Your Social Skills
Exercise helps you improve your social skills, or the ways you behave with other people. Social exercises help you learn to make and keep friends. They also help you to become a good neighbor and a good citizen.

Working and playing with others are two ways to improve your social skills. Playing a game of volleyball or working with classmates to prepare a health report helps you learn cooperation. When you cooperate, you want to do your best for the team or the group — and for yourself. Then you feel good. Games and other kinds of teamwork help you learn to play fair and to lose gracefully. The more you work at improving your skills, the more successful you'll be.

Health

UNDERSTANDING

A. Answer the following questions.
1. What does the word *exercise* mean?
   Possible answers: to keep busy; practicing to improve

2. What three kinds of exercise does everyone need?
   mental   physical   social

B. List three ways that mental exercise helps you.
1. Possible answers: It keeps your mind working well. It helps you think clearly.
2. It helps you solve problems. It helps you understand your feelings.
3. It helps you study and learn.

C. List three ways that physical exercise helps you.
1. Possible answers: It keeps your body healthy. It makes your muscles strong.
2. It helps you sleep and work better.
3. It helps control your weight. It helps improve your blood flow.

D. List three ways that social exercise helps you.
1. Possible answers: It helps you make and keep friends.
2. It helps you learn to cooperate with others.
3. It helps you learn to play fair and lose gracefully.

E. Read each sentence below. Check the answers that correctly complete the sentence.
1. You can improve your social skills by _____ with others.
   ✓ playing   _____ fighting   ✓ working
2. You cooperate with others when you _____.
   ✓ follow the rules   ✓ play fair   _____ have to win

Reading and Writing Wrap-Up

THINKING

A. Draw a line to match each word on the left with its meaning on the right.
1. mental — d. having to do with the mind
2. physical — b. having to do with the body
3. social — a. having to do with the personality
4. cooperation — c. working with others for the good of all

B. Read each phrase below. Write *mental*, *physical*, or *social* to tell what kind of exercise is described. Some phrases may describe more than one kind of exercise. Write all the answers that fit each description. The first one has been done for you.
1. mental, physical, social — marching in the band
2. physical — jumping rope
3. physical — riding a bicycle
4. physical, social — washing cars with your scout group to raise money
5. mental — reading the front page of the newspaper
6. social — introducing a new student to your classmates
7. mental — working math problems
8. mental, physical, social — playing basketball
9. mental — doing a crossword puzzle

C. Choose one of the numbered items in Part B and tell why you gave the answer or answers you did. Tell exactly how the exercise would improve a person's mind, body, or social skills.
   Answers will vary.

Health

WRITING

My Exercise Journal

Every day for a week, write down the exercises you do for your mind, your body, and your personality. Try to do each kind of exercise every day.
Answers will vary.

SUNDAY Mental _____
Physical _____
Social _____

MONDAY Mental _____
Physical _____
Social _____

TUESDAY Mental _____
Physical _____
Social _____

WEDNESDAY Mental _____
Physical _____
Social _____

THURSDAY Mental _____
Physical _____
Social _____

FRIDAY Mental _____
Physical _____
Social _____

SATURDAY Mental _____
Physical _____
Social _____

214

Guide Words

The two words at the top of a dictionary page are called guide words. The first guide word is the same as the first word listed on the page. The second guide word is the same as the last word listed on the page. To find a word in the dictionary, decide if it comes in alphabetical order between the guide words on a page. If it does, you will find the word on that page. For example, the word **home** falls between the guide words **hollow** and **hop.**

Read each pair of guide words and the words that are listed below them. Circle the words in each list that could be found on a page that has that pair of guide words.

bass / bobcat	burro / cobra	caterpillar / crow	dog / elephant
(beaver)	copperhead	(catfish)	dinosaur
baboon	cow	(cricket)	(dove)
boxer	bulldog	cuckoo	(dragonfly)
(bat)	(buzzard)	cardinal	deer
bobwhite	(cat)	(crocodile)	(eagle)
(bluegill)	(camel)	(collie)	(dolphin)
(beagle)	(canary)	(chipmunk)	elk
(bluebird)	buffalo	(chimpanzee)	(duck)

Read the words below. Then look at the guide words above. For each word below, write the guide words between which the word would be found in a dictionary.

1. butterfly   burro / cobra
2. eel   dog / elephant
3. coyote   caterpillar / crow
4. bloodhound   bass / bobcat
5. donkey   dog / elephant
6. bear   bass / bobcat
7. bobcat   bass / bobcat
8. button   burro / cobra
9. chickadee   caterpillar / crow

Read the six pairs of guide words and their dictionary page numbers. Then read the list of words that follow. Write the page number on which each list word would be found in the dictionary.

damage / disease - p. 130	**doubt / faucet** - p. 152	**flavor / hotel** - p. 188
human / jealous - p. 234	**jingle / lantern** - p. 257	**leather / lodge** - p. 270

1. giraffe   p. 188
2. locomotive   p. 270
3. design   p. 130
4. language   p. 257
5. envelope   p. 152
6. invention   p. 234

7. jungle   p. 257
8. lemon   p. 270
9. hesitate   p. 188
10. instrument   p. 234
11. dinosaur   p. 130
12. electricity   p. 152

Read the sentences and word choices below. Using the guide words above, complete each sentence by writing the word that would be found on the dictionary page whose number is shown beside the word choices.

1. It is ___dangerous___ to dive into a shallow pond.
   (p. 130 - unsafe, dangerous)
2. Grandma taught me how to play a folk song on the ___guitar___.
   (p. 188 - guitar, banjo)
3. Spot is afraid of ___lightning___, so he hides under my bed during a storm.
   (p. 270 - lightning, thunder)
4. It was fortunate that no lives were lost during the ___hurricane___.
   (p. 234 - hurricane, tornado)
5. Two people paddled down the river in a ___kayak___.
   (p. 257 - kayak, canoe)
6. I bought this ___jacket___ on sale at Kale's Department Store.
   (p. 234 - jewelry, jacket)
7. Miguel plans to be a ___dentist___ after he graduates from college.
   (p. 130 - doctor, dentist)
8. There were ___forty___ people at the holiday party.
   (p. 188 - forty, fifty)

Read the list of words below. Then read the guide words that follow. Write each word or phrase below the correct pair of guide words. Then number each list of words to show how they would be listed in alphabetical order.

respiration	saliva	blood	appendix	artery	vitamin
biceps	tissue	pupil	stomach	cell	breath
pulse	bladder	reflex	capillary	vein	
cartilage	aorta	cerebrum	tendon	calcium	
blood vessel	cerebellum	spine	bacteria	breathe	
taste	red blood cell	skeleton	ventricle	retina	

1. abdomen / bone

aorta	1
biceps	5
blood vessel	8
bladder	6
blood	7
appendix	2
bacteria	4
artery	3

2. brain / cornea

cartilage	5
cerebellum	7
cerebrum	8
capillary	4
cell	6
calcium	3
breathe	2
breath	1

3. plasma / skin

pulse	1
saliva	7
respiration	5
red blood cell	3
pupil	2
reflex	4
skeleton	8
retina	6

4. skull / vocal cord

taste	3
tissue	5
spine	1
stomach	2
tendon	4
ventricle	7
vein	6
vitamin	8

Entry Words

Name _____

The word you look up in a dictionary is called an entry word. An entry word shows the spelling of the word and its syllables. Entry words are printed in dark type at the left of each column on the dictionary page. An entry word together with its meanings is called an entry.

cit y /sit′ ē/ n, pl **cit ies** **1** a large town: Chicago is a large city. **2** the people of a city: The city elected a new mayor in this year's election.

drea ry /drir′ ē/ adj **drea ri er; drea ri est 1** gloomy: The room looked dreary without any windows. **2** causing feelings of sadness: The rainy weather put me in a dreary mood. —**drea ri ly** adv —**drea ri ness** n

When you look for a word in a dictionary, look for the base word. For example, if you want to find **cities**, look for **city**. If you want to find **drearily**, look for **dreary**. Any spelling changes for different forms of the entry word are usually listed at the beginning or end of the entry.

An abbreviation for an entry word's part of speech is usually listed at the beginning or end of the entry. In the first example above, **n** means that **city** is a noun. Abbreviations for other forms of the entry word are usually listed beside those forms. In the second example, **adv** means that **drearily** is an adverb.

Read each word below. In the first blank, write the entry word you would look for to find the word in a dictionary. Then look up the entry word in a dictionary. In the second blank, write the dictionary abbreviation for the entry word's part of speech.

1. starved ___starve___ ___v___
2. politely ___polite___ ___adj___
3. simplest ___simple___ ___adj or n___
4. improves ___improve___ ___v___
5. punishing ___punish___ ___v___
6. orchards ___orchard___ ___n or adj___
7. uglier ___ugly___ ___adj___
8. victories ___victory___ ___n or adj___
9. defenseless ___defense___ ___n, adj, or v___
10. admired ___admire___ ___v___
11. territories ___territory___ ___n___
12. shaggiest ___shaggy___ ___adj___
13. radishes ___radish___ ___n or adj___
14. multiplied ___multiply___ ___v___
15. preparing ___prepare___ ___v___
16. sadder ___sad___ ___adj___
17. speeches ___speech___ ___n or adj___
18. sombreros ___sombrero___ ___n___
19. irrigated ___irrigate___ ___v___
20. amazing ___amaze___ ___v___
21. gratefulness ___grateful___ ___adj___
22. scarcely ___scarce___ ___adj or adv___
23. marshes ___marsh___ ___n or adj___
24. shallowest ___shallow___ ___adj or n___

Entry Words and Dictionary Meanings

Name _____

Read the dictionary entries below. Then read the sentences that follow. Complete each sentence by writing the correct entry word. You will use some entry words more than once. In the blank that follows the sentence, write the number of the word's correct meaning.

bulb /bulb/ n **1** the underground resting stage of a plant, consisting of a short stern base enclosed in thick leaves **2** a round glass object that glows when put into the socket of an electric light
calf /kaf/ n, pl **calves 1** a baby cow **2** the back of the leg between the knee and the ankle
free /frē/ adj **1** having liberty **2** without cost
iron /′ïrn, ï′ ərn/ n **1** metal used in making a large number of building materials, tools, and machinery: The rail is made of iron. **2** an electrical hand tool used for pressing or smoothing cloth

key /kē/ n **1** a tool made to open locks **2** a lever on a musical instrument or machine that is pushed down by the fingers: This piano key plays a C note. **3** something that helps with finding the answer: We found the key to the problem.
lace /lās/ n **1** a decoration used on clothing or a string used for bringing two edges together, such as a lace for tying a shoe
nail /nāl/ n **1** a thin, pointed piece of metal used to hold pieces of wood together **2** something that grows on a finger or toe: The nail on Kay's little finger is broken.

1. Rosa wore a red velvet dress with ___lace___ around the collar. __1__
2. The fish I caught wasn't big enough to eat, so I set it ___free___ __1__
3. Mr. Wise had to break a window to get into his apartment because he locked his ___key___ inside. __1__
4. Plant this ___bulb___ in the fall, and in the spring you'll have a beautiful red tulip. __1__
5. Terry broke the ___nail___ on her big toe when she stubbed it. __2__
6. By pouring water into an ___iron___, you can use steam to press the wrinkles out of your clothes. __2__
7. The runner had to drop out of the race because she had a painful cramp in the ___calf___ of her left leg. __2__
8. One ___key___ on the typewriter is stuck. __2__
9. That lamp doesn't work because the ___bulb___ is burned out. __2__
10. The department store is giving ___free___ theater tickets to each customer who buys twenty-five dollars' worth of goods. __2__
11. Cindy tied her ice skate with twine because the ___lace___ broke. __2__

Dictionary Meanings and Word Histories

Name

Many words in the English language have been borrowed from other languages. Some have come from the names of people or places. A few are made of letters from two or more words. Most dictionaries list a word history, or etymology, for some entry words. A word history tells what language the entry word comes from. It shows how the word is spelled in that language and what it means. Usually, a word history is shown before or after the meaning.

al li ga tor /al' ə gāt' ər/ n [from Spanish *el lagarto*, meaning "the lizard"] a large animal that lives in rivers and has a long body, short legs, thick skin, and a long tail

chop su ey /chop sü' ē/ n [from Chinese *tsap sui*, meaning "odds and ends"] a food made from bamboo shoots, bean sprouts, onions, mushrooms, and meat or fish cut up, cooked in a sauce, and often served over rice or fried noodles

Fer ris wheel /fer' əs hwēl/ n [named after George Ferris, the American engineer who invented it] an amusement park ride made of a large revolving wheel that has seats hanging from it

jum bo /jum' bō/ adj. [from *Jumbo*, the name of a large elephant in P.T. Barnum's circus] very big

ra dar /rā' där/ n [from the beginning letters of *radio detecting and ranging*] an electronic detector that sends out a powerful beam that reflects off a distant object to show its position and direction of movement

tu lip /tü' lip, tyü' lip/ n [from Turkish *tülbend*, meaning "turban"] a plant with a thick stem, long narrow leaves, and a cup-shaped flower

Answer each question by using the sample entries above.

1. From what language does the word *alligator* come? _____Spanish_____ What do the words from which *alligator* comes mean? _____the lizard_____

2. After whom was the Ferris wheel named? _____George Ferris_____

3. The word *radar* comes from a combination of what four words? _____radio detecting and ranging_____

4. From what language do the words *chop suey* come? _____Chinese_____ What do the words mean? _____odds and ends_____

5. After what was the word *jumbo* named? _____Jumbo, the large elephant_____

6. What is the Turkish word from which *tulip* comes? _____tülbend_____ What is the meaning of this word? _____turban_____ Was the tulip probably named for the shape of the stem, the leaves, or the flower? _____flower_____

7. Which three entry words began as English words? _____jumbo, Ferris wheel, radar_____

Review and Apply: Comprehension

Name

Read the dictionary entries below. Use them to answer the questions that follow.

¹**inch** /inch/ n, pl **inch es** [from Old English *ynce*, which came from Latin *uncia*, meaning "one twelfth"] one of twelve equal parts of a foot (about 2.5 cm): *The baby's finger is an inch long.*

²**inch** v to move very slowly, a little at a time: *The line of people waiting to purchase theater tickets inched toward the ticket booth.*

rul er /rü' lər/ n **1** one who governs or rules: *Queen Elizabeth is the ruler of Great Britain.* **2** a marked strip of wood or metal for drawing lines or measuring

spa ghet ti /spə get' ē/ n, pl [from Italian, from the plural of *spaghetto*, meaning "little strings"] a food made of wheat dough that is formed into long, thin strands and boiled in water before eating

1. Circle the pair of words that would be guide words for each dictionary entry shown in dark print below.

   a. **inch**   instead / invisible   (inactive / income)   idea / imagine
   b. **ruler**   rust / saddle   royal / rug   (ruin / rush)
   c. **spaghetti**   slipper / spacecraft   sparrow / squirt   (sour / statue)

2. Which entry word can be used as either a noun or a verb? _____inch_____

3. From what two languages did the word *inch* come? _____Old English, Latin_____

4. Which entry word is the plural form of an Italian word? _____spaghetti_____ What was the Italian meaning of this word? _____little strings_____

5. What was the meaning of the word from which the word *inch* came? _____one twelfth_____

6. Look at the underlined word in each sentence below. Write the number of the word's meaning.

   a. Before buying a picture frame, Rachael measured the length and width of the picture with a <u>ruler</u>. __2__

   b. From 1862 to 1908, Tz'u-hsi, one of the most powerful women in history, was the <u>ruler</u> of China. __1__

7. Look at the underlined word in each sentence below. Write the dictionary abbreviation for the word's part of speech.

   a. An <u>inch</u> of snow fell while we were sleeping last night. __n__

   b. Antonio watched a caterpillar <u>inch</u> its way across a tree limb. __v__

8. What other form of the word *inch* is listed in the entry for *inch*? _____inches_____

Review and Apply: Composition

Name

This is your chance to invent the wackiest word in the English language. No one else knows the word, so it's your job to write a dictionary entry for it. Follow the directions below.

1. Think of a wacky word and write it here. _____Answers will vary._____

2. Write two guide words (real words) between which your word would fall.
   _____Answers will vary._____

3. Write the meaning of your wacky word. _____Answers will vary._____

4. As what part of speech would your word be used? Use one of these abbreviations to name its part of speech: n, v, adj, adv, conj, prep, pron, int. _____Answers will vary._____

5. Think of a second meaning for your word. It should have the same part of speech as the first meaning. _____Answers will vary._____

6. For each meaning, write a sentence using the word. _____Answers will vary._____

7. Did you form your wacky word from another word or words? Tell how it got its name. _____Answers will vary._____

8. Does your word have an unusual plural or an **-ed**, **-ing**, **-er**, or **-est** form? Write any forms of your word. _____Answers will vary._____

9. Using the examples below, write a complete dictionary entry for your wacky word.

anchor   **astronaut**

ar rive v **ar rived; ar riv ing** [from Latin *arripare*, meaning "to come to shore"] **1** to reach a place to which one is going: *Ricardo will arrive in New York today.* **2** to come: *I can't wait for my birthday to arrive.*

as sem bly n, pl **as sem blies 1** a group of people meeting together for some purpose: *Our mayor talked to us at the assembly today.* **2** a collection of parts that make up a unit: *The airplane had lost its tail assembly.*

_____Answers will vary._____

Pronunciation Key and Respellings

Name

Words to use: /sā/, /nēd/, /is/, /kōt/, /yüz/, /lük/, /rül/, /kär/, /hwi/

A dictionary can show you how words are pronounced. An entry word is followed by a respelling. The respelling is made up of letters and special symbols. The words in the dictionary's pronunciation key show you how to pronounce each letter or symbol. By combining the sounds for each symbol and letter, you can pronounce the word.

Pronunciation Key

/a/ = apple, tap	/k/ = kick, can	/th/ = thing, both
/ā/ = ate, say	/l/ = laugh, pail	/u/ = up, cut
/är/ = car, heart	/m/ = mouse, ham	/ü/ = soon, rule
/âr/ = hair, care	/n/ = nice, ran	/ù/ = look, put
/b/ = bat, cab	/ng/ = ring, song	/v/ = vine, live
/ch/ = chain, chair	/o/ = father, hot	/w/ = wet, away
/d/ = door, sad	/ō/ = old, so	/y/ = yes, you
/e/ = get, egg	/ò/ = ball, dog	/yü/ = use, cute
/ē/ = even, bee	/oi/ = boy, oil	/yù/ = cure, pure
/f/ = fan, off	/ou/ = house, cow	/z/ = zoo, zero
/g/ = goat, big	/p/ = pan, nap	/zh/ = pleasure, beige
/h/ = her, happy	/r/ = ran, race	/ə/ = a (ground)
/hw/ = wheel, why	/s/ = sun, mess	e (better)
/i/ = is, fit	/sh/ = she, rush	i (rabbit)
/ī/ = ice, tie	/t/ = toy, mat	o (doctor)
/j/ = jump, gentle	/th/ = they, smooth	u (upon)

Use the pronunciation key above to pronounce each respelling below. Then read the words in the row. Circle the word that matches the respelling.

1. /ə pēl'/	apple	uphill	(appeal)	appear
2. /dēd/	(deed)	did	dead	deep
3. /gaj' ət/	engage	jagged	garage	(gadget)
4. /ring' kəl/	ring	(wrinkle)	wriggle	ringlet
5. /kə nü'/	(canoe)	can	kennel	canyon
6. /bam bü'/	bandage	banana	balloon	(bamboo)
7. /feŦH' ər/	father	(feather)	future	farther
8. /haz' ənt/	haze	hesitate	(hasn't)	has
9. /hüm/	(whom)	hum	who	humid
10. /nōn/	none	noon	(known)	noun
11. /jē og' rə fē/	jogging	jealousy	(geography)	geology
12. /shan' də lir'/	sandier	champion	shabby	(chandelier)

Pronunciation Key and Respellings

Words to use: /nīt/, /plezh' ər/, /fút/, /kär/, /krōl/, /fyü/, /bred/, /kəch/, /pärt/

Name _____

In most dictionaries, a short form of the pronunciation key can be found on each page.

Pronunciation Key

/a/ = apple, tap; /ā/ = ate, say; /är/ = car, heart; /âr/ = hair, care; /ch/ = chain, chair; /e/ = get, egg; /ē/ = even, bee; /hw/ = wheel, why; /i/ = is, fit; /ī/ = ice, tie; /ng/ = ring, song; /o/ = father, hot; /ō/ = old, so; /o/ = ball, dog; /oi/ = boy, oil; /ou/ = house, cow; /sh/ = she, rush; /ŦH/ = they, smooth; /th/ = thing, both; /u/ = up, cut; /ü/ = soon, rule; /ú/ = look, put; /yü/ = use, cute; /yu/ = cure, pure; /zh/ = pleasure, beige; /ə/ = a (ground), e (better), i (rabbit), o (doctor), u (upon)

Read the first word in each row below. Then read the respellings in the row. Use the key to pronounce the respellings. Circle the one that matches the word.

1.	launch	(/lônch/)	/lənch/	/lach/
2.	petal	/ped' əl/	(/pet' əl/)	/pórt' ə bəl/
3.	house	(/hórs/)	/hüz/	(/hous/)
4.	quiet	(/kwī' ət/)	/kwit/	/kwīt/
5.	cherries	/cher' ish/	(/cher' ēz/)	/chēz/
6.	swarm	/swòmp/	/swam/	(/swôrm/)
7.	delicate	(/del' i kət/)	/del' i gāt/	/ded' i kāt/

Read each respelling below. Then read the sentence and the words shown in parentheses. Complete the sentence by writing the word that matches the respelling.

1. /rā' zər/ My brother bought a new _____razor_____ because he lost his old one.
   (eraser, razor)

2. /sik' əl/ The garden hose is hanging in the garage near Mom's _____sickle_____.
   (sickle, cycle)

3. /sēd' ər/ One of the things I like most is the smell of _____cedar_____.
   (cedar, cider)

4. /bi nēth'/ Scamper's favorite place to sleep is _____beneath_____ my bed.
   (beside, beneath)

5. /ri sēt'/ The woman wasn't able to read the _____receipt_____ without her glasses.
   (receipt, recipe)

6. /kus' təmz/ Rita's report was about the _____customs_____ of other countries.
   (costumes, customs)

Accent Marks

Words to use: co zy, No vem ber, ad van tage, pur pose, di vide, but ton, cir cus, de cide, gov ern ment, friend li ness, en cour age ment

Name _____

Dictionary respellings of words that have two or more syllables show the syllables by putting a space or mark between them. When a word has more than one syllable, one syllable is usually said with more stress than the others. In the respelling /fin' ish/, the accent mark after the first syllable shows that **fin** is said with more stress than **ish.** In some words, the syllables in the entry word are not the same as the ones in the respelling.

Use the key to pronounce each respelling in List A. Then read the words in List B. Write the word from List B that matches each respelling. Leave a space between its syllables. Then put an accent mark after the syllable that is said with more stress.

Pronunciation Key

/a/ = apple, tap; /ā/ = ate, say; /är/ = car, heart; /âr/ = hair, care; /ch/ = chain, chair; /e/ = get, egg; /ē/ = even, bee; /hw/ = wheel, why; /i/ = is, fit; /ī/ = ice, tie; /ng/ = ring, song; /o/ = father, hot; /ō/ = old, so; /o/ = ball, dog; /oi/ = boy, oil; /ou/ = house, cow; /sh/ = she, rush; /ŦH/ = they, smooth; /th/ = thing, both; /u/ = up, cut; /ü/ = soon, rule; /ú/ = look, put; /yü/ = use, cute; /yu/ = cure, pure; /zh/ = pleasure, beige; /ə/ = a (ground), e (better), i (rabbit), o (doctor), u (upon)

	List A		List B
1.	/fē es' tə/	fi es' ta	ma roon
2.	/bā' ləf/	bai' liff	pa ren the sis
3.	/kar' ik tər/	char' ac ter	e mo tion
4.	/i mō' shən/	e mo' tion	ci der
5.	/sīd' ər/	ci' der	fi es ta
6.	/mə rün'/	ma roon'	ki mo no
7.	/kə mō' nə/	ki mo' no	bai liff
8.	/pə ren' thə səs/	pa ren' the sis	char ac ter

The words below have been divided into syllables. Say each word and listen for the stressed syllable. Put an accent mark after the stressed syllable in each word.

1.	bliz'zard	5.	beau ti ful	9.	car pen ter
2.	dis turb'	6.	a wake'	10.	par rot
3.	vol ca'no	7.	cal'en dar	11.	ge og ra phy
4.	si'ren	8.	fu'ri ous	12.	gov'ern ment

Accent Marks

Words to use: ob ject (thing), ob ject (complain), pres ent (gift), pre sent (introduce), pro duce (make), prod uce (fruits and vegetables)

Name _____

Two-syllable words that are spelled alike may have different respellings. They may be pronounced with the stress on different syllables. Read the dictionary entries below. Use the accent marks to say each word and listen for the stressed syllable.

¹con tent /kən tent'/ *adj* pleased; satisfied: *Mrs. Meyers is content with her son's grades in school.*

²con tent /kon' tent/ *n* **1** something that is contained—often used in the plural, **contents:** *The contents of the box fell out on the floor.* **2** the subject matter treated: *The content of her speech made everyone unhappy.* **3** amount held: *These jars have a content of one gallon each.*

des ert /dez' ərt/ *n* a hot, sandy area with few trees and little water: *We were thirsty and hot in the desert.*

²de sert /di zərt'/ *v* **de sert ed; de sert ing** to leave or abandon a person or thing that one should stay with

min ute /min' ət/ *n* one of sixty equal units of time in an hour: *Let the water boil for one minute.*

²mi nute /mi nüt'/ *adj* **1** very small; tiny

re fuse /ri fyüz'/ *v* **re fused; re fus ing** **1** to say no to: *She tried to refuse my offer of help.* **2** to decline to do: *The horse might refuse to jump.*

²ref use /ref' yüs, ref' yüz/ *n* something to be thrown away; trash

Read each sentence below. Write the underlined word, leaving a space between its syllables. Put an accent mark after the stressed syllable in each word. Use the entries to help you.

1. On cold winter days, Luis is <u>content</u> to stay indoors and read. ___con tent'___

2. Some insects are so <u>minute</u>, they can't be seen by the naked eye. ___mi nute'___

3. Although it would have been easy, Michael did not <u>desert</u> his old friends after he became a well-known singer. ___de sert'___

4. It is hard to <u>refuse</u> one's favorite foods while dieting. ___re fuse'___

5. Our team scored a touchdown in the last <u>minute</u> of the game. ___min' ute___

6. Once a week, city workers on a truck take away the <u>refuse</u> from the bins behind our apartment building. ___ref' use___

7. The teacher liked the <u>content</u> of my report but said that the handwriting could be improved. ___con' tent___

8. A cactus can survive in the <u>desert</u> because it needs little water. ___des' ert___

9. A soldier who chooses to <u>desert</u> the army will be punished. ___de sert'___

10. Our new aquarium has a larger <u>content</u> than the one that broke. ___con' tent___

11. The Sahara, in Africa, is the largest <u>desert</u> in the world. ___des' ert___

Name _____

Read the list of words below. Then read the paragraph and the respellings shown below the blanks. Use the pronunciation key to pronounce the respellings. In each blank, write the list word that matches the respelling. You will use only twelve of the list words.

libraries	native	capsule	carriage	stroll	variety	tutors	Hobby
wouldn't	Acquire	capital	vanity	courses	horseback	Happy	wooden
lawbreakers	nature	Aquarium	stroke	garage	tourists	houseboat	coarse

Pronunciation Key

/a/ = apple, tap; /ā/ = ate, say; /är/ = car, heart; /âr/ = hair, care; /ch/ = chain, chair; /e/ = get, egg; /ē/ = even, bee; /hw/ = wheel, why; /i/ = is, fit; /ī/ = ice, tie; /ng/ = ring, song; /o/ = father, hot; /ō/ = old, so; /o/ = ball, dog; /oi/ = boy, oil; /ou/ = house, cow; /sh/ = she, rush; /ŦH/ = they, smooth; /th/ = thing, both; /u/ = up, cut; /ü/ = soon, rule; /ú/ = look, put; /yü/ = use, cute; /yu/ = cure, pure; /zh/ = pleasure, beige; /ə/ = a (ground), e (better), i (rabbit), o (doctor), u (upon)

Bermuda is a tiny island in the Atlantic Ocean. The east side of the island is well known for its historic sights. In the town of St. George's, heavy _____wooden_____ frames /wúd' ən/ that were once used to hold _____lawbreakers_____ are on display. Outside St. George's, /lo' brāk ərz/ _____nature_____ lovers enjoy visiting the Bermuda _____Aquarium_____, where /nā' chər/ /ə kwer' ē əm/ they can see 150 kinds of sea life. In the _____capital_____ city, Hamilton, visitors can /kap' ət əl/ ride around town in a _____carriage_____ drawn by horses. Or they may /kar' ij/ _____stroll_____ through the beautiful Par-la Ville Gardens. The west side of /strōl/ Bermuda, with its famous pink, sandy beaches, attracts sports lovers. Besides swimming and

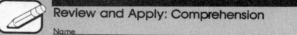

diving, visitors can choose from a wide _____variety_____ of sports. They /və rī' ət ē/ may play golf on the finest _____courses_____ or play tennis on /kórs' əz/ all-weather courts. They take a morning _____horseback_____ ride along the /hórs' bak/ beach before breakfast. No wonder so many _____tourists_____ have agreed with /tür' əsts/ Mark Twain, who called Bermuda "The _____Happy_____ Island." /hap' ē/

Review and Apply: Composition

Name _____

Use the pronunciation key to pronounce each respelling below. In the first blank, write the word that matches the respelling. In the blanks that follow, write a riddle that uses the word for an answer. If you need to, you may change the spelling of your answer to better fit the riddle, as has been done in the example.

Pronunciation Key

/a/ = apple, tap; /ā/ = ate, say; /är/ = car, heart; /âr/ = hair, care; /ch/ = chain, chair; /e/ = get, egg; /ē/ = even, bee; /hw/ = wheel, why; /i/ = is, fit; /ī/ = ice, tie; /ng/ = ring, song; /o/ = father, hot; /ō/ = old, so; /ô/ = ball, dog; /oi/ = boy, oil; /ou/ = house, cow; /sh/ = she, rush; /th/ = they, smooth; /th/ = thing, both; /u/ = up, cut; /ū/ = soon, rule; /u̇/ = look, put; /yū/ = use, cute; /yu̇/ = cure, pure; /zh/ = pleasure, beige; /ə/ = a (ground), e (better), i (rabbit), o (doctor), u (upon)

1. /mü′ vē/ _____ movie _____ Where do cows take their dates on Saturday nights?
   Answer: To the drive-in MOOOOOOOOvies!

2. /ā′ körn/ _____ acorn _____ Riddles will vary.

3. /krak′ ərz/ _____ crackers _____

4. /gō′ fər/ _____ gopher _____

5. /ə las′ kə/ _____ Alaska _____

6. /bat′ ə rēz/ _____ batteries _____

7. /nā′ bər hüd/ _____ neighborhood _____

8. /tə bog′ ən/ _____ toboggan _____

9. /fur′ ni chər/ _____ furniture _____

Review of pronunciation key, respellings, and accent marks

169

Check-Up Test 7: Dictionary Skills

Name _____

Read the sample dictionary entries below. Use them to answer the questions that follow.

plum /plum/ n **1** a round, purple juicy fruit that grows on a tree **2** a dark bluish-purple color

¹pres ent /prez′ ənt/ n something given; a gift

²pre sent /pri zent′/ v **1** to hand over; give: *We will present the prize today.* **2** to bring before the public: *Our class will present a play next month.*

rest /rest/ v **1** to lie down **2** to stop work or activity

sand wich /san′ wich, san′ dwich/ n, pl **sand wich es** [named for the fourth Earl of Sandwich, a British official who invented it so he could continue to play a card game without stopping for a meal] two pieces of bread with meat, cheese, jam, or another filling between them

um brel la /um′ brel′ ə/ n [from Italian *ombrella*, meaning "parasol," from Latin *umbra*, meaning "shade"] a folding frame covered with cloth or plastic, used for protection against weather

1. Circle the pair of words that would be guide words for the dictionary entries above.
   (pledge/unusual)   parrot/ugly   plural/under

2. Which entry word is listed as both a noun and a verb? _____ present

3. What is the plural form of *sandwich*? _____ sandwiches

4. Name the two languages and words from which *umbrella* came.
   Italian *ombrella* and Latin *umbra*

5. What were the meanings of the two words from which *umbrella* came?
   "parasol" and "shade"

6. Look at the underlined word in each sentence below. In the blank, write the word, leaving a space between its syllables. Put an accent mark after the stressed syllable.

   Our club will <u>present</u> a slide show of our trip to the Grand Canyon. _____ pre sent′

   I made a brass letter opener as a birthday <u>present</u> for Dad. _____ pres′ ent

   The committee will <u>present</u> a silver medal to the athlete. _____ pre sent′

7. Look at the underlined word in each sentence below. In the blank, write the number of the word's meaning.

   After digging the hole for the fence post, Gina sat down to <u>rest</u>. _2_

   Noise from the nearby midnight train made it hard for me to <u>rest</u> last night. _1_

   Mom wants to decorate the room in lavender, but I prefer <u>plum</u>. _2_

   I have a bologna sandwich, carrot sticks, and a <u>plum</u> for lunch. _1_

170

Assessment of dictionary skills

Check-Up Test 8: Dictionary Skills

Name _____

Look at the pronunciation key and read the list of words that follow. Use the pronunciation key to pronounce each respelling. Write the word the respelling stands for.

Pronunciation Key

/a/ = apple, tap; /ā/ = ate, say; /är/ = car, heart; /âr/ = hair, care; /ch/ = chain, chair; /e/ = get, egg; /ē/ = even, bee; /hw/ = wheel, why; /i/ = is, fit; /ī/ = ice, tie; /ng/ = ring, song; /o/ = father, hot; /ō/ = old, so; /ô/ = ball, dog; /oi/ = boy, oil; /ou/ = house, cow; /sh/ = she, rush; /th/ = they, smooth; /th/ = thing, both; /u/ = up, cut; /ū/ = soon, rule; /u̇/ = look, put; /yū/ = use, cute; /yu̇/ = cure, pure; /zh/ = pleasure, beige; /ə/ = a (ground), e (better), i (rabbit), o (doctor), u (upon)

graceful   employment   cushion   aisle   shower   education   cautious   saucer

1. /sô′ sər/ _____ saucer
2. /shou′ ər/ _____ shower
3. /im ploi′ mənt/ _____ employment
4. /ej′ ə kā′ shən/ _____ education
5. /grās′ fəl/ _____ graceful
6. /kô′ shəs/ _____ cautious
7. /kush′ ən/ _____ cushion
8. /īl/ _____ aisle

Use the dictionary entries below to answer the questions that follow.

crust /krust/ n **1** the hard, dark surface of a piece of bread **2** the pastry portion of a pie **3** the outer part of the earth

ga rage /gə rozh′, gə roj′/ n **1** a building where cars are kept **2** a repair shop for cars

wade /wād/ v **wad ed; wad ing 1** to step through water, mud, or sand **2** to make progress, but with great difficulty

Write the number of the meaning of the underlined word in each sentence.

1. Mom took the car to the <u>garage</u> so a mechanic could change the engine oil. _2_
2. After the thunderstorm, the workers had to <u>wade</u> through puddles in the parking lot. _1_
3. Chun cut the <u>crusts</u> off the sandwiches and cut them into small pieces. _1_
4. The lawyers will <u>wade</u> through the list of questions in order to find some answers. _2_
5. Molly finished mowing the lawn and then stored the lawn mower in the <u>garage</u>. _1_
6. Scientists found rare fossils buried within the <u>crust</u> of the earth. _3_
7. What other forms of the word *wade* are listed in the entry for *wade*?
   _____ waded _____ wading
8. What part of speech is the word *garage*? Write the dictionary abbreviation. _n_

Assessment of dictionary skills

171

Reading and Writing Wrap-Up

Name _____

READING

Three Kinds of Rocks

Do all rocks look alike to you? They aren't. Rocks are different in the way they are formed and in how they look. Take a close look at the next rock you see.

Igneous Rocks

How Igneous Rocks Are Formed Deep inside the earth's crust is a hot liquid called magma. When magma cools, it becomes rock. Some magma cools very slowly while it is still deep inside the earth. Magma that rises to the surface of the earth cools more quickly. All rocks formed from magma—whether they cool slowly or quickly—are called igneous rocks. *Igneous* means "fiery."

Kinds of Igneous Rocks Magma that cools slowly forms a rock called granite. Granite is used in making buildings and monuments. Lava is magma that comes from volcanoes. It cools quickly. The Hawaiian Islands are largely made up of this kind of rock. Obsidian is another kind of rock formed from lava. It looks like black glass and is often used in making rings, pins, and other kinds of jewelry.

Sedimentary Rocks

How Sedimentary Rocks Are Formed Some rocks are formed from other rocks that have broken up into pieces of gravel or sand. These pieces of gravel and sand are called sediment. In the bottoms of lakes and rivers, many deposits of sediment are squeezed together to form sedimentary rocks.

Kinds of Sedimentary Rocks Rocks that have been ground into sand may be squeezed together to form sandstone. When you look at sandstone, you can see the tiny grains of sand that have formed the rock.

When mud and clay are mixed with water and pressed together, a rock called shale is formed. Shale appears to be made up of very thin slabs.

Animal bones and shells crushed into fine pieces by heavy ocean water may form a rock called limestone. Much of this rock is found in Ohio and Kentucky.

Metamorphic Rocks

How Metamorphic Rocks Are Formed Metamorphic rocks are rocks that have been changed in some way. Heat and pressure can act on both igneous and sedimentary rocks to change them into metamorphic rocks. You can see bands of light and dark color in some metamorphic rocks but not in others.

Kinds of Metamorphic Rocks Heat and pressure can change shale into slate. Slate may be used for chalkboards and floors. Limestone can be changed to marble. Many statues are carved from marble, and some furniture is also made from marble.

172

Application of reading skills in a science context

Science

Name _____

A. Draw a line to connect the name of each type of rock to the word or words it comes from.

1. igneous
2. sedimentary
3. metamorphic

a. *sedimentum*, meaning "settling"
b. *meta*, meaning "change," and *morph*, meaning "form"
c. *ignis*, meaning "fire"

B. Write the name of each rock you read about on page 172 under the correct heading below.

Kinds of Igneous Rocks	Kinds of Sedimentary Rocks	Kinds of Metamorphic Rocks
granite	sandstone	slate
lava	shale	marble
obsidian	limestone	

C. Beside the name of each kind of rock, list one of its uses.

1. granite ____ buildings *or* monuments ____
2. slate ____ chalkboards *or* floors ____
3. marble ____ statues *or* furniture ____
4. obsidian ____ jewelry ____

D. Under each picture, write *igneous*, *sedimentary*, or *metamorphic* to show which kind of rock would probably be used to make the object.

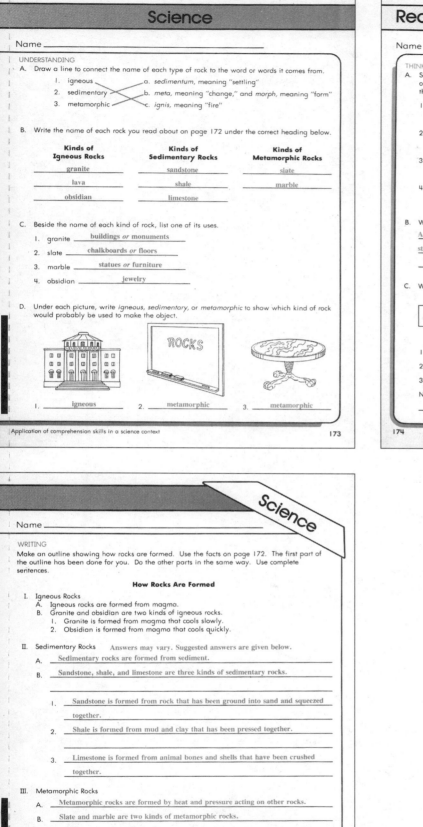

1. ____ igneous ____
2. ____ metamorphic ____
3. ____ metamorphic ____

Application of comprehension skills in a science context   173

Reading and Writing Wrap-Up

Name _____

A. Several students have collected rocks. Each student has written a description of the rock he or she found. Study each description below, and then write the best name for the rock that the student found.

1. This rock is sandy and rough to the touch. You can almost see little grains of sand in it.
   This rock is likely to be ____ sandstone ____

2. This rock is shiny and black. You can almost see yourself in it.
   This rock is likely to be ____ obsidian ____

3. You can see small pieces of shell in this rock.
   This rock is likely to be ____ limestone ____

4. This rock looks as if it had been formed in sheets. You can write on it with chalk.
   This rock is likely to be ____ shale *or* slate ____

B. Why might scientists think that an ocean once covered parts of Ohio and Kentucky?
   Answers may vary but should be similar to the following: Much limestone is found in these
   states, and limestone is formed when ocean water crushes animal bones and shells.
   _____

C. Write a word from the box to complete each analogy below.

floors	metamorphic	marble

1. *Limestone* is to *sedimentary* as *marble* is to ____ metamorphic ____
2. *Granite* is to *buildings* as *slate* is to ____ floors ____
3. *Shale* is to *slate* as *limestone* is to ____ marble ____

Now write an analogy of your own. Use facts from page 172. Answers will vary.

____ is to ____ as ____ is to ____

174   Application of thinking skills in a science context

Science

Name _____

Make an outline showing how rocks are formed. Use the facts on page 172. The first part of the outline has been done for you. Do the other parts in the same way. Use complete sentences.

How Rocks Are Formed

I. Igneous Rocks
   A. Igneous rocks are formed from magma.
   B. Granite and obsidian are two kinds of igneous rocks.
      1. Granite is formed from magma that cools slowly.
      2. Obsidian is formed from magma that cools quickly.

II. Sedimentary Rocks   Answers may vary. Suggested answers are given below.
   A. ____ Sedimentary rocks are formed from sediment. ____
   B. ____ Sandstone, shale, and limestone are three kinds of sedimentary rocks. ____
      1. ____ Sandstone is formed from rock that has been ground into sand and squeezed together. ____
      2. ____ Shale is formed from mud and clay that has been pressed together. ____
      3. ____ Limestone is formed from animal bones and shells that have been crushed together. ____

III. Metamorphic Rocks
   A. ____ Metamorphic rocks are formed by heat and pressure acting on other rocks. ____
   B. ____ Slate and marble are two kinds of metamorphic rocks. ____
      1. ____ Slate is formed by heat and pressure acting on shale. ____
      2. ____ Marble is formed by heat and pressure acting on limestone. ____

Application of writing skills in a science context   175

NOTES

NOTES

SPECTRUM

All our workbooks meet school curriculum guidelines and correspond to
The McGraw-Hill Companies classroom textbooks.

DOLCH Sight Word Activities

The DOLCH Sight Word Activities workbooks use the classic Dolch list of 220 basic vocabulary words that make up from 50% to 75% of all reading matter that children ordinarily encounter. Since these words are ordinarily recognized on sight, they are called *sight words*. Volume 1 includes 110 sight words. Volume 2 covers the remainder of the list. 160 pages. Answer key included.

TITLE	ISBN	PRICE
Grades K-1 Vol. 1	1-56189-917-8	$9.95
Grades K-1 Vol. 2	1-56189-918-6	$9.95

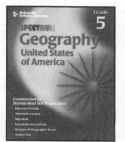

GEOGRAPHY

Full-color, three-part lessons strengthen geography knowledge and map reading skills. Focusing on five geographic themes including location, place, human/environmental interaction, movement, and regions. Over 150 pages. Glossary of geographical terms and answer key included.

TITLE	ISBN	PRICE
Grade 3, Communities	1-56189-963-1	$8.95
Grade 4, Regions	1-56189-964-X	$8.95
Grade 5, USA	1-56189-965-8	$8.95
Grade 6, World	1-56189-966-6	$8.95

MATH

Features easy-to-follow instructions that give students a clear path to success. This series has comprehensive coverage of the basic skills, helping children to master math fundamentals. Over 150 pages. Answer key included.

TITLE	ISBN	PRICE
Grade K	1-56189-900-3	$8.95
Grade 1	1-56189-901-1	$8.95
Grade 2	1-56189-902-X	$8.95
Grade 3	1-56189-903-8	$8.95
Grade 4	1-56189-904-6	$8.95
Grade 5	1-56189-905-4	$8.95
Grade 6	1-56189-906-2	$8.95
Grade 7	1-56189-907-0	$8.95
Grade 8	1-56189-908-9	$8.95

PHONICS/WORD STUDY

Provides everything children need to build multiple skills in language. Focusing on phonics, structural analysis, and dictionary skills, this series also offers creative ideas for using phonics and word study skills in other language areas. Over 200 pages. Answer key included.

TITLE	ISBN	PRICE
Grade K	1-56189-940-2	$8.95
Grade 1	1-56189-941-0	$8.95
Grade 2	1-56189-942-9	$8.95
Grade 3	1-56189-943-7	$8.95
Grade 4	1-56189-944-5	$8.95
Grade 5	1-56189-945-3	$8.95
Grade 6	1-56189-946-1	$8.95

ENRICHMENT MATH AND READING

Books in this series offer advanced math and reading for students excelling in grades 3–6. Lessons follow the same curriculum children are being taught in school while presenting the material in a way that children feel challenged. 160 pages. Answer key included.

TITLE	ISBN	PRICE
Grade 3	1-57768-503-2	$8.95
Grade 4	1-57768-504-0	$8.95
Grade 5	1-57768-505-9	$8.95
Grade 6	1-57768-506-7	$8.95

Prices subject to change without notice.

READING

This full-color series creates an enjoyable reading environment, even for below-average readers. Each book contains captivating content, colorful characters, and compelling illustrations, so children are eager to find out what happens next. Over 150 pages. Answer key included.

TITLE	ISBN	PRICE
Grade K	1-56189-910-0	$8.95
Grade 1	1-56189-911-9	$8.95
Grade 2	1-56189-912-7	$8.95
Grade 3	1-56189-913-5	$8.95
Grade 4	1-56189-914-3	$8.95
Grade 5	1-56189-915-1	$8.95
Grade 6	1-56189-916-X	$8.95

SPELLING

This full-color series links spelling to reading and writing, and increases skills in words and meanings, consonant and vowel spellings, and proofreading practice. Over 200 pages. Speller dictionary and answer key included.

TITLE	ISBN	PRICE
Grade 1	1-56189-921-6	$8.95
Grade 2	1-56189-922-4	$8.95
Grade 3	1-56189-923-2	$8.95
Grade 4	1-56189-924-0	$8.95
Grade 5	1-56189-925-9	$8.95
Grade 6	1-56189-926-7	$8.95

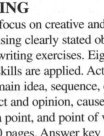

WRITING

Lessons focus on creative and expository writing using clearly stated objectives and pre-writing exercises. Eight essential reading skills are applied. Activities include main idea, sequence, comparison, detail, fact and opinion, cause and effect, making a point, and point of view. Over 130 pages. Answer key included.

TITLE	ISBN	PRICE
Grade 1	1-56189-931-3	$8.95
Grade 2	1-56189-932-1	$8.95
Grade 3	1-56189-933-X	$8.95
Grade 4	1-56189-934-8	$8.95
Grade 5	1-56189-935-6	$8.95
Grade 6	1-56189-936-4	$8.95
Grade 7	1-56189-937-2	$8.95
Grade 8	1-56189-938-0	$8.95

TEST PREP

Prepares children to do their best on current editions of the five major standardized tests. Activities reinforce test-taking skills through examples, tips, practice, and timed exercises. Subjects include reading, math, language arts, writing, social studies, and science. Over 150 pages. Answer key included.

TITLE	ISBN	PRICE
Grades 1-2	1-57768-672-1	$9.95
Grade 3	1-57768-673-X	$9.95
Grade 4	1-57768-674-8	$9.95
Grade 5	1-57768-675-6	$9.95
Grade 6	1-57768-676-4	$9.95
Grade 7	1-57768-677-2	$9.95
Grade 8	1-57768-678-0	$9.95

LANGUAGE ARTS

Encourages creativity and builds confidence by making writing fun! Seventy-two four-part lessons strengthen writing skills by focusing on parts of speech, word usage, sentence structure, punctuation, and proofreading. Each level includes a Writer's Handbook at the end of the book that offers writing tips. This series is based on the highly respected SRA/McGraw-Hill language arts series. More than 180 full-color pages. Answer key included.

TITLE	ISBN	PRICE
Grade 2	1-56189-952-6	$8.95
Grade 3	1-56189-953-4	$8.95
Grade 4	1-56189-954-2	$8.95
Grade 5	1-56189-955-0	$8.95
Grade 6	1-56189-956-9	$8.95

Prices subject to change without notice.

PRESCHOOL

Learning Letters offers comprehensive instruction and practice in following directions, recognizing and writing upper- and lowercase letters, and beginning phonics. Math Readiness features activities that teach such important skills as counting, identifying numbers, creating patterns, and recognizing "same and different." Basic Concepts and Skills offers exercises that help preschoolers identify colors, read and write words, identify simple shapes, and more. 160 pages.

TITLE	ISBN	PRICE
Learning Letters	1-57768-329-3	$8.95
Math Readiness	1-57768-339-0	$8.95
Basic Concepts and Skills	1-57768-349-8	$8.95